INTERESTING CANTONESE COLLOQUIAL EXPRESSIONS

Interesting Cantonese Colloquial Expressions

Lo Wood Wai and Tam Fee Yin

中文大學出版社

© **The Chinese University of Hong Kong** 1996

All Rights Reserved. No part of this publication may
be reproduced or transmitted in any form or by any
means, electronic or mechanical, including photocopying,
recording, or any information storage and retrieval
system, without permission in writing from
The Chinese University of Hong Kong.

ISBN 962-201-666-9

The Chinese University Press
The Chinese University of Hong Kong
Sha Tin, N.T., Hong Kong

Fax: +852 2603 6692
E-mail: cup@cuhk.edu.hk
Web-site: http://www.cuhk.edu.hk/cupress/w1.htm

Printed in Hong Kong

Contents

Preface vii

A Brief Introduction to Cantonese Pronunciation xi

Explanatory Notes xv

List of Entries xvii

Years of the Dynasties in Chinese History 217

References 219

Index of Expressions by Pronunciation 221

Index of Expressions in Chinese 231

Preface

This book is written for non-Chinese speaking people, especially for those foreigners who know some Cantonese and are interested in learning more about the cultural implications of some Cantonese expressions.

In Hong Kong, Cantonese has become the main spoken form intelligible to the largest proportion of the population. However, many Cantonese words are not easy to understand. Even native speakers do not know why some words are said the way they are or where they come from. They, too, wonder why Ngàhyīn means dangerous, Chyun means disgustingly bad attitude and Hàahmsāp is the word for a nasty man, etc.

Actually, many Cantonese words or expressions are not only colloquial, but also historical. We have tried to find out their origins, but what we have found may not be their exact geneses. In fact, readers may encounter difficulties in determining which one of the hypotheses is more convincing when they are confronted with two explanations for a word or an expression. Through this book, it is hoped that foreigners can learn more about our culture, which is the main objective of our venture. Indeed, language learning implies and embraces culture learning. [1] The latter plays a role in the acquisition of a new language. If you learn an additional language, you may as well learn the culture, which is also in close connection with the history of the country that speaks your target language.

On the other hand, some Cantonese words, expressions as well as slang may sound vulgar in their present-day spoken form out of no linguistic reasons. A word in itself is neither refined nor coarse from a strictly linguistic point of view, but its decency or foulness is just a reflection of social views. However, it is interesting to note that some Cantonese words or expressions can be retrieved from the Chinese classics written two or three millenniums ago while some are derived from the language that the ancient educated Chinese used in literary writing. Some of them are the exact words spoken by people in former times. Cantonese, as a "dialect" in its general sense, is a spoken variety as against the standardized written form of the Chinese national language.[2] Nowadays, people are not supposed to use Cantonese words or expressions in modern written Chinese, but all of the Cantonese words or expressions have universally recognized written parallels, which, though refined, as opposed to the former, should not be assumed as a superior form. On the one hand, we should esteem our national language, the major part of which is based on the Northern dialect, as a nation-wide uniformity in language. On the other hand, all regionalects and dialects in the family of Chinese language[3] ought to be regarded equal as well.

During the twelfth century in Chinese history, there was a mass exodus of the Han people from the Middle Plain to the south, due to the invasion of the non-Han Tartars in the northern half of China.[4] Following the migration of the imperial clan and the Han common people, it is recognized by some of the phonologists and linguists that a certain amount of the ancient accents in speech and also the ancient characters in the written script were retained in the Cantonese dialect. In Hong Kong, in addition to the formal characters used in modern written Chinese, people use one more type of characters, i.e. the Cantonese script, which is adopted in this book, too. Some of the characters of the so-called Cantonese script are recently forged by the Hong Kong people, while quite a lot of them are ancient graphics that survived till today. So by studying the colloquial expressions, foreign learners of Cantonese are at the same time gaining an insight of the historical link with the Cantonese dialect.

Part of the colloquial expressions collected in this book originated from historical episodes, well-known legends, folk-tales or just hearsay. Part of them are associated with famous personages in the Chinese history. Some have undergone phonological or morphological changes before they have acquired their current form, while some have successfully preserved their ancient pronunciations over the centuries. The make-up of some of the idiomatic expressions, whether the key words in them are hidden or are supplemented by parallel phrases or clauses, is also explained in some of the entries. Through the study of colloquialisms, readers may also learn how modern people are affected by the customs or by the way the ancient people had lived. Once you realize what is behind the words that people say, you will register them in your mind without difficulty.

The colloquial expressions collected in this book are people's utterances which can easily be found in our daily speech. A few of them are not used frequently, but we would like to have them recorded too for reference. There are also a few expressions marked with a "#", which means it is not advisable for the readers to say them, especially for the female readers (since there is difference between the spoken varieties of men and women as found in some sociolinguistic surveys.) Just like books of similar kind, the presentation of the colloquial expressions and slang is of descriptive nature. A piece of slang in one language may not necessarily be considered slang in another language. The relation between the phonetic representation and the meaning it signifies is arbitrary. However, the aim of introducing such sayings in this book is not to advocate the use of them, but that readers can tell that they are abusive terms or they mean something filthy once they hear them, though in fact, they constitute part of the repertoire of the speech community of Hong Kong people. The interpretations of the expressions, which is the major feature of the book, are given in both Chinese and English. The Chinese text is prepared for the readers who can read Chinese.

The literal meanings of the words or expressions are also given to render more help to the readers in apprehending their significance. Examples are cited too using the plain language[5] of the Hong Kong people. They are intended as a supplementary constituent to indicate in what situations these expressions are to be used.

Cantonese script is given under the romanized words correspondingly for the convenience of those with no knowledge of the Yale romanization. The entries are categorized into ten groups: (1) appellations about people (women first); (2) descriptions about human personality; (3) about nature; (4) about language (from single or simple words to sophisticated structured sentences); (5) about Canton; (6) culture and customs; (7) historical figures; (8) myths and folklore; (9) about animals; and (10) argots used among triads. The entries in groups 2, 7 and some in group 6 are arranged on a chronological basis.

This book is not an academic one, nor is it a textual research. Instead, we have tried to make it terse, comprehensible and more interesting through the use of the short story illustrations. The kind of register, or style of writing, adopted in this book is the one that can be easily understood by the readers whose mother tongues are not Chinese or English. The errors and the shortcomings of this book are all our responsibilities. We are grateful to Julie Zuzanne Beley, Virginia Khong Go, Antoine Law, David Lee-hin, Nicholas Macfie, Ann Mah, Dawkin Tania Marshall, Benigna Menezes, Philip Mielke, Ericka Lynn Quock, Joy Marie Turner, Maylan Wong and Nathaniel Madarang who gave us much help in going through the English translations. We are particularly grateful to Rev. Fr. Ciaran Kane for checking through the whole manuscript. We also thank the office staff of the Chinese Language Centre, CUHK for offering us stationery convenience for the preparation of the book. The encouragement of our friends and students, whose growing need to learn the Cantonese colloquial expressions in a more specific and systematic manner has been our vital inspiration. It was first compiled by Lo Wood Wai and was then translated into English by Tam Fee Yin. Last of all, comments and suggestions for improvement will be greatly appreciated.

Tam Fee Yin
Lo Wood Wai
August 1995

---

[1] Louise Damen, chaps. 1–2.
[2] Joseph H. Greenberg, p. 65.
[3] John Defrancis, Part I.3
[4] Ch'en Shou-yi, chap. 18.
[5] Note 3, Part IV 15, p. 243.

A Brief Introduction to Cantonese Pronunciation

A Cantonese syllable is composed of three parts: an initial, a final and a tone.

Initials

An initial is the starting-off sound of a syllable. There are 19 initials.

1. Aspirated stops:	P	T	K	CH	KW
2. Non-aspirated stops:	B	D	G	J	GW
3. Nasals:	M	N	NG		
4. Fricative and Continuants:	F	L*	H	S	
5. Semi-vowels:	Y	W			

* L is in free variation with N. To replace N with L does not involve differentiation between meanings.

Finals

A final is the ending sound of a word. There are 51 finals. The main vowel is the most essential part of a final. The vowels may be either long or short.

*L.	S.	L.	S.	L.	S.	L.	S.	L.	S.	L.
A		E		EU		I		O		U		YU
AAI	AI	ENG	EI	EUNG	EUI	IU	ING	OI	OU	UI	UNG	YUN
AAU	AU	EK		EUK	EUN	IM	IK	ON		UN	UK	YUT
AAM	AM				EUT	IN		ONG		UT		
AAN	AN					IP		OT				
AANG	ANG					IT		OK				
AAP	AP											
AAT	AT											
AAK	AK											

* L. is for a long vowel whereas S. is for a short one.

Tones

There are seven tones in Cantonese. They may have a musical significance.

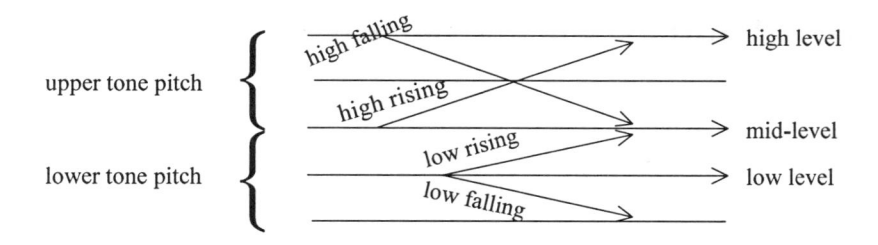

```
upper tone pitch  {  high falling ─────→ high level
                     high rising ─────→ mid-level
lower tone pitch  {  low rising  ─────→ 
                     low falling ─────→ low level
```

Tones are distinguished by a tone mark which is put on top of the vowel or the first vowel. The letter H is used to signify the lower tones. It should be placed after the vowel or the vowels and go before the consonants. For example:

Fà	High falling	Yùhn	Low falling
Hóu	High rising	Ngáahn	Low rising
Taai	Mid-level	Louh	Low level
Hēung	High level		

Comparative Chart of Four Romanization Systems

Initials

Yale	IPA	Sidney Lau	Meyer-Wempe
p	p'	p	p'
b	p	b	p
t	t'	t	t'
d	t	d	t
k	k'	k	k'
g	k	g	k
ch	ts	ch	ch', ts'
j	dz	j	ch, ts
kw	k'w	kw	k'w
gw	kw	gw	kw
m	m	m	m
n	n	n	n
ng	ŋ	ng	ng
f	f	f	f
l	l	l	l
h	h	h	h
s	s	s	s, sh
y	j	y	i, y
w	w	w	oo, w

Finals

Yale	IPA	Sidney Lau	Meyer-Wempe
a	aː	a	a
aai	aːi	aai	aai
aau	aːu	aau	aau
aam	aːm	aam	aam
aan	aːn	aan	aan
aang	aːŋ	aang	aang
aap	aːp	aap	aap
aat	aːt	aat	aat
aak	aːk	aak	aak
ai	ai	ai	ai
au	au	au	au
am	am	am	am, om
an	an	an	an
ang	aŋ	ang	ang
ap	ap	ap	ap, op
at	at	at	at
ak	ak	ak	ak
e	ɛː	e	e
eng	ɛːŋ	eng	eng
ek	ɛːk	ek	ek
ei	ei	ei	ei
eu	œː	euh	oeh
eung	œːŋ	eung	eung
euk	œːk	euk	euk
eui	œi	ui	ui
eun	œn	un	un
eut	œt	ut	ut
i	iː	i	i
iu	iːu	iu	iu
im	iːm	im	im
in	iːn	in	in
ing	iŋ	ing	ing
ip	iːp	ip	ip
it	iːt	it	it
ik	ik	ik	ik
o	o	oh	oh
oi	oːi	oi	oi

on	oːn	on	on
ong	oːŋ	ong	ong
ot	oːt	ot	ot
ok	oːk	ok	ok
ou	ou	o	o
u	u	oo	oo
ui	uːi	ooi	ooi
un	uːn	oon	oon
ung	uːŋ	ung	ung
ut	uːt	oot	oot
uk	uːk	uk	uk
yu	yː	ue	ue
yun	yːn	uen	uen
yut	yːt	uet	uet

Tones

Yale		Sidney Lau			Meyer-Wempe	
high falling	à	high falling	1	a¹	upper even	a
high rising	á	middle rising	2	a²	upper rising	á
middle level	a, at	middle level	3	a³	upper going	à
					middle entering	àt
high level	ā, āt	high level	1°	a¹⁰	upper even	a
					upper entering	at
low falling	àh	low falling	4	a⁴	low even	ā
low rising	áh	low rising	5	a⁵	lower rising	ă
low level	ah, aht	low level	6	a⁶	lower going	â
					lower entering	ât

Explanatory Notes

1. The Cantonese words, expressions and proper names are given in Yale romanization except "Canton", "Swatow", "Peking", "Hong Kong", "Taiwan", "Taipei" and the names of different dynasties in Chinese history which will remain in their conventional spellings excluding tone marks.
2. The entries are illustrated by examples.
3. The passage on the origins of the entires are given in English followed by their Chinese translation.
4. The parts of speech and their functions as used in this book are as follows:

Abbreviation	Parts of speech	Function
A	Adverb	modifying a verb or a stative verb
ADJ.PH	Adjectival phrase	modifying a noun; manner of action
ADV.PH	Adverbial phrase	modifying a verb
FV	Functive verb	indicating a function of an action
I.E.	idiomatic expression	
M	Measure	classifier of a noun
N	Noun	(a) subject or object of a verb; (b) can modify another noun; (c) can be modified by another noun
NU	Number	
PH	Phrase	(a) as a predicate; (b) may stand alone
PN	pronoun	
SV	Stative verb	expressing quality or condition
VO	Verb-object	forming one single concept in English

5. Different usages of different measures as used in this book:

bāan	a group of people
bāt	a case of
bún	for a book
būi	a cup of
bouh	for a book or a vehicle
chi	for time or an occasion
dī	modifying plural nouns
dihk	a drop of
dūk	for excrement
ga	for a vehicle
gàan	for a certain place or a building
gàn	a catty of
gihn	for clothes

go	for people
gyún	a roll of
jek	for animal or people
jēun	a bottle of
jèung	a sheet of
tìuh	(slang) for people
tùhng	a roll of
wái	(polite form) for a person

6. Others:

e.g.	for example
i.e.	that is
lit.	literally
/	or
;	different meanings or separating two different entries
(...)	enclosing: (1) English explanation; (2) an optional Cantonese word; (3) an optional English word; (4) a Chinese character for illustration; (5) a romanization for illustration
"..."	for a dialogue or quotations from books
→	inserted between the paired clauses of a HIT or: leads to another meaning
,	(1) inserted between paired clauses; (2) used to indicate two separate syllables in the romanization
Hit	(Hithauhyúh / Kithauhyúh) enigmatic parallelism, tail-less pun
《 》	enclosing the name of a book in Chinese
「...」	emphasizing a special term
[ ]	enclosed within brackets

7. Expressions which are considered vulgar or insulting are marked with a # after the expression and readers are advised not to use them.

List of Entries

1. Appellations about people

Wùhlèihjìng 狐狸精 1

Daaihgū 大姑 2

Taaitáai 太太 2

Sàamgū Luhkpòh 三姑六婆 4

Baatpòh 八婆 4

Sailouh 細路 6

Sailóu 細佬 6

Daaihlóu 大佬 6

Dauhdēng 豆丁 8

Fógei 伙記 10

Fótáu 伙頭 10

Sìfó 私伙 10

Màhlātlóu 麻甩佬 12

Yihsaijóu 二世祖 13

Wòhsihlóuh 和事老 14

A-Fūk 阿福 16

Fūktàuh 福頭 16

Yàuhpéhng Jái / Néui 油瓶仔/女 17

A-Chà 阿差 18

Mōlōchà (Mōlōchàai) 摩囉差 18

Daaihyíhlūng 大耳窿 18

2. Human personality

Jìyàuh 滋油 20

Wùlúng 烏龍 21

Fáandáu 反斗 22

Wán Jàugùng 搵周公 22

Sūkgwāt 縮骨 24

Màhngsāk 萌塞 26

Jìujik 招嘖 27

Gùhòhn 孤寒 28

Yìhhèi 兒戲(兒嬉) 30

Ngaahnggéng 硬頸 32

Séingàuh Yātbihn Géng 死牛一便頸 32

Ngàuhgéng 牛頸 32

Gòudau 高竇 34

Lahkdau 簕竇 34

Hàahmsāp 鹹濕 36

Māfù 馬虎 38

3. About nature

Ńghhàhng Him Dá 五行欠打 39

Yātmaht Jih Yātmaht, Nohmáih Jih Muhksāt
   一物治一物，糯米治木虱 40

Baatgwa 八卦 42

Jìsih 滋事 42

Jìsih Baatgwa 滋事八卦 42

M̀sàam M̀sei 唇三唇四	44
Jai M̀jai 濟唔濟	46
Jaidākgwo 濟得過	46
Jaim̀gwo 濟唔過	46
Deihséui 地水	48

4. About language

Gwādauh 瓜豆	49
Gwāchàaih 瓜柴	49
Gwā Lóuhchan 瓜老襯	49
Sàamchèuhng Léuhngdyún 三長兩短	50
Dùnggwā Dauhfuh 冬瓜豆腐	50
Lódáu 攞豆	51
Singgwā 勝瓜	52
Jyūleih 豬脷	52
Gātngūk 吉屋	52
Yàyàwū (Yàhyàhwū) 吔吔烏	54
Dínggwāgwā 頂呱呱	54
Fèihlóu 肥佬	56
Sàjí 沙紙	56
Jaahpbālāng (Jaahpbālāang) 雜崩能	58
Hahmbahlaahng 冚辦冷	58
Lāausūnglóu 咾鬆佬	59
Ngoihgōnglóu 外江佬	59
Lóuhgéui 老舉	60
Sàmpóuh 心抱	62

Pòuhtàuh 浦頭	62
Séuipèih 水皮	64
Ngàuhyāt 牛一	64
Gùnjih Léuhnggo Háu 官字兩個口	66
Sīk Jih Tàuhseuhng Yātbá Dōu 色字頭上一把刀	66
Sàanyàhn Jih Yáuh Miuhgai 山人自有妙計	68
Chyun 串/寸	70
Chè Daaihpaau 車大炮	71
Chètīn Chèdeih 車天車地	71
Yāttàuh Mouhséui 一頭霧水	72
Tòuh Gújéng 淘古井	74
Sòujàusí 蘇州屎	75
Sáuméih 手尾	75
Yáuh Mòuh Yáuh Yihk 有毛有翼	76
Syùngēungkíuh 酸薑蕎	78
Màauhgānjūk 茅根竹	78
Sihdaahn 是但	80
Bunyeh Chèuhn (Chàh) 半夜巡(茶)	80
Gàmtùhng Yuhk (Néuih) 金童玉(女)	80
Pèitàuh Sáan (Faat) 披頭散(髮)	80
Yìngtòuh Síu (Háu) 櫻桃小(口)	80
Lóuhyìhbāt 老而不	82
Wàih Lóuh Bātjyùn, Gaauwaaih Jísyùn 爲老不尊，敎壞子孫	82
Lóuhsyú Làaigwāi→Móuhdehng Màaihsáu 老鼠拉龜→冇定埋手	83

List of Entries   xxi

Nàih Pòuhsaat Gwogōng→Jihsàn Nàahnbóu
  泥菩薩過江→自身難保 85
Sihyàuh Lòufaahn→Jíngsīk (Jíng) Séui
  豉油撈飯→整色（整）水 87
Wòhng Daaih Sīn→Yáuh Kàuh Bīt Ying 黃大仙→有求必應 .. 89
Dálaahn Sàpùhn Mahndou Dūk 打爛砂盤問（璺）到篤 90
Fuhngjí Sìhngfàn 奉子（旨）成婚 90
Sih Gāp Máh Hàahng Tìhn 事（士）急馬行田 90
Jáugāi 走雞（機） 90
Chìhntòuh Chíh Gám 前途似噉（錦） 90
Maaihyùhlóu Sáisàn→Móuhsaai Sènghei
  賣魚佬洗身→冇晒腥（聲）氣 92
Fósìu Kèihgōn→Chèuhng Taan 火燒旗桿→長炭（嘆） 92
Daahngālóu Dájiu→Móuh Tàahn 蛋家佬打醮→冇壇（彈） 92
Sauchói Sáugān→Bàau Syù 秀才手巾→包書（輸） 92

5. About Canton

Jyūyihsíng 朱義盛 94
Paaktō 拍拖 95
Jáamlaahm 斬纜 95
Lāttō 甩拖 95
Hàau Jūkgong 敲竹杠 96
Sàinàahm Yih Baakfú 西南二伯父 98
Bòlòhgāi→Kaau Chì 波羅雞→靠黐 99
Maaih Jyūjái 賣豬仔 100
Wūlēi Dàandōu 烏利單刀 102

6. Culture and customs

Jeukhéi Lùhngpòuh Dōu M̀chíh Taaijí
著起龍袍都唔似太子 104

Sihk Gáu Daaih Gwái 食九大簋 104

Ngàhyīn 牙煙 106

Sihk Chāt Gam Sihk 食七咁食 108

Daaihmòuh Sīyeuhng 大模尸樣 110

Jāplāp 執笠 111

Jouhdūng 做東 112

Tipcho Mùhnsàhn 貼錯門神 114

Jí Héui Jàugùn Fongfó, Bātjéun Baaksing Dímdāng
只許州官放火，不准百姓點燈 115

Yātlàuh 一流 117

Gáulàuh 九流 117

Sahpnìhn (Dōu) M̀fùhng Yātyeuhn 十年(都)唔逢一閏 118

Lohksáu Dá Sàamgāang 落手打三更 119

Lohkbāt Dá Sàamgāang 落筆打三更 119

Néih Jouh Chòyāt, Ngóh Jouh Sahpńgh
你做初一，我做十五 121

Bīuchēng 標青 123

Gèngchēng 驚青 123

Kàhmchēng (Kàhmkàhmchēng) (Kàhmkámchēng) 噙青 123

Wán Kaausàan 搵靠山 125

Séui Wàih Chòih 水爲財 126

Mahnbūi 問杯 127

Jouh Galéung 做架樑 128

List of Entries   xxiii

Giuh Chèuhnggeuk 撬牆腳 129

Jèung (PN) Gwàn 將(某人)軍 130

Dàudūk Jèunggwān 兜篤將軍 130

Haapchou 呷醋 132

Gànhùhng Díngbaahk 跟紅頂白 133

Wòhng Máh'kwá 黃馬褂 134

Baahk Beihgō 白鼻哥 134

Sá Fàchēung 耍花槍 135

Hahpsaai Hòhchē 合晒合尺 136

Lèihpóu 離譜 136

Johngbáan 撞板 136

Dohkkíu 度喬 138

7. Historical figures

M̀sái Mahn A-Gwai 唔使問阿貴 140

Yahpmàaih (PN) Sou 入埋(某人)數 142

Yáuh Fànsou 有分數 143

Yáuh Fànchyun 有分寸 143

Jouhdou Jek Kehk Gám 做到隻屐噉 144

M̀jicháu 唔知醜 146

Yāt Bātjouh, Yih Bātyàu 一不做，二不休 148

Lìhngse 零舍 150

Lìhngse M̀tùhng 零舍唔同 150

Dáiséi 抵死 152

Dái (PN) Séi 抵(某人)死 152

Jítìn Dūkdeih 指天篤地 154

Yātméi Kaau Jí 一味靠指 154

Jadai 詐帝 156

Gīgī Gahtgaht 嘰嘰吃吃 157

Háu Gahtgaht 口吃吃 157

Báauséi 飽死 158

Báauséi Hòhlāan Dáu 飽死荷蘭豆 158

Jengdáu 正斗 160

Sīk Yìnghùhng Juhng Yìnghùhng 識英雄重英雄 162

Jouh Chēungsáu 做槍手 164

Chéngchēung 請槍 164

Kèh Làuhwòhngmáh 騎劉皇馬 166

Yātgo Yuhn Dá, Yātgo Yuhn Ngàaih 一個願打，一個願捱 .. 168

Lātsōu 甩鬚 170

Diugá 丟架 170

Āauwū/Ngāauwū 丫烏 171

Tok Daaihgeuk 托大腳 172

Chaathàaih 擦鞋 172

Jáu Hauhmún 走後門 173

Louhchēut Máhgeuk 露出馬腳 175

Chóh Láahngbáandang 坐冷板櫈 177

8. Myths and folklore

Wahtdaht 核突 178

Baingai 蔽翳 179

Taaiseui Tàuhseuhng Duhng Tóu 太歲頭上動土 181

Lóuhfú Tàuhseuhng Dèng Sātná 老虎頭上釘虱乸 181

List of Entries

Chésin 扯線 183
Ngàaihdou Gàmjìng Fó'ngáahn 捱到金睛火眼 184
Fèiṁchēut Ngóh Sáujíla 飛唔出我手指罅 185
Chìhnsai 前世 186
Chìhnsai M̀sàu 前世唔修 186
Gwojó Hói Jauh Haih Sàhnsīn 過咗海就係神仙 187
Chídeih Mòuh Ngàhn Sàambaak Léung 此地無銀三百兩 189
Séuigwái Sìng Sìhng'wòhng 水鬼升城隍 191

9. About animals

Mōkgwòng Jyū / Mōk Gwòngjyū 剝光豬 193
Waihsihkmāau 爲食貓 194
Sihk Séimāau 食死貓 194
Laaimāau 賴貓 194
Chēutmāau 出貓 197
Ngàuh Séi Sung Ngàuh Sōng 牛死送牛喪 199
Gagāi Chèuih Gāi, Gagáu Chèuih Gáu 嫁雞隨雞，嫁狗隨狗 . . 200
Yātyàhn Dākdouh, Gài'hyún Gàai Sìng
  一人得道，雞犬皆升 201
Sihk Mòuhchìhnggāi 食無情雞 203
Cháau Yàuhyú 炒魷魚 203
Chèuigūk 催谷 205
Tìhnngáap 塡鴨 205
Yàhnsàm Bātjūk Sèh Tàn Jeuhng 人心不足蛇吞象 207
Yàhnsàm Móuh Yimjūk 人心冇厭足 207
Hàahmyú Fàansàang 鹹魚翻生 209

Daaihtàuhhā 大頭蝦 210

Sātwàhnyú 失魂魚 210

Yātháaih Bātyùh Yātháaih 一蟹不如一蟹 211

Gwa Yèuhngtàuh Maaih Gáuyuhk 掛羊頭賣狗肉 212

10. Argots used among triads

Màhnjéuk 文雀 213

Sàamjeksáu 三隻手 213

Tiufūi 跳灰 214

Tòhdéi 陀地 214

Gam Jegū 撳鷓鴣 215

Jūk Wòhnggeuk Gāi 捉黃腳雞 215

Wùhlèihjìng 狐狸精#

Wùhlèihjìng

N   woman of easy virtue, an enchantress (lit. a fox demon) [M: jek, go]
擅於迷惑男人的女人

e.g. Gójek wùhlèihjìng ngāuyáhn ngóh lóuhgùng.
嗰隻 狐狸精 勾引 我 老公。
(That bad woman seduced my husband.)
（那壞女人引誘我丈夫。）

Legend has it that the last ruler of the Shang dynasty was very fond of pretty women. He indulged in the beauty of Táan Géi. She led him into such evil ways that he only lived for the pleasure of women and wine day and night. She even instigated him to kill loyal officals. People suffered from tyranny so much that they were all angry with him.

Gèi Faat revolted against the tyrant and overthrew the Shang dynasty. After Táan Géi was executed, her body turned into its real shape, a thousand-year-old fox which had nine tails.

The above story can be found in *The Metamorphoses of the Gods*, a very famous novel of the Ming dynasty. There is another well-known novel *Strange Stories from a Chinese Studio*, in which many stories are about foxes which can turn themselves into beautiful women to seduce men.

據小說《封神榜》說，商代的紂王好色，他被美女妲己迷惑。妲己教他日夜飲酒玩樂，又慫恿他殺害忠臣，虐待百姓，弄得天怒人怨。姬發起兵革命，滅了商朝。當妲己被斬殺時，她的屍首化為一隻九尾狐狸。

在小說《聊齋志異》裏，也有許多狐妖化身美女迷惑男人的故事。

Daaihgū 大姑；Taaitáai 太太

Daaihgū

N   an address for an elderly woman [M: wái, go]
通常用以稱呼五六十歲的女人

e.g.   Síufáan heung séuhngjó nìhngéi ge néuihyán dàu sàangyi ge
小販　向　上咗　年紀嘅　女人　兜　生意　嘅

sìhhauh wúih wah, "Daaihgū, yáuh māt bòngchan a?"
時候　會　話「大姑，有　乜　幫襯　呀？」

(A hawker calling out for patronage will say to an elderly woman, "Hey daaihgū, may I help you?")
（小販向上了年紀的婦女招徠生意的時候會說：「大嬸，你有甚麼買嗎？」）

Taaitáai

N   Mrs. (originally a title of respect for the wives of the officials in ancient China); wife [M: wái, go]
古代是對官員的妻子的尊稱，今日則稱呼結了婚的女士

e.g.   Nīgo haih ngóhge taaitáai.
呢個　係　我嘅　太太。

(This is my wife.)
（這位是我的妻子。）

In the Han dynasty, there was a lady who excelled in both learning and conduct named Bàan Chìu (A.D. 25–88). Her elder brother, Bàan Gu, was the author of *The History of the Han Dynasty* which he did not complete before dying. The emperor then assigned the task to Bàan Chìu. She finished it successfully. Later, she was invited by the emperor to teach the ladies in the palace. They respected her so much that they all addressed her as Daaihgū which originally meant "a learned woman". However, these days in Hong Kong, ladies, especially those in the upper class, do not like to be called Daaihgū. They prefer to be addressed as Taaitáai.

在漢代，有一位學問和品格都極好的女子，名叫班昭（公元25-88）。她的哥哥是寫作《漢書》的班固。但是班固死時，《漢書》還未完全寫成。皇帝命令班昭接手寫，結果完成了。皇帝又請班昭進皇宮教導宮中的婦女，各人都尊稱班昭為「大家」（這裏「家」讀「姑」），意思是有學問的人。

在香港，有些女士（尤其上流社會的女士）不喜歡被人稱作「大姑」。不如叫聲「太太」好了。

Sàamgū Luhkpòh 三姑六婆；Baatpòh 八婆#

Sàamgū Luhkpòh

N women who are low in social status and morality [M: dī, bāan]
一些身分低下、品格行為也不太好的婦女

e.g. Góbāan sàamgū luhkpòh, néih m̀hóu kwàhnmàaih kéuihdeih a!
嗰班 三姑 六婆，你 唔好 羣埋 佢哋 呀！
(Don't associate with those bad women.)
（那幫壞女人，你不要跟她們來往。）

Baatpòh

N a vulgar term of abuse addressed to a woman [M: go, tìuh]
辱罵婦女的話語

e.g. Séi baatpòh!
死 八婆！
(Damn you!)
（潑婦，臭婆娘）

Sàamgū: 1. Buddhist nun; 2. Taoist nun; 3. female diviner.
Luhkpòh: 1. a slave broker; 2. a match-maker; 3. a witch; 4. a procuress, a woman in charge of a brothel; 5. a woman doctor; 6. a midwife.

In the Yuan dynasty, people were classified into ten grades: 1. officials; 2. civil officers; 3. Buddhist monks; 4. Taoist monks; 5. doctors; 6. workmen and labourers; 7. craftsmen; 8. prostitutes; 9. scholars; 10. beggars. Being in the eighth grade, prostitutes were abused as Baatpòh.

三姑： 1. 尼姑（比丘尼）、2. 道姑（女道士）、3. 卦姑（主持占卜的）。

六婆： 1. 牙婆（販賣人口的中間人）、2. 媒婆（媒人）、3. 師婆（巫婆）、4. 虔婆（鴇母，即妓院的主持）、 5. 藥婆（醫生之類）、6. 穩婆（接生婦）。

八婆，原義是娼婦。元代把人民按職業分為十等：官、吏、僧、道、醫、工、匠、娼、儒、丐。排在第八的是娼。

Sailouh 細路；Sailóu 細佬；Daaihlóu 大佬

Sailouh

N   children, kids [M: go]
小孩

Sailóu

N   younger brother [M: go]
弟弟

Daaihlóu

N   elder brother [M: go, wái]
兄長

The head of a triad gang is also addressed as Daaihlóu. He will call the man under him Sailóu.
黑社會頭目也稱手下為「細佬」，手下則稱頭目為「大佬」。

e.g.   Kéuih haih ngóh sailóu, ngóh haih kéuih daaihlóu.
佢　係　我　細佬，我　係　佢　大佬。

(He is my younger brother and I'm his elder brother.)
（他是我的弟弟，我是他的哥哥。）

Both Sailouh and Sailóu meant "little boy" in ancient China. We can find in *The Book of History* that when King Móuh, the first ruler of the Chou dynasty, introduced his younger brother, he said, "This little boy is my younger brother named Fùng." The recent implication of Sailouh (i.e. little boy) can also be used as an intimate term for one's own younger brother by changing Louh into Lóu.

In *The Mencius*, it says, "Both Baak Yìh and Taai Gùng are the two venerable elders below heaven." Obviously, Daaihlóuh (i.e. the venerable elders) is a respectful term for the aged. It is very common for the Cantonese people to change the tone of Lóuh into Lóu. Thus, a new Cantonese character was created for it.

細路、細佬，本應寫作「細孥」，古漢語是「小子」。《尚書》：「朕其弟，小子封。」（周武王說：「這是我的弟弟阿封。」）小子，指小孩子，但兄長也用來稱呼成年的弟弟，表示親愛。

　　大佬，本作「大老」，古代用來尊稱年歲、輩份最高的人。《孟子》：「（伯夷、太公）二老者，天下之大老也。」

　　「老」（lóuh）讀「佬」（lóu），是「變調」，廣東話口語詞常有這種現象。

Dauhdēng 豆丁

Dauhdēng

N: small children [M: go]

e.g. M̀hóu hà dī dauhdēng saigo, yáuhsìh kéuihdeih juhng lēkgwo
唔好 蝦啲 豆丁 細個，有時 佢哋 仲 叻過
daaihyàhn.
大人。

(Don't bully children because they are small [and naive]. Sometimes they can do better than adults.)
（不要欺負小孩年紀小，有時候他們比大人更能幹。）

Do you know how to solve Chinese riddles? I would like to give you two word puzzles to work out:

1. 他們失了踪

   (They are found missing.)

   Tips: "missing" refers to "people". The solution would be the name of a country in Asia.

   Can you guess it? It is Yemen (i.e. 也門 with their radical "人" dropped).

2. 豆丁

   (The solution is supposed to be a special kind of people.)

   Can you guess it? It is "a child" (i.e. 豎子, an appellation of children in ancient times. If you cut out the upper part of both characters, you will get the form of 豆丁(Dauhdēng), which means "small children".

你懂猜中國謎語嗎？現在請你猜兩個字謎：

1. 謎面：他們失了踪。（猜一個亞洲國家的名字）
   提示：「失了踪」即是「人」不見了。
   猜到嗎？謎底是「也門」。

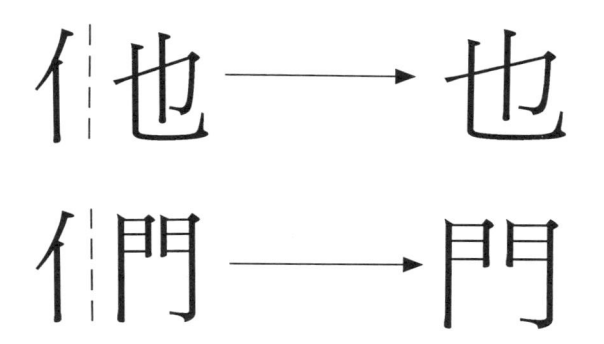

   他 ⟶ 也
   們 ⟶ 門

2. 謎面：豆丁（猜某一類人）
   猜到嗎？謎底是「小孩子」。
   原來古代叫小童做「豎子」，「豆丁」就是半個豎子，也就是很矮的小孩。

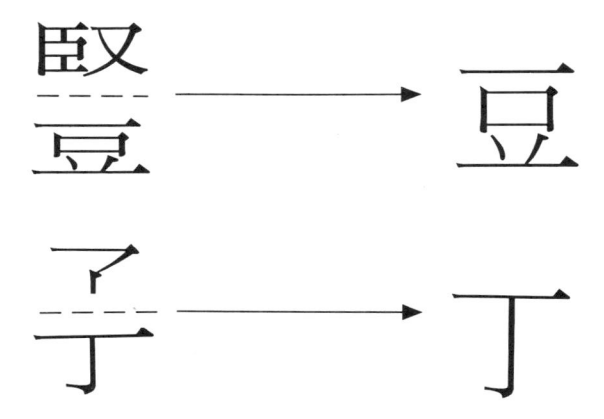

   豎 ⟶ 豆
   子 ⟶ 丁

Fógei 伙記；Fótáu 伙頭；Sìfó 私伙

Fógei

N waiter (in a teahouse); employee (in a shop); address used among policemen [M: go]
茶樓裏的服務員；店鋪的僱員；警察對同伴的稱呼

e.g. Hái chàhlàuh màaihdāan ge sìhhauh, ngóhdeih wah, "Fógei, màaihdāan."
喺 茶樓 埋單 嘅 時候 我哋 話 「伙記，埋單。」

(When we are going to leave the teahouse, we'll say, "Waiter, my bill please.")
（在茶樓要結賬時說：「服務員，結賬。」）

Fótáu

N a cook [M: go]
廚子

e.g. Dī fógei sìyìh go fótáu dá fútàuh.
啲 伙記 思疑 個伙頭 打 釜頭。

(The cook was suspected of keeping some of the money for buying food by his colleagues.)
（僱員懷疑廚子吞佔了部分菜錢。）

Sìfó

N private belongings [M: dī]
屬於私人的財物

e.g. Yātgo dihnsih ngaihyùhn deui dī yùhlohk geijé wah, "Ngóh hái nītou kehkjaahp sódaai ge sáusik, dōuhaih sìfó yéh làih ga."
一個 電視 藝員 對 啲 娛樂 記者 話 「我 喺 呢套 劇集 所戴 嘅 首飾 都係 私伙 嘢 嚟 㗎。」

(A TV actress told the entertainment reporters, "All the jewels that I wore in this serial are my own [things].")
（一個電視藝員對娛樂記者說：「我在這劇集中所戴的首飾全都是自己的。」）

Fó is a unit of ten soldiers in ancient China. The one who is responsible for cooking is called Fótáu. Soldiers in the same unit will call one another Fógei. Gei is an empty morpheme* serving as a suffix in this word. Things that can be used by everyone in the same unit are called "gàfó", and things belonging to one's own self are sìfó.

There was a man called Sit Yàhn Gwai in the Tang dynasty. He was born to be strong and brave. Because he had to eat so much, no one wanted to hire him. He then joined the army and worked as a cook. Later, he achieved great distinction and became a general. Therefore, we also say that a cook is a "fótáu jèunggwàn".

在古代，軍士每十人一組，稱爲「火」。「火」有管生火煮食的人，就是「火頭」。同火的人是「伙記」。「記」字沒有意思，是個詞綴。「伙記」等於說「同火啊」。同一火的人，許多物件是共用的，這些工具就叫「傢伙」。而不屬於眾人的財物，就是「私伙」。

唐朝有個叫薛仁貴的人，天生神力，但是食量太大，沒有人肯僱用他。他便投軍當伙頭，後來立了大功，升爲將軍。所以「伙頭將軍」便是「廚子」。

---

* empty morpheme: a word that has no meaning of its own, see Y. R. Chao, *A Grammar of Spoken Chinese* (University of California Press, Berkeley and Los Angeles, 1968), p. 196.
見任學良，《漢語造詞法》(中國社會科學出版社，北京，1981)，pp. 31-33。

Màhlātlóu 麻甩佬#

Màhlātlóu

N   a man one despises [M: go, tìuh]
對男人的鄙視的稱呼

e.g.   Dī màhlātlóu háu fàfà, hóu hātyàhnjàng.
啲　麻甩佬　口花花，好　乞人憎。
(Those men who flirt all the time are disgusting.)
（那些男人說輕佻話，眞討厭。）

There is a famous Jyuhn K èih* of the Tang dynasty called *A Slave from Kwānlèuhn* or *The Negrito Slave*. It tells about a young man falling in love with a beautiful concubine of a high official. The old servant of the young man was from Kwānlèuhn. One night, he carried the young man on his back and climbed over the wall. They crept into the official's residence to meet the beautiful lady. Later, the old servant helped the lady to get out of the official's residence to marry the young man. In the Tang dynasty, rich people liked to make slaves of people from the country of Kwānlèuhn (i.e. India or Malaya). They had curly hair and dark skin. Canton has always been the main entrance of business and trading with Southeast Asia. Some of the Malayans wandered to China. They made a living by working as servants. Formerly they were called Kwānlèuhn lòuh. Lòuh means slave or servant. But Cantonese people knew that they were Malayan. Thus, they called them Màhlātlóu (lóu: a man, fellow).

　　　唐代有篇著名的傳奇小說《崑崙奴》，大意說有個青年愛上了大官家裏的美女，青年的老僕人 —— 崑崙奴 —— 就在夜裏背着青年翻過牆頭，潛進官第和美女相會。後來老僕人救出美女，她和青年結了婚。

　　　唐代富豪喜歡以「崑崙國」人作奴隸，他們頭髮卷曲，皮膚黝黑。原來他們來自今日的印度或馬來亞。廣州一向是中國對東南亞商業貿易的大門，有些馬來人流浪來到中國，就做人家的奴僕。以前叫他們「崑崙奴」，但是廣州人知道他們是馬來人（Malayan），就叫他們做「麻甩佬」。

* Jyuhn kèih(síusyut): novel, a type of prose romance in the Tang dynasty.

Yihsaijóu 二世祖[#]

Yihsaijóu

N   a descendant of the rich who only enjoys himself by squandering money [M: go]
終日玩樂和揮霍金錢的富家子弟

e.g.   Gógo yihsaijóu baaihsaai kéuih lóuhdauh fu sàngà.
嗰個 二世祖，敗晒 佢 老豆 副 身家。

(That richman's son threw away all the wealth of his father.)
（那不肖子把他父親的家產都亂花光了。）

Chinese people esteem their ancestors very much. In the past, famous clans all had their own pedigree to keep a record of every male in the clan, excluding the female. The first ancestor was called "chíjóu" or "yātsaijóu". His heir was "yihsaijóu" (i.e. the second), and then "sàamsaijóu" (i.e. the third), "seisaijóu" (i.e. the fourth) ... and so forth.

    Yihsaijóu was not a derogatory term. But in Chinese history, there was a good-for-nothing emperor who was the second. The First Emperor of Chin (reigned: 221-210 B.C.) was an extremely capable ruler. He conquered the other six states and unified China. He was the founder of the Chin dynasty. He hoped that his achievements could last forever up to many many generations. Therefore he called himself Chí Wòhngdai. When his son succeeded him to the throne, he was called Yihsai Wòhngdai (i.e. Chin Emperor II). Who was to know that he was a stupid man? The Chin dynasty was destroyed within a few years.

    中國人重視「根」。以往，大家族都有自己的族譜，記載家族中每一名男丁（女子不予記錄）。家族的開創者稱爲「始祖」或「一世祖」，他的繼承者稱爲「二世祖」，以後是三世祖、四世祖……「二世祖」原來沒有貶義，可是歷史上出現過一個很不肖的二世皇帝。

    話說雄才大畧的秦始皇帝（公元前221-210在位）掃平了六國，統一天下，開創秦朝。他以爲自己的功業可以傳至萬代的子孫，於是他自稱「始皇帝」，而他的兒子繼位則稱「二世皇帝」。誰知二世皇帝是個白痴，幾年間就把國家亡了。

Wòhsihlóuh 和事老

Wòhsihlóuh

N   a mediator, a peacemaker [M: go]
爲他人解決紛爭的中間人

e.g. Kéuihdeih léuhng gùngpó ngaaigāau, néih heui jouh wòhsihlóuh lā.
佢哋　兩　公婆　嗌交，你　去　做　和事老　啦。

(The couple had a quarrel. Please go and help them make up.)
（他們夫婦倆吵架，你去做個中間人調解一下吧。）

During the Warring States Period, there was a chivalrous man called Lóuh Juhng Lìhn who was very fond of being a mediator. The state of Chèuhn sent its army to attack the state of Jiuh. Jiuh then asked for the help of other feudal kings. But they were all so afraid of Chèuhn that they dared not intervene. The king of the state of Ngaih even sent an envoy to advise Jiuh that it would be better to recognize Chèuhn as emperor. When Lóuh Juhng Lìhn heard that, he went to see the envoy. He succeeded in persuading him that Chèuhn was unreliable. Later, the king of Chèuhn realized that the feudal kings had united, so he gave up the invasion against Jiuh and withdrew his troops.

Wòhsihlóuh may refer to Lóuh Juhng Lìhn. Some people say it may refer to Sàam Lóuh, the title of an official in ancient China. The government appointed some old men of good moral standing and reputation in a village to be the Sàam Lóuh. Actually they were peacemakers, responsible for all the affairs of the village and for mediating and judging the arguments of the villagers. Now we do not have such officials. But it is still a custom that the head of a clan or the seniors of a village will be requested to act as mediator.

戰國時代，有個俠士叫魯仲連，專好替人排難解紛。當時秦國出兵攻打趙國，趙國向其他諸侯求救，但諸侯怕秦國而不敢行動，魏王甚至派使者勸趙奉秦為帝。魯仲連去見魏使者，說服了他，令他明白秦國是不可信任的。秦國知道諸侯團結起來，也就捨棄趙國而退兵。

　　「和事老」可能指魯仲連。另一個說法，是指「三老」官。古代政府在鄉村選派一些德高望重的老人任「三老」，負責排解糾紛。鄉村的大小事務、鄉民的爭執對錯，都由「三老」調停或判決。現代雖然沒有「三老」官，但鄉村人請族長父老作中間人的風俗仍然存在。

A-Fūk 阿福#/Fūktàuh 福頭#

A-Fūk/Fūktàuh

N   sucker, a fool (lit. a blessed man) [M: go]
愚蠢人

e.g.   Gàmchi béi yàhn wán lóuhchan, jouhjó a-fūk.
今次 俾 人 搵 老襯, 做咗 阿福。

(This time I'm a fool because others have taken advantage of me.)
（這次被人家騙了，做了笨蛋。）

Sōu Dùng Bō (A.D. 1036-1101), a famous poet in the Sung dynasty, was a man of genius. He could write smoothly and fluently in a short time. But he was not successful in his political career and was demoted and exiled quite a number of times. Three days after his son was born, he wrote a poem:

> All people wish that their sons will grow up to be extremely clever,
> But just because I'm clever I've been suffering all my life.
> I want only a stupid and foolish son,
> And I hope he will become a court minister in stability.

As the saying goes, "A fool is always a blessed man." As we know, Wahn Deuhn (see p. 178) was much happier before he got his eyes, ears, nose and mouth. As soon as he got all the organs on his face, he became clever. Yet he died shortly after. So, can you understand the irony that Sōu Dùng Bō employed in composing the above poem?*

宋朝詩人蘇東坡（公元1036-1101）生性聰明，寫文章如行雲流水，但他在仕途上頗不得意，屢遭貶謫。他在兒子出生三日時寫了首詩：

> 人皆養子望聰明，我被聰明誤一生。
> 唯願孩兒愚且魯，無災無難到公卿。

所謂「庸人厚福」，所以笨蛋等於福頭。你看，渾沌（見頁178）未有眼耳口鼻之前是多麼快樂，到他給鑿了七竅，耳目聰明，就立即死了！

---

* See Ronald C. Egan, p. 250.

Yàuhpéhng Jái/Néui 油瓶仔/女#

Yàuhpéhng jái/néui

N   stepchild on mother's side [M: go]
一個失婚婦人帶同子女再嫁，那些小孩就被稱爲「油瓶仔/女」

e.g. Gógo gwáfúh tò léuhnggo yàuhpéhng jái gabéi Chánbaak.
嗰個 寡婦 拖 兩個 油瓶 仔 嫁俾 陳伯。

(That widow, along with her two sons of her dead husband, married old Mr. Chan.)

（那寡婦帶着兩個跟前夫所生的小孩，嫁進陳伯伯家。）

Yàuhpéhng is an oil bottle given free when one goes to buy oil from a hawker. Thus, it is a metaphor for those children who are brought to a man by his wife from her first marriage.

    There is another more interesting interpretation. In the past, people regarded marriage as a kind of trade. Once a poor man was dead, his widow would be sold by his family in order to get money to live on. The buyer and the seller had to sign a contract, and usually, it would be written in the contract that the child/children of the widow was "yáuh behng" (sick) for fear that the old kinfolks of the child/children would try blackmail in case of their sudden death. After a long time, people pronounced it as Yàuhpéhng by mistake. Note that Yàuhpéhng jái/néui is derogatory. However, it is not so for the stepchild/stepchildren on the father's side.

    油瓶，是盛油的瓶，在買油的時侯，由小販免費附送，於是比喻娶妻時，由妻子「送」來的現成的孩子。

    另一個說法較有趣：舊時流行買賣式的婚姻，假如某窮人家的兒子死了，爲了過活，就把死者的寡妻賣給另一戶人。買主和賣主要簽署文件。在那份文件上，常常將寡婦帶來的小孩稱爲「有病」的小孩。那樣寫，是預防將來小孩夭折，而小孩的舊日親屬來追究要挾。時日久遠，人們把「有病」訛作「油瓶」，就出現了所謂「油瓶仔」或「油瓶女」。

A-Chà 阿差#/Mōlōchà(Mōlōchàai) 摩囉差#；Daaihyíhlūng 大耳窿

A-Chà/Mōlōchà(Mōlōchàai)

N   Indians or Pakistanis [M: go]
      印度人或巴基斯坦人

e.g. Mōlōchà baaisàhn→tái tìn/mohng tìn dágwa.
      摩囉差　拜神→　　睇天/望　天 打卦。

(lit. when the Indians worship their god, they look at the sky. But actually it is a hithauhyúh (see p. 83) meaning all depends on the weather or to boringly long for a chance to come.)

Daaihyíhlūng

N   loan-shark [M: go]
      放高利貸的人

e.g. Chìnkèih m̀hóu je daaihyíhlūng dī chín a!
      千祈　唔好 借　大耳窿　啲　錢　呀！

(Be sure not to borrow money from the loan-sharks.)
（千萬別借高利貸。）

Early in Hong Kong history (1842-1949), the British government employed a lot of Indians to work as policemen. People called them Mōlōchàai. Mōlō is the changed sound of the first two syllables of "Pòhlòhmùhn" (Brahmanism). In ancient times, India was also called "Pòhlòhmùhn gwok". Chàai is the short form of "chàaiyàhn" (i.e. a policeman). Today in Hong Kong, there are very few Indian policemen, but we still call the Indians A-Chà, having the Chàai changed into Chà.

    The first loan-sharks in Hong Kong were also Indians. Because they liked to wear big round earrings, they were called Daaihyíhlūng (lit. big ear hole). Usually when people borrowed money from others, they had to pay 10-20% interest. But the Indian loan-sharks would demand 13 dollars back when the time was due for just lending you nine dollars. Now there are very very few of them. Instead, most of the Daaihyíhlūng are Chinese triad gangs.

香港開埠初期（1842-1949），英政府找來許多印度人當警察，俗稱「摩囉差」。「摩囉」是「婆羅門」Brahmanism的變音，以前印度也稱為「婆羅門國」。而「差」是「差人」，即警察。今天已很少印度人在香港當警察，但我們習慣上仍叫印度人做「阿差」。

　　香港早期放高利貸的人，也是印度人。由於他們喜歡戴上有大圓圈的耳環，所以就稱為「大耳窿」。民間一般的借貸，利息約一至二分（10-20%），但大耳窿要「九出十三歸」，即貸出九元，到期要收回十三元。今日已很少印度人放高利貸，「大耳窿」多是華籍黑社會分子。

Jìyàuh 滋油

Jìyàuh

SV   unhurriedly, leisurely, slowly
處事從容不迫

e.g.   Waih, jouhyéh sóngsáudī, m̀hóu gam jìyàuh lā!
喂，做嘢爽手啲，唔好咁滋油啦！

(Hey! Hurry up. Don't be so slow.)
（唏！做事要快，不好慢吞吞的！）

It is said in *The Book of Changes* that one would be considered marvelous if one appreciated the subtleties and the wonder of all things. Even a small change would be a good omen. When a clever man sees a small change, he is able to predict the occurrence of a great event. When he "knows" (i.e. jì) the "weak" (i.e. yàuh), he can predict the "strong". Such a wise man is qualified to be the leader of all people.

    Small twigs will grow into thick branches. Everything is very weak and soft at the beginning. But it will become stronger and stronger, just like the growth of a tree. When a person realizes the development of all the things and know what is going to happen, he can prepare well for it. He can just do it leisurely. He is said to be Jìyàuh. But the two characters were replaced by another two which literally mean "to lubricate [with] oils".

    滋油，本寫作「知柔」。

    《易經》說：「知幾其神乎！……幾者動之微，吉之先見者也。……君子知微知彰，知柔知剛，萬夫之望。」大意說：知曉事理的微妙之處真是了不起啊！微妙的變化就是吉祥的先兆。聰明人看見了小事，就預測到大事；知曉了柔弱，就預測到剛強。這樣的聰明人就是萬民的領袖。

    正如一株樹的生長，由柔嫩的小枝到粗壯的樹幹，事物都是由柔到剛的。「知柔」就是掌握了事物發展的原則，成竹在胸，所以處事從容不迫。

Wùlúng 烏龍

Wùlúng

SV/N   muddled [M: chi, go]
       糊塗

e.g. Kéuih jingyāt wùlúngwòhng, sìhngyaht báai wùlúng.
     佢   正一   烏龍王，   成日   擺   烏龍。

(He's really a muddled person. He always gets everything mixed up.)
（他是個糊塗蟲，整天弄錯事情。）

The family of Confucius considered rites very important. Habitually, a son should mourn a dead mother who had married someone else. But Jí Sì, the grandson of Confucius, did not allow his son to mourn his dead mother who had divorced Jí Sì. Someone asked him about this and he replied, "A virtuous man will take it very seriously (i.e. to 'lùhng' which now changed to Lúng). But as for me, I'm not that virtuous, so I just take it casually (i.e. to Wù)."

So we can see the original meaning of Wùlúng is to be adaptable and try not to be stubborn. But people may misunderstand you and think you are too muddled.

    孔子的家族是很重視禮的，習慣上，兒子會爲改嫁別姓的母親守喪。但是子思（孔子的孫）的前妻死了，子思卻不叫兒子爲她守喪。有人拿這事問子思，他答：「道隆則從而隆，道污則從而污。」意思是道德好的人認眞做，道德差的人馬虎點。

    烏龍，本寫作「污隆」，意思是看情況而有所升降，並不執着。但是這樣做事容易引起誤會，人家以爲你太糊塗了！

Fáandáu 反斗；Wán Jàugùng 搵周公

Fáandáu

SV   mischievous, naughty
指小孩子貪玩頑皮

e.g.   Sailóugō m̀hóu gam fáandáu.
細路哥 唔好 咁 反斗。

(Don't be so naughty, you little boy.)
（小孩不要頑皮。）

Wán Jàugùng

VO   go to bed
去睡覺

e.g.   Ngóh heui wán Jàugùng kìnggái.
我 去 搵 周公 傾偈。

(I'm going to bed.) (lit. I'm going to have a chat with Jàugùng.)
（我去睡覺。）

Both expressions have something to do with Confucius (551–479 B.C.). We can read in *The Historical Records*, or *Records of the Historian*, that when he was a child, he liked to play the game of the sacrificial ceremony. He needed a ceremonial vessel called "Dauh" to play with. Nowadays Fáandáu is used to mean "naughty", while originally it meant to learn through games. Note that the pronunciation has been changed. Cantonese people would say Fáandáu rather than "wáandauh".

Since childhood, Confucius liked to learn and practise all kinds of rites for different ceremonies. He greatly admired Jàugùng (or the Duke of Chou, around 1122 B.C.) who established rules and customs for the people of the Chou dynasty. Even when Confucius was asleep, he always dreamt of Jàugùng. Therefore, Wán Jàugùng became an expression meaning "to go to bed".

這兩個詞語都和孔子有關。《史記》說孔子（公元前551-479）小孩時玩耍，常擺設豆，作行祭禮的樣子。我們叫小孩「玩豆」，原本是說他像孔子一樣，從遊戲中學習。後來被誤作頑皮貪玩的意思。

　　孔子喜歡習禮，而周公（約公元前1122）是周代創製禮的人，所以孔子很崇拜周公，甚至睡覺時也常夢見周公。他在《論語》中說：「久矣吾不復夢見周公！」於是「搵周公」成了「睡覺」的代詞。

Dauh: a ceremonial apparatus used in a worshipping ceremony
豆：祭祀用具

Sūkgwāt 縮骨

Sūkgwāt

SV   selfish and cunning (lit. shrinkable bones)
     狡猾

e.g. Kéuih sìhngyaht wán yàhn jeuhksou, yíngjàn sūkgwāt.
     佢　成日　搵　人　着數，　認眞　縮骨。

   (He always thinks of taking advantage of others. He's really selfish and cunning.)
   （他整天想着佔便宜，眞靠不住。）

A man of broad figure surely has longer bones. A man of shorter bones must be short. A short man may lose in fighting, but he will always use tricks.

During the time of the Spring and Autumn Annals, there had been a prime minister in the state of Chàih called Ngaanjí. He was less than five feet tall, but he was a man of strategy. There were three warriors in Chàih. They were famous for their bravery, and they were quite dangerous because they were likely to rebel. Ngaanjí sent somebody to give them two peaches and told them to share the peaches according to their bravery.

Two of the warriors snatched the peaches. The third one took out his sword and was ready to fight. The two warriors said, "We are not as brave as you, but we are still brave enough to kill ourselves." After saying these words, they killed themselves. Regretting that the two warriors died just because of two peaches, the third warrior also killed himself.

Ngaanjí killed three warriors just by using two peaches. How terrible he is!

骨骼長的一定身材高大，骨骼短了的當然是矮子。矮子在打架時吃虧，但他往往會使用狡計。

　　春秋時代齊國的宰相晏子身高不滿五尺，但很有計謀；那時齊國有三個武士，以有勇氣聞名，而且有作亂的危險。晏子便派人送給三人兩個桃子，叫他們自己按勇氣的大小來分吃。

　　第一、二個武士都搶着拿了桃。第三個武士拔劍站起來，準備打鬥。兩個武士說：「我們的勇氣不及你，但是我們還有自殺的勇氣。」兩人說完就自殺死了。第三個武士見爲爭桃子而害了兩條性命，心裏悔恨，也跟着自殺了。

　　晏子祇花費兩個桃子便殺掉三個武士，多麼厲害！

Màhngsāk 萌塞

Màhngsāk

SV   stubborn and not flexible
     頭腦不靈活，古板

e.g. Yìgā jouh yàhn yiu hòitùngdī, m̀hóu gam màhngsāk.
     伊家做人要開通啲，唔好咁萌塞。

(Be open-minded and flexible. Don't be so stubborn.)
（如今做人要開通點，不要太古板。）

Mencius (372-289 B.C.) said that men are born with four good natures. They are: mercy, feeling of shame, humility and the ability to distinguish right from wrong. These four good human natures can develop into four virtues, i.e. humanity, righteousness, propriety and wisdom.*

But if a man does not care about them, these four good natures will be hidden and will disappear. He gave us a parable, "The path on the hill will remain a road[+] if people walk on it often. But if nobody goes by that road for a long time, couch grass (i.e. Maàuhchóu, which has become Màhng) will grow on it and the path will be covered. Mind that your heart is not filled with couch grass!"

Màhngsāk refers to the growth of the couch grass which suffocates (i.e. sāk) our hearts. In that case, there is no room in our hearts and we shall not be clever then.

孟子（約公元前372-289）說人有四種天生的善性，就是惻隱之心（同情心）、羞惡之心（憎厭罪惡的心）、辭讓之心（謙讓的心）和是非之心（辨別對錯的心）。這四種善性可以發展成「仁、義、禮、智」四種美德。可是人不注意修養，這四種善性就會被蒙蔽、埋沒。孟子打了個比喻：「山間的小路，常常有人走在上面就成了路，但有一段時日沒有人走過，茅草就塞住了它。現在茅草塞了你的心呢！」

「萌塞」，就是說茅草萌生，塞住了人的心，那麼人就太不聰明了。

* the translation is taken from *Tai Chen on Mencius*, p. 154.
[+] "road" or "path" can be viewed as the symbolic term for "the Confucian way", "the way of man" or "the way of Heaven".

Jìujik 招嘖

Jìujik

SV   disgustingly proud in one's speech or behaviour
     態度囂張，行為過分

e.g. Nīgo yàhn góngyéh hóu jìujik, tèngdou ngóh jokngáu.
     呢個 人　 講嘢　好 招嘖，聽到　 我　作嘔。

(This man talked too proudly and made me sick.)
（這人說話態度囂張，討人厭。）

In ancient times, there was a filial girl named Fà Muhk Làahn. Once, her father was drafted by the government for military service because there was a war. She was very worried because her father was already old. It was written in the *Song of Muhk Làahn*:

> We can't hear the sound of the shuttle of the loom
>   when Muhk Làahn is weaving,
> But Jīkjīk again and again
>   We can hear her sighing.

Later, there was a folk-tale about her disguising herself as a man and going to battle on behalf of her father. Jīkjīk is the sound of someone sighing, implying sadness, lament or dissatisfaction. When a person behaves too proudly, he will Jìu (lit. arouse, invite) the Jīk (i.e. sigh of dissatisfaction) of others.

　　古時有個女子叫花木蘭的，她的父親被朝廷徵召去打仗，木蘭見父親年紀已老，就很替父親擔心。《木蘭辭》裏這樣寫着：「唧唧復唧唧，木蘭當戶織，不聞機杼聲，唯聞女歎息。」後來就有了「花木蘭代父從軍」的故事。

　　「唧唧」是歎息的聲音，內裏也包含愁苦、悲痛和不滿的情緒。「唧」也可以寫作「嘖」。

　　廣州話裏的「招嘖」，是說某人的所作所為太過分了，招致大眾不滿的歎息聲。

Gùhòhn 孤寒

Gùhòhn

SV   miserly, mean, stingy
十分孤寒

e.g. Jīngyāt gùhòhngwái, sái yātgo sīn dōu m̀sédāk.
正一 孤寒鬼，使 一個 仙 都 唔捨得！

(What a miser! He is not willing to spend even one cent.)
（孤寒鬼，一文錢也不肯花。）

The above example is especially used for rich misers. According to its original form, it meant to pretend to be poor in order to fool other people. During the Warring States Period, a man called Sèui Gá was sent to the state of Chèuhn as an ambassador. In an inn, he met his former subordinate Faahn Jèui who was wearing shabby clothes and looked very poor. Sèui Gá sighed and said, "Mr. Faahn, are you really that poor? I just can't believe it." He treated him to a meal and gave him a robe.

    The next day, Sèui Gá paid an official visit to the prime minister of Chèuhn. To his great surprise, the prime minister turned out to be Faahn Jèui. Once when Faahn Jèui worked under Sèui Gá, he was nearly beaten to death just because he did something wrong. Later, he fled to Chèuhn and changed his name. He convinced the king of Chèuhn and became the prime minister. He learned that Sèui Gá would come and wanted to kill him. So, in the disguise of a poor man, he went to the inn to test him. Seeing that Sèui Gá was so kind to him, Faahn Jèui changed his mind and let him go. Now we can see the development of Gùhòhn: pretend to be poor → miserly.

孤寒，原應寫作「沽寒」。沽是出賣，也帶有欺騙的意思。沽寒即擺出寒酸的樣子去騙人，引申成一毛不拔。

　　戰國時，須賈出使到秦國，在客舍裏遇見以前的一個舊部下范睢。范睢衣衫襤褸，樣子很可憐。須賈留他吃飯，感歎地說：「范叔貧寒到這個地步嗎！」於是取一件袍送給范睢。

　　第二天，須賈謁見秦國宰相，出乎意料，秦相竟然是范睢。原來范睢以前當須賈的部下時，因爲小誤會，須賈使人打范睢，打得半死。范睢輾轉逃來秦國，更換姓名，游說秦王，竟然當了秦相。范睢知須賈來出使，便故意裝貧寒去試探須賈。范睢本想殺掉須賈，但見他肯念舊情和送衣袍，便放過了他。

Yìhhèi 兒戲（兒嬉）

Yìhhèi

SV   unreliable, not serious (lit. playing like the kids)
　　不認眞，像小孩子玩耍

e.g. Nīgàan muhk ngūk héidāk hóu yìhhèi, dáfùng jauh wúih lam.
　　　呢間 木 屋 起得 好 兒嬉，打風 就 會 冧。

（This wooden house is not safely built. It will fall if there is a typhoon.）
（這間木造的房子建造得不堅固，颱風來時便會塌下。）

Emperor Màhn, the third ruler of the Han dynasty who reigned from 179 to 156 B.C., wanted to know more about his troops. So he personally went to conduct an inspection of the two barracks Bah Seuhng and Gīk Mùhn. When he and his attendants rode to the two barracks by horse, no one stopped them, and they entered very smoothly.

　　Later, he went to the Sai Láuh Barracks. The soldiers there were all armed and were intensively on guard. He wanted to go in but the guard at the entrance would not let him in. He then sent a man to give the military warrant to the commander general and told him that the emperor would like to conduct an inspection of the barracks. After a while, the commander general ordered the soldiers to open the gate, but they would not allow the emperor to ride on his horse inside the barracks because of their regulations. Then Emperor Màhn and his attendants had to dismount their horses and walk. Finally, Emperor Màhn saw the commander general. He greatly appreciated his strict discipline. He sighed and said, "Oh, this is what a real commander general should be! The soldiers of the two barracks that I went to before were just like kids playing."

漢文帝（公元前179-156在位）要了解軍隊的情況，親自去到霸上和棘門兩處軍營視察，他和侍從騎馬直入營內，完全沒有受到攔阻。稍後，他來到細柳營，這處的軍士都全副武裝，高度戒備。文帝想進營裏，但守門的軍士不放他進來，他只好派使者拿信物見將軍，說明是皇帝來巡視。一會兒，將軍傳令開門，但軍士又不准文帝等人騎馬進營，說是軍營的規矩。他們只好下馬步行。文帝最後見到將軍，對他治軍的嚴格很讚賞。「啊，這位才是真正的將軍！先前霸上、棘門的軍隊，只是兒戲罷了！」文帝感慨地說。

Ngaahnggéng 硬頸/
Séingàuh Yātbihn Géng 死牛一便頸/
Ngàuhgéng 牛頸

Ngaahnggéng/Séingàuh Yātbihn Géng/Ngàuhgéng

SV/PH   stubborn, tough, unyielding
個性倔強，不肯屈服

e.g. Néih yiu tèng yàhn hyun, m̀hóu gam ngaahnggéng/séingàuh yātbihn
你 要 聽 人 勸，唔好 咁 硬頸/ 死牛 一便
géng lā.
頸 啦。

(You should listen to the advice of others. Don't be so stubborn.)
（你要聽取人家的勸告，不要那麼倔強。）

Ngaahnggéng (lit. stiff neck) is the modern way of saying "stubborn", while in ancient times, it would have been "kèuhnghohng" (lit. strong neck). There is a story about a "strong neck" official in *The History of the Later Han*.

    A man called Dúng Syùn was the governor of Lok Yèuhng, somewhat equivalent to the present day mayor of Peking. One of the servants of the Wùh Yèuhng princess killed a person and then hid in her palace. Thus the police responsible for this case was unable to catch him. One day the princess had to go out. She told that servant to accompany her on the carriage. Dúng Syùn went and stopped her carriage. He criticized the princess for protecting her servant and killed the servant right in front of her. The princess went to the emperor in tears to complain. The emperor became angry and called for Dúng Syùn. He wanted to flog him to death. Dúng Syùn said to the emperor, "How can you rule the country if Your Majesty spoil the wicked people and kill the good ones?" After saying that, he banged his head against a pillar and his face was covered with blood. The emperor told the guards to stop him. He then told Dúng Syùn to apologize to the princess and kowtow, but Dúng Syùn refused to obey. The guards pressed his head and forced him to kowtow. Dúng Syùn propped his head up by strongly pressing the ground with his hands and did not yield at all. Finally, the emperor set him free and bestowed on him three hundred thousand coins.

「硬頸」是現代口語詞，古代叫「強項」。《後漢書》有個「強項令」的故事：

董宣是洛陽令（相當於今日的北京市長）。有次湖陽公主的家奴殺了人，匿藏在公主家裏，辦案的衙差捉不到他。一次，公主出外，叫那家奴在車上陪伴，董宣就在半路上攔住車子，斥責公主的過失，當場殺了家奴。公主向皇帝哭訴，皇帝大怒，召董宣來，想鞭死他。董宣說：「皇上縱容惡人殺好人，怎能治理天下？」說着就自己用頭撞楹柱，血流披面。皇帝叫侍衛制止他，又叫董宣向公主叩頭道歉，但董宣不肯。侍衛用力按着董宣的頸，逼他叩頭，董宣就用兩手拼命撐住地面，不肯屈服。最後，皇帝釋放了這個「強項令」，還賜了三十萬錢給他。

Gòudau 高竇；Lahkdau 簕竇

Gòudau

SV proud of oneself and look down upon others
自高自大，看不起人

e.g. Gógàan baakfo gùngsī dī sauhfoyùhn hóu gòudau,
嗰間 百貨 公司 啲 售貨員 好 高竇，

gin néih jeukdāk chàdī jauh m̀haih géi jìufù néih.
見 你 着得 差啲 就 唔係 幾 招呼 你。

(The salesmen in that department store would look down upon you and not give you satisfactory service if you dress too casually.)
（那百貨公司的售貨員瞧不起人，看見你穿的衣服差一點就不大理睬你。）

Lahkdau

SV tough, hard to cope with
難於對付的人

e.g. Kéuih go yàhn hóu lahkdau.
佢 個 人 好 簕竇。

(He's a very tough man.)
（他這人很難對付。）

Dau is a cavity and by extension, a place where one lives. Some eccentric people do not like to associate with others. They grow many thorny plants outside their houses so that people cannot easily get close to them. This is what we call Lahk (lit. thorn) Dau.

During the last years of the Eastern Han dynasty, there was a very famous scholar called Chàhn Dāng. He was a learned and capable man. He was always ready to render service to the country and to the people. Once, a man visited him, but he despised the visitor because he was so vulgar. So Chàhn Dāng slept on a high bed and let his guest sleep on a low bed. Since then, Gòudau became the alternative for "proud".

竇，本指洞穴，引申為棲身的地方。有些人性情孤僻，不喜歡和別人來往，就在竇（家）的外面種許多有刺的植物，阻止外人接近，這就是「範竇」。

　　東漢末年，有位名士叫陳登，他很有才華，常想為國家民族做點事。一次，有客人造訪他，但他看不起這客人的鄙俗。於是他自己睡在高的大床上，讓客人睡矮的床。從此「高竇」就成了驕傲的代詞。

Hàahmsāp 鹹濕

Hàahmsāp

SV   (said of a man) dirty, nasty, randy, lascivious (lit. salty and wet)
（男人）好色

e.g. Deihtit yáuh hóudò hàahmsāp lóu, sìhnggèi bokmúng.
地鐵　有　好多　鹹濕　佬，乘機　博懵。

(There are many nasty men on the MTR, waiting for chances to molest women.)
（地下鐵路的車廂裏有許多色迷迷的男人，伺機佔女乘客便宜／非禮女乘客。）

Hàahmsāp might be regarded as the implicit way of saying Hahlàuh, which means "morally bad". *The Book of History* tells us the nature of water, which goes, "Yeuhn *hah* jok hàahm." (When it flows down, it nourishes everything that grows on earth and gives us salt.) In the *I Ching*, we learn from the explanatory notes by Confucius that "Séui *làuh* sāp." (Water runs to low land and makes it wet.) People just picked the last word of the two sentences to refer to those nasty men.

There is a Hithauhyúh (see p. 83) "yìhmchōng tóudéi" (lit. the god of the storehouse for salt)→"Hàahmsāp Baakfú" (i.e. a dirty old man).

Salt may has something to do with Hàahmsāp. Let us read a story:

During A.D. 265, the northern part of China was the kingdom of Jeun and the southern part, Ǹgh. The emperor of Ǹgh kept three thousand beautiful girls in his palace. Later, Ǹgh was destroyed by Jeun and those beautiful girls were all taken over by the new emperor. Having so many women, he did not know which one to choose. He rode on a cart driven by a goat. He would spend the night at the girl's place where the goat stopped. All the girls sprinkled salty water on the ground to make the goat come and stop at their place. So the emperor can be regarded as the first Hàahmsāp Lóu!

「鹹濕」是「下流」的隱語。《書・洪範》：「潤下作鹹。」《易・乾文言》：「水流濕。」水向下流動時會帶來鹽分，而水也會聚於低濕之處。

有句歇後語叫「鹽倉土地→鹹濕伯父」。不過「鹹濕」可能是「鹽水」的隱語，它有個故事：

在公元265年，中國北方是晉國，南方是吳國。吳王後宮有三千個美女。後來晉武帝滅吳，把美女都接收過來。因爲宮中女人太多了，他不知挑哪個，就乘坐羊車，羊走到那處停下來他就在該處過一夜。宮女紛紛在路面灑上鹽水，引羊舔着走來。所以晉武帝是第一個「鹹濕佬」。

Māfù 馬虎

Māfù

SV   careless or not serious in doing things
做事糊塗，不認眞

e.g.   Kéuih jouhyéh māfù, béi lóuhbáan cháau kéuih yàuhyú.
佢 做嘢 馬虎，俾 老闆 炒 佢 魷魚。

(He was not serious in his work and so he was fired by his boss.)
（他工作不認眞，被東主解僱了。）

Once there was a painter who liked to draw tigers. One day, just as he finished drawing a tiger's head, a man came to commission a picture of a horse from him. So he painted the body of a horse beneath the tiger's head. The man asked him what it was. The painter said, "If you think that it looks like a horse, then it is a horse. If you think that it looks like a tiger, then it is a tiger. Ha Ha! A horse or a tiger; it makes no difference!"

The man did not want to buy that painting. So the painter put it in the living room of his house. When his elder son saw it, he asked what it was. The painter replied casually, "It's a horse." Then, his younger son saw the picture and also asked what it was. The painter answered carelessly, "It's a tiger." Later, his younger son saw a horse on the street. He thought it was a tiger and shot it dead with an arrow. When his elder son saw a tiger in the woods, he thought it was a horse. He wanted to ride on it, but he was killed by the tiger. From then on, people called the painter Mr. Māfù.

　　據說古時有個畫家，很喜歡畫虎。一天，他剛畫了個虎頭，有客人來求他畫馬，他就在虎頭下加了個馬身。客人問牠是甚麼，畫家答：「你看牠似馬，牠就是馬；你看牠似虎，牠就是虎。哈哈！馬馬虎虎。」客人不肯買那幅畫，畫家就把它掛在自家的廳堂。畫家的大兒子見了，問是甚麼，畫家隨口答：「是馬。」過了一會，畫家的小兒子見了，問是甚麼，畫家又隨口答：「是虎。」後來，小兒子在街上看見匹馬，以為是老虎，就用箭把牠射死了。大兒子在樹林看見老虎，以為是馬，就想去騎牠，結果給咬死了。從此，大家就稱畫家為「馬虎先生」。

Nǵhhàhng Him Dá 五行欠打

Nǵhhàhng Him Dá

I.E. Someone should be given a beating because of his bad attitude
指某人的態度惡劣，令人惱怒得想揍他一頓

e.g. Kéuih gam jiujik, gánghaih nǵhhàhng him dá la.
佢　咁　招噴，梗係　　五行　欠 打 嚕。

(He is so boastful that I just want to give him a beating.)
（他那麼囂張，真想揍他。）

Chinese people observe that there are five common elements in the universe: metal, wood, water, fire and earth. They are as a whole called Nǵhhàhng: "the Five Elements" or "the Five States of Being". They are very much interrelated. When metal is heated, it melts into liquid. Water can make plants grow. We get fire when we burn twigs. After the wood is burnt, it becomes ashes which will become soil or earth. From the earth, we can dig out gold. This special cyclical relation among them is called "the mutual growth of the Five Elements". It will be considered as imperfect if any one of them is missing. If we say that you lack (i.e. Him) gold or water, we mean that you are in need of money. If someone wants to beat (i.e. Dá) you, then he will say that you are Nǵhhàhng Him Dá.

　　古人留意到天地間有五種最常見的事物，就是：金、木、水、火、土，合稱「五行」。它們彼此關係密切。金（金屬）受熱熔化爲液體，水滋潤樹木生長，樹木燃燒就生火，火會生灰，灰屬於泥土，而泥土中可以掘出金礦。

　　古人叫這種關係做「五行相生」。如果五行中欠了某一樣，就不完美。「五行欠金/水」，意思是沒有錢。再轉一種說法，就產生「五行欠打」這俗語。

Yātmaht Jih Yātmaht, Nohmáih Jih Muhksāt
一物治一物，糯米治木虱

Yātmaht Jih Yātmaht, Nohmáih Jih Muhksāt

I.E. One thing is controlled by something else, and so it is with people too. (lit. meaning of the latter part: glutinous rice can kill wood louse)
某種東西（或人）總有它的剋星

e.g. Tái m̀chēut kéuih gam daaihjek, daahnhaih gam pa lóuhpòh, jànhaih
　　 睇　唔出　佢　咁　大隻，　但係　　咁怕　老婆，　　眞係

yātmaht jih yātmaht, nohmáih jih muhksāt lo.
「一物　治　一物，　糯米　治 木虱」咯。

(He's so strong, yet he's so afraid of his wife. Truly he has his wife to control him.)
（沒想到他身型高大，卻那麼怕太太，眞是「一物治一物」了。）

We have talked about the mutual growth of the Five Elements. Now I would like to talk about the mutual control of them. As you know, the hatchet made of metal can cut wood. The roots of the trees can grasp the earth. A dam is built up of earth to prevent a flood. We can put out fire with water and we can also use fire to melt metal.

　　Chinese people believe that there is nothing in the world that is uncontrollable or unbeatable. Everything is controlled (i.e. jih) by some other thing. But can a wood louse be killed by glutinous rice? The answer is "No". People just put rhymes to these two sentences and make them easier to say and easier to remember.

　　前面談過「五行相生」，今次談談「五行相剋」。我們知道，金屬製的斧頭可以砍樹木，樹木的根抓着泥土，用土築堤可以防止水淹，水可以滅火，而火可以燒熔金屬。

　　中國人相信，世上沒有無敵的東西，反之，任何東西都有它的剋星。但是糯米是不是眞的可以消滅木虱？答案是：不可以。人們只是隨便把兩句押韻（物、虱）的話連起來，好唸好記吧了。

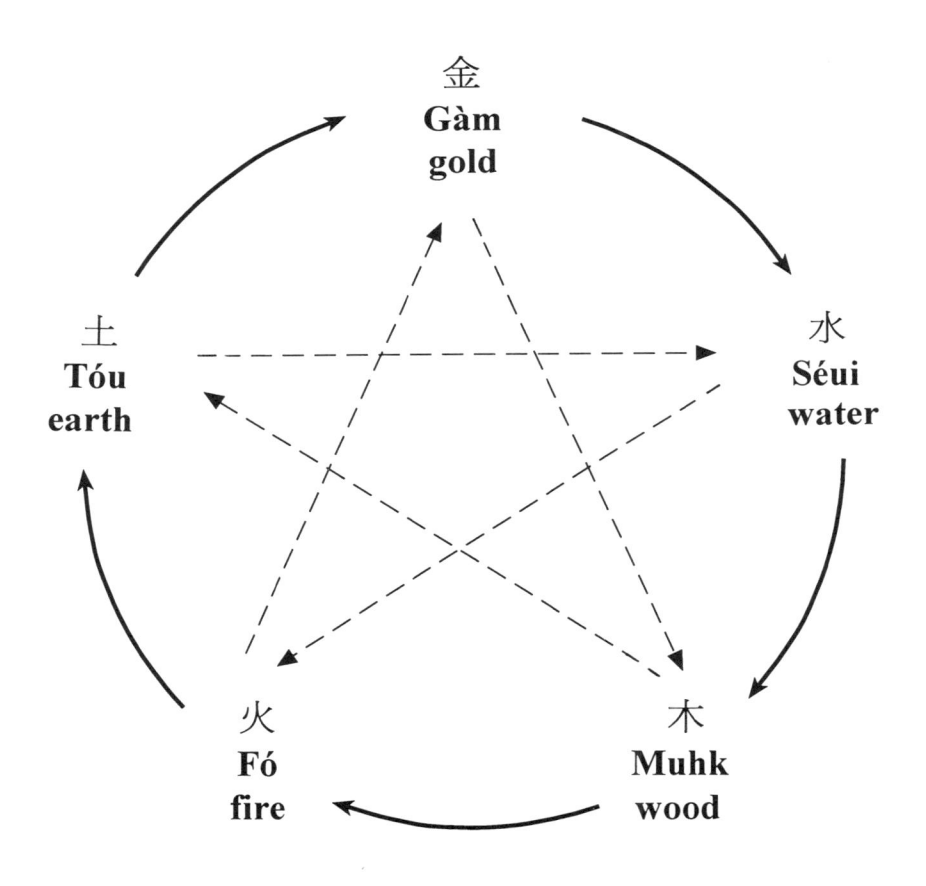

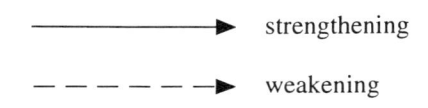

```
         金
         Gàm
         gold

 土                           水
 Tóu                         Séui
 earth                       water


    火                     木
    Fó                    Muhk
    fire                  wood
```

———▶ strengthening

- - - ▶ weakening

Baatgwa 八卦/Jìsih 滋事/
Jìsih Baatgwa 滋事八卦

Baatgwa/Jìsih/Jìsih Baatgwa

SV   nosy, too curious to know the secrets of others
即好奇心強，愛打探人家的祕密

e.g.   1. Sailouhjái, m̀hóu jìsih baatgwa.
      細路仔，唔好 滋事 八卦。

(When a child is admonished by an adult, he will be told, "Don't be nosy, you little boy.")
（小孩子不要多管閒事。）

e.g.   2. Kéuih hóu jùngyi tái dī baatgwa jaahpji.
      佢　好　中意 睇啲　八卦　雜誌。

(She likes to read gossip magazines.)
（她很喜歡看報導名人及藝員新聞的雜誌。）

e.g.   3. baatgwapó or simply: baatpòh
      八卦婆　　　　　八婆

(a vulgar term for nosy woman)
好管閒事的婦女

The original meaning of Baatgwa is the eight trigrams which can be found in *The Book of Changes* or *I Ching*, the oldest oracle book in ancient China. Each of the eight trigrams is composed of three broken or unbroken lines. They symbolize different things in the world (see the figure on next page). Ancient Chinese people matched them up to make 8 × 8 = 64 hexagrams, each of which had six lines. Furthermore, 384 (i.e. 64 × 6) changes of all the things in the universe are indicated according to the arrangement of the hexagrams. Many Chinese will consult a fortune-teller if they are anxious to know about their fate or to decide whether to do something. Thus, Baatgwa/Jìsih/Jìsih Baatgwa leads to what we mean today: nosy, too curious (to know).

中國最古老的一本占卜書──《易經》，記載了八卦，分別象徵天地間不同的事物：天、澤、火、雷、木、水、山、地（見圖）。中國人把八卦重疊排列（8×8），得出64卦，每卦又有6爻，於是代表（64×6 = 384）種宇宙事物變化的情況，可以推測未來，占問吉凶。由於八卦有衍生知事的作用，所以出現「滋事八卦」。

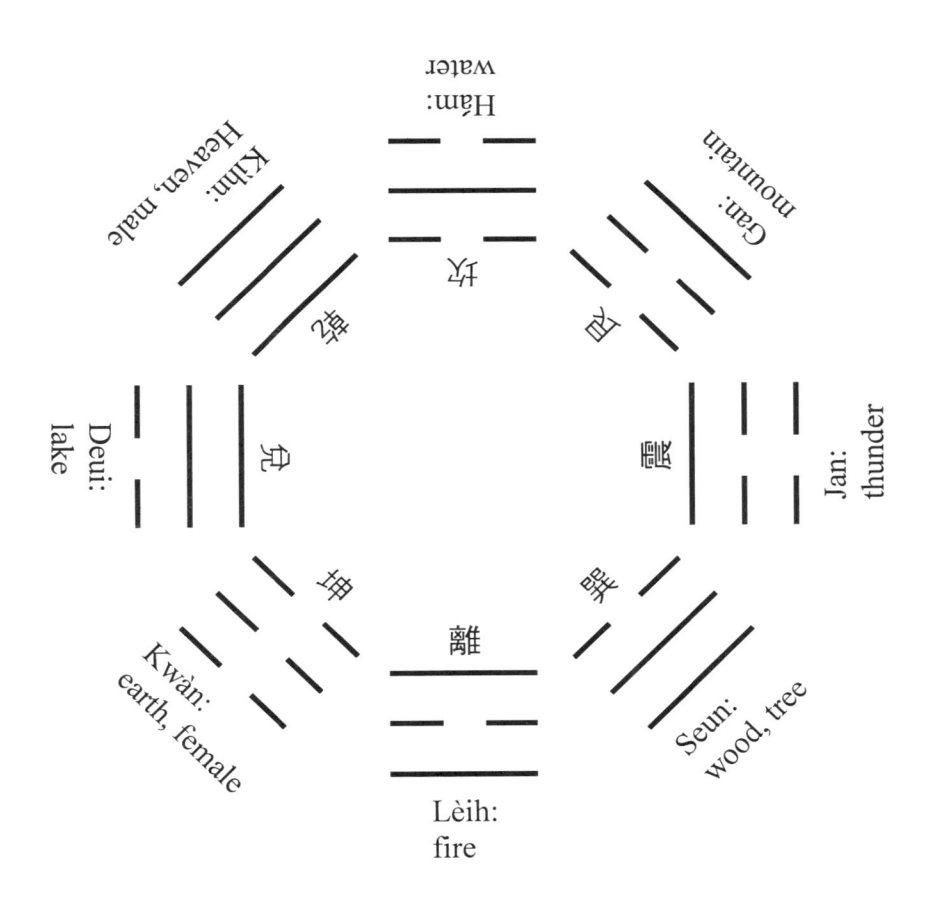

八卦圖：

- Kìhn: Heaven, male（乾）
- Hām: water（坎）
- Gan: mountain（艮）
- Deui: lake（兌）
- Jan: thunder（震）
- Kwǎn: earth, female（坤）
- Seun: wood, tree（巽）
- Lèih: fire（離）

M̀sàam M̀sei 唔三唔四

M̀sàam M̀sei

ADJ.PH　improper
　　　　即不三不四，指人不安於本份

e.g.　M̀hóu tùhng dī m̀sàam m̀sei ge yàhn lòihwóhng a!
　　　唔好　同　啲　唔三 唔四嘅　人　　來往　　呀！
　　　(Don't associate with those improper people.)
　　　（不要跟壞分子來往哩！）

In *The Book of Changes* or *I Ching*, there are 64 hexagrams each of which is composed of six lines. The lines symbolize different social status. The first and the top one is the symbol of the powerless people. The second line stands for a young official who has a promising future. The third represents a provincial governor. Looking forward to being a court official, he becomes impatient. He tries many good and bad ways to achieve his goal. The fourth is for a prime minister. He is the most powerful man just under the king. But he is also the one who will very easily offend the king. The fifth line symbolizes the ruler who has the absolute power of his kingdom. It says in the *I Ching* that the fourth line will make the prime minister worried (about the risk of offending the king) while the third one indicates the unfavourable situation of the provincial governor. So it is hard being in the third or in the fourth place as revealed in the hexagrams. People who are not satisfied with their present position and who will try many improper ways to attain their goal are criticized as M̀sàam M̀sei.

《易經》有六十四卦，每卦有六爻，每爻可以象徵一種身分地位。

　　初爻和上爻都是代表沒有權力的人。第二爻代表一個剛踏進仕途的青年人，前途光明。第三爻代表一個地方長官，常想著進身中央政府。第四爻代表宰相，他權力很大，但卻容易得罪國君。第五爻是掌握絕對權力的國君。

　　《易經》又說：「四多懼……三多凶。」可知處身在這兩個位置令人不好過。「唔三唔四」就是說：「三」那人不甘心做「三」，「四」那人不安於做「四」，引申爲心術不正、行爲差劣。

```
上：老人 Lóuhyàhn ―― the top: the aged
五：國君 Gwokgwān ―― the fifth: the ruler
四：宰相 Jóiseung ―― the fourth: the prime minister
三：省長 Sáangjéung ―― the third: the provincial governor
二：縣令 Yuhnlihng ―― the second: the governor of a county
初：平民 Pìhngmàhn ―― the first: common people
```

Jai M̀jai 濟唔濟；Jaidākgwo 濟得過；Jaim̀gwo 濟唔過

Jai M̀jai

PH   willing/agree to do it or not
願不願意做

Jaidākgwo

PH   worth doing
值得幹

Jaim̀gwo

PH   not worth doing
不值得幹

e.g. Kéuih séung tùhng ngóh gaapfán jouh sàangyi, mahn ngóh jai m̀jai.
佢 想 同 我 夾份 做 生意，問 我 濟唔濟，

Daahnhaih nījúng sàangyi bún dò leih síu, jaim̀gwo ge.
但係 呢種 生意 本 多 利 少，濟唔過嘅。

(He asks me if I am willing to join him to do business. But it's not worth doing the business that he wants to do because it needs much capital but can make only little profit.)
（他問我肯不肯跟他合作做生意？可是他想做的生意需要很多資金，利錢又少，我看還是不值得幹。）

The last two hexagrams in the *I Ching* are geijai (䷾) and meihjai (䷿). The former indicates "have already crossed the river" while the latter "have not yet crossed the river".

In ancient times, people regarded it as a great event to cross the river. Imagine in ancient times a person at the bank of a very rapid river and he had only very simple means, all he had in his mind is whether to go ahead and cross the river (i.e. Jai) or not (i.e. M̀jai). If he had confidence and considered it worth doing, he would give it a try. That is Jaidākgwo. Otherwise, it would be Jaim̀gwo.

《周易》六十四卦裏最後的兩卦是「既濟」（☲☵）和「未濟」（☵☲）。「既濟」是說「過了河」，「未濟」是「還沒有過河」。

　　在古代，渡河是大事。我們可以想像一下，古人面對洶湧湍急的河水，而只有簡單的渡河工具，這時，要冒險渡河呢？還是暫且不渡河呢？他們腦裏恐怕只有三個字「濟（渡河）？唔濟（不渡河）？」

　　如果考慮過，有信心一試，就是「濟得過」（願意去幹）。如果覺得不適宜做，就是「濟唔過」了。

Deihséui 地水

Deihséui

N   blind man [M: go]
　　盲人

e.g. Gógo deihséui cheung dī nàahmyām hóu hóutèng.
　　　嗰個　地水　唱　啲　南音　好　好聽。

(The blind man sings folk songs well.)
（那個盲人唱的歌很好聽。）

In Gwóngdùng province, there is a special kind of folk song called "Deihséui nàahmyām". Nàahmyām (lit. south tune) is a kind of folk song in Gwóngdùng. Deihséui is a blind (man) musician. There is one hexagram in the *I Ching* called "sī" which is composed of Deih (i.e. earth) and Séui (i.e. water). The arrangement of this hexagram is ䷆ and the explanation of it says, "There is water under the ground. So, this is the significance of sī." Sī can refer to "teacher", "troop" or "musician". In ancient times, almost all music masters* were blind men. The famous musicians Master Kwong* and Master Gyūn of the Warring States Period were blind.

Thus, Deihséui is a blind (man) musician and is now used to refer to all blind men.

　　在廣東，有一種由盲人唱的民謠，叫「地水南音」。「南音」意即中國南方的音樂。「地水」是盲人音樂師。《周易》六十四卦裏有個「師」卦（䷆），它由坎和坤組成（坎下坤上），坤是地，坎是水。卦象說：「地中有水，師。」

　　「師」字可解爲老師、軍隊，或音樂師。而在古代，音樂師都是由盲人擔任的，著名的音樂師如戰國時的師曠和師涓，都是盲人。

　　所以，「地水」指「師」，就是盲人樂師。今日也指盲人。

* See Vincent Yu-chung Shih, p. 77.

Gwādauh 瓜豆/Gwāchàaih 瓜柴/ Gwā Lóuhchan 瓜老襯

Gwādauh/Gwāchàaih/Gwā Lóuhchan

VO   to die
「死」的意思

e.g. Kéuih gwājó lóuhchan lo.
佢　瓜咗　老襯　囉。

(He is dead.)
（他死了。）

Cantonese people do not like to say the word "séi"* (i.e. to die). We try to use another word for it. The component "Gwā" in these three expressions is supposed to be "gwài", which means to go back, to return to a place. Gwādauh is the changed sound of "gwàidau" which means to go back to one's old home or to the hole under the earth. It also suggests that the dead should go back to the world before they were born or be buried under the earth. Gwāchàaih is also the changed sound of "gwàichòih" which means to go (back) to a coffin and lie in it. Gwā Lóuhchan is the third example of sound changing. Originally it should be "gwài lóuhchān", to go back to one's old kinfolks who are already dead.

　　中國人不喜歡提到「死」*，常常用其他話語代替。「瓜豆」是「歸竇」的轉音，即是回到老家或地穴的意思。暗示人死後回到未出生前的世界，或埋在地裏。

　　「瓜柴」是「歸材」的轉音，即是進棺材裏。

　　「瓜老襯」是「歸老親」的轉音，即是回到(已逝去的)年老親人的身邊。

* a taboo word in Chinese, 中文的禁忌語

Sàamchèuhng Léuhngdyún 三長兩短/
Dùnggwā Dauhfuh 冬瓜豆腐

Sàamchèuhng Léuhngdyún/ Dùnggwā Dauhfuh

I.E. to die
「死」的意思

e.g. Yùhgwó kéuih hái nīchi yingoih jījùng yáuh mātyéh
如果　佢　喺呢次　意外　之中　有　乜嘢

sàamchèuhng léuhngdyún/dùnggwā dauhfuh, gám jauh cháam lo.
三長　　兩短/　冬瓜　豆腐，咁　就　慘　咯。

(It would be too bad if he is dead in this accident.)
（假如他在此次意外中死了，就可憐啦。）

To avoid saying "séi" (i.e. to die), we will use some other indirect words for it.* We have talked about Gwādauh before. Dùnggwā Dauhfuh is a development of it. Some people say that Dùnggwā (i.e. winter gourd) and Dauhfuh (i.e. bean curd) are the offerings to the dead.

Sàamchèuhng Léuhngdyún is another way of saying coffin. People can see three long pieces (i.e. Sàamcheùhng) of wood and two short ones (i.e. Léuhngdyún) when the coffin is not yet covered with the lid.

為了避免說「死」，我們會轉個彎來表達意思。*

前面已談過「瓜豆」。「冬瓜豆腐」就從「瓜豆」變來，意思是「死」。另一種解法，冬瓜和豆腐都是拜祭死者的祭品。

至於「三長兩短」，說的是棺材。棺材蓋未蓋上前，人們看見三塊長木板和兩塊短木板。

* They are euphemisms, 委婉語

Lódáu 擺豆

Lódáu

FV   to die
　　　死

e.g. Go baakyēgūng heuijó lódáu lo!
　　　嗰　伯爺公　　去咗　擺豆　囉！

(The old man died.)
（老公公死了。）

The last ruler of the Shang dynasty (around 1066 B.C.) was a tyrant. Gèi Faat led the people to revolt against him. Baak Yìh and Sūk Chàih, the two old men, stopped him from doing so when he was on his way to fight with the tyrant. They remonstrated with him that he should not rebel against the ruler. At first, Gèi Faat wanted to kill them but finally he let them go owing to their loyalty.

Later, Gèi Faat overthrew the Shang dynasty and set up the Chou dynasty. The two old men refused to work under him. They hid themselves on a mountain and lived as hermits. They fed themselves with some wild peas they picked. Unfortunately, they died of hunger. So you can see the original implication of Lódáu (lit. to get peas) is to seek one's own death and by extension, to die.

商代末年（約公元前1066），紂王無道，姬發帶領人民革命。當時有兩個老人叫伯夷、叔齊的，攔着路勸阻，他們說姬發是紂王的臣子，不應該作反。姬發原本想殺了他們，但因爲尊重他們對商朝的忠心而放他們走。

後來姬發滅了商朝，建立周朝。伯夷、叔齊不肯做姬發的臣子，就躲到首陽山上，採拾野生薇豆來吃，結果餓死了。

「擺豆」，擺是拿取，豆指野薇豆。這語詞原義是自尋死路，轉化爲「死」。

Singgwā (sīgwā) 勝瓜；
Jyūleih (jyūsiht) 豬脷；
Gātngūk (hùngngūk) 吉屋

Singgwā (sīgwā)

N   luffa cylindrica, a kind of gourd which one can buy during summer season [M: go, gàn]
絲瓜

Jyūleih (jyūsiht)

N   the pig's tongue [M: tiuh]
豬舌

Gātngūk (hùngngūk)

N   an unoccupied house [M:gàan]
空置（沒人住）的房子

Cantonese people will avoid using a word which sounds like one suggesting something bad. Instead, they will use another word which has a good meaning. For example, the "sī" in "sīgwā" or the "syù" in "tùngsyù"* are phonetically similar to or even identical with the word "syù" meaning "to lose (in gambling)". "Tùngsyù" sounds like you will lose all. Therefore, they are changed to "sing" which means "victory". "Siht", the word for tongue, is pronounced the same as "siht", "to lose money (in business)". Businessmen do not like losing money. So we have "leih", profit, to replace "siht" for the tongue.

An unoccupied house or car is originally called a "hùngngūk" or a "hùngchè". "Hùng" is pronounced the same as "hùng" which means unlucky or haunted. Therefore, it has to be changed into "Gāt" (which means lucky, auspicious), the opposite of "hùng".

In Hong Kong, Lantau Island is called Daaih Yùh Sàan which sounds like "a big fish mountain" while the exact way of saying it is Daaih Jeuih Sàan which sounds like "a major sin mountain".

廣東人說話時，常常避用一些「不吉利」的字眼，改用「好意頭」的詞。絲瓜，讀音近於「輸瓜」，對於賭徒很不吉利。於是改爲「勝瓜」。同樣地，通書*改稱「通勝」。

　　舌，讀音同「蝕」。做生意最怕蝕本，所以豬舌改稱「豬脷」，牛舌稱「牛脷」，人的舌頭就叫「脷」。

　　空與「凶」同音，所以空屋改說「吉屋」，空車改說「吉車」。

　　香港有處地方叫「大嶼山」，原本應讀「大罪山」，但香港人取「與」字讀成「大魚山」算了。

* Tùngsyù: Chinese lunar calendar compiled in a book form.
　通書：中國民間所用的曆書

YàyàwūźYàhyàhwūć 吔吔烏；
Dínggwāgwā 頂呱呱

Yàyàwū źYàhyàhwū)

ADJ.PH　very low standard; not serious
　　　　很低劣的；不認眞

e.g.　Gógàan hohkhaauh béi gam síu yàhngūng, m̀gwaaidāk dī sìnsàang
　　　嗰間　學校　俾咁　少　人工，　唔怪得　啲　先生

　　　gaausyù yàhyàhwū lā!
　　　教書　吔吔烏　啦！

　　　(That school pays so low a salary that teachers do not teach seriously.)
　　　（那學校的薪水那麼低，難怪教師們教書不認眞了。）

Dínggwāgwā

PH　very good
　　最好的，非常好

e.g.　Kéuihge yìngmàhn dínggwāgwā.
　　　佢嘅　英文　頂呱呱。

　　　(His English is very good.)
　　　（他的英文非常好。）

Yàyàwū (Yàhyàhwū) is an exclamation originating in the northern part of China. It expresses disapproval or something not worth talking about. In Chapter 32 of *Gùnchèuhng Yihnyìhng Gei** (The Bureaucracy Exposed), a novel of the Ching dynasty, in which the author made sarcastic descriptions of the practices of officialdom, we can read this: (A man sighed and said,) "Yàyàwū, it's not worthwhile to buy a job in the government." But now, we just use it as an ADJ.PH to mean "very poor".

　　Dínggwāgwā may be a word jointly created by Westerners and the people who worked as interpreters in Canton. Díng means "the top". Gwāgwā may be the Cantonese transliteration of the English word "good, good". Let us imagine: an English merchant came to Canton to buy tea. He asked, "Is it good?" The interpreter put his thumb up and answered on behalf of the seller, "Díng (it's the best). Good! Good!"

「吔吔烏」原是個由北方傳來的歎詞,表示不同意、不值得談。清代的小說《官場現形記》第三十二回:「呀呀呼(即吔吔烏)!差事那里好捐!」但是現在我們只用作形容詞。

「頂呱呱」大概是西人與早期在廣州任翻譯的人合創的詞語。「頂」指最上,最高級。呱呱是「Good — Good」的中國字譯音。我們不妨想像一下:有位英國商人來廣州買茶葉,他問:「Good?」翻譯的人豎起大拇指,代貨主答:「頂,Good — Good!」

* William Nienhauser, *Indiana Companion to Traditional Chinese Literature* (Bloomington: Indiana University Press, 1986).

Fèihlóu 肥佬；Sàjí 沙紙

Fèihlóu

N/FV   a fat man; fail in the examination [M: go]
考試不及格

Sàjí

N   sandpaper; certificate [M: jèung]
畢業證書

e.g.   Kéuih háausi fèihlóu, lómdóu jèung sàjí.
佢 考試 肥佬，攞唔到 張 沙紙。

(He failed in the examination and could not get the certificate.)
（他考試不及格，拿不到畢業證書。）

Hong Kong is a unique place in the world where the East meets the West. The two dominant languages spoken in Hong Kong are Cantonese and English. As we can see, there is a large amount of language borrowing from English into Cantonese, a very common phenomenon resulting from bilingualism and language contact. The loan-words, or borrowed items, enter Cantonese in three ways: 1. transliteration, a kind of assimilation in which foreign sounds are replaced by native sounds*; 2. loan translation* by coining new expressions (for the borrowed items); 3. transliteration further supplemented by a word to denote category.

Fèihlóu is the transliteration for "to fail" while the original meaning of it is "a fat man". Sàjí, sandpaper, is a kind of rough paper with sand stuck on it, used for rubbing things. Sà is the transliteration for "cert(ificate)", and Jí is adopted to denote that it is "a sheet of paper".

Both Fèihlóu and Sàjí are the examples to illustrate the Cantonese loan-words from English in the above-mentioned 1. and 3., the two categories that we are concerned with here.

香港是中西文化交流的地方，因語言接觸的關係，香港流行的粵語裏，借入了很多英語詞彙，這些借詞，通過 1.音譯 2.意譯 3.音義兼譯的形式進入粵語中[+]。我們來看看第一及第三類。「肥佬」是第一類，它本來指肥胖的男人，又是英文"fail"的音譯，意即考試落第。「沙紙」是第三類，它本是一種打磨用的、黏着細沙的紙，「沙」也是英文"cert(ificate)"的音譯，「紙」是用來指稱它的類別。

其他的例子如：
Other examples:

Sēutsāam:	N	shirt [M: gihn] 恤衫
Sēutfaat:	VO	set the hair 恤髮
Gafē :	N	coffee [M: dī, būi, jēun, dihk] 咖啡
Gūlēi :	N	coolie [M: go] 咕喱
Chèfēi :	N	"fare", ticket of bus or train [M: jèung] 車「飛」
Heifēi :	N	ticket in a cinema or theatre [M: jèung] 戲「飛」
Jáubā :	N/PW	bar [M: gàan] 酒吧
Fēksí :	N/FV	fax [M: jèung] 圖文傳真
Fèilám :	N	film [M: tùhng, gyún, jèung] 菲林
Fùhlūk:	SV	fluke 符碌（僥倖成功）
Kūséun:	N	cushion [M: go] 咕啞（墊子）

* see R. A. Hudson, *Sociolinguistics* (Cambridge University Press, Malta, 1993), chapter 2.5.2.
+ 見張日昇〈香港廣州話英語音譯借詞的聲調規律〉，《中國語文》，第一期(1986)，頁42–50。

Jaahpbālāng(Jaahpbālāang) 雜崩能；
Hahmbahlaahng 冚辦冷

Jaahpbālāng (Jaahpbālāang)

ADJ.PH   not pure; mixed; inferior; miscellaneous
　　　　　雜亂而不純的

Hahmbahlaahng

A   all
　　　全部

e.g. Nīdī jaahpbālāang fosīk, hahmbahlaahng dámlohk laahpsaaptúng lā.
　　　呢啲　雜崩能　貨色，　冚辦冷　　泵落　　垃圾桶　　啦。

(These are goods of inferior quality. You can just throw them all into the litter bin.)
（這些雜牌次貨，全部扔進垃圾箱吧。）

The Cantonese dialect is of multi-origins. It originated partly from the ancient language of the Han people, partly from the dialects of northern China, and partly from foreign languages. Both Jaahpbālāng and Hahmbahlaahng came from the spoken language of northern China during the Yuan dynasty.

　　"Bālā" was the spoken word of the Yuan people. It is an empty morpheme, a word that does not have a meaning by itself. It always goes after an adjective, e.g. dìnbālā (i.e. romantic) and pobālā (i.e. broken).

　　Jaahpbālāng actually was "jaahpbālā" which means nothing but "jaahp" (mixed, not pure or inferior). Hahmbahlaahng was "hahpbālā". "Hahp" means all.

　　廣東話的來源很複雜，有源於古代漢語的，有源於北方話的，有源於外來語的。「雜崩能」和「冚辦冷」由元代的北方口語變來。

　　元人口語有「不剌」，這個口語本身沒有意義，它多附在形容詞的後面，例如「顛不剌」（人很風流）和「破不剌」（破爛的）。

　　「雜崩能」其實是「雜不剌」，意思就是「雜」。「冚辦冷」其實是「闔不剌」，「闔」的意思是「全部」。

Lāausūnglóu 咯鬆佬#/Ngoihgōnglóu 外江佬#

Lāausūnglóu/Ngoihgōnglóu

N　quite an impolite term for the people who come to Gwóngdūng from other provinces of China [M: go, tiuh]
對非廣東省人的不很客氣的稱呼

Some spoken words in Cantonese are taken from Mandarin. Lāausūng actually is the changed sound of "lao xiōng" which is a general term of greeting between men in the northern part of China. But it is used by the Cantonese people to refer to non-Cantonese. There is a big river called Jyūgōng (i.e. Pearl River) in Gwóngdūng province. Those people who do not come from any place in Gwóngdūng are referred to as Ngoihgōnglóu.

　　廣東話裏面有些口語詞是由普通話轉變而來的。「咯鬆」其實是「老兄」的普通話變音。「老兄」普通話唸lao xiong，它原是北方人見面時互相稱呼的用語，但被廣東人用來借指外省人。

　　另外，廣東省內有一條著名的河流叫珠江，「外江佬」就是指本來不屬於珠江流域的外省人。

Lóuhgéui 老舉#

Lóuhgéui

N　　a prostitute [M: go, tiuh]
　　　妓女

e.g.　Kéuih béi yàhn maaihheui geihjáai jouh lóuhgéui.
　　　佢　俾　人　　賣去　　妓寨　做　　老舉。
　　　(She was sold to a brothel to be a prostitute there.)
　　　（她被賣到妓院當娼妓。）

To sell rice is written 粜 which is a rarely used character. But how do we say it in Cantonese? You can find the answer in the dictionary which says 粜：替叫切. There is an old phonetic system in Chinese dictionaries called "fàanchit". It is quite similar to the phonetic spelling of English. In the "fàanchit" system, two characters are picked as phonetic symbols. The pronunciation of a character will be indicated by the initial of the first character combined with the final of the second one. For example 粜 :

　　　替　tai　　t
　　　叫　giu　　iu

So 粜 should be read as "tiu".

　　Usually, the rising, falling or level tone is the same as that of the second character while the tone pitch will be determined by that of the first one. People also play word games by using fàanchit. Now let us apply this phonetic system to Geihnéuih, the original term for "prostitute". We will then get Géuih as expected. But there is not a Cantonese word having such a pronunciation, so people just switched it to a high rising tone and picked the character 舉 to stand for it. To change tone is a very common practice among Cantonese people. Furthermore, the tone change* to high rising from other low tones can easily be found in the Cantonese dialect[+]. Lóuh is an empty morpheme, serving as a prefix in this combination.

賣米叫做「粜」。它是個僻字,怎麼唸?字典說:「替叫切」。

中國字典舊有的一種標音方法,叫「反切」,等於英文的拼音。反切時總有上下兩個字,上字取聲母(發聲),下字取韻母(收韻),合讀成一字音。例如:

替(反切上字),取t
叫(反切下字),取iu

由此拼讀出tiu的音。所以「粜」音跳(tiu)。

通常反切的第一字定陰陽調,第二字顯示平、上、去、入。人們也利用反切來進行文字遊戲[#],把「妓女」兩字反切,嚴格來說得出Géuih,讀陽上聲,是有聲無字,所以人們拿了陰上聲舉(Géui)字來代替;而變調,是粵語中頗爲常見的現象。[+]

---

[*] See Stephen Matthews and Virginia Yip, p. 23.
[+] See S. L. Wong.
[#] 見俞敏〈反語〉,《中國大百科全書之語言文字》(中國大百科全書出版社,北京・上海,1988),頁73。

Sàmpóuh 心抱；Pòuhtàuh 浦頭

Sàmpóuh

N   daughter-in-law [M: go]
       媳婦

e.g. Chéui sàmpóuh
       娶　　心抱

(to get a daughter-in-law or: my son is getting married)
（娶新媳婦）

Pòuhtàuh

FV (said of a person) turn up
       露面

e.g. Ngóhdeih buhkjó hóu noih dōu juhng m̀gin kéuih pòuhtàuh.
       我哋　伏咗　好　耐　都　仲　唔見　佢　　浦頭。

(We hid ourselves and waited for so long, and yet he didn't show up.)
（我們埋伏了很久也還不見他露面。）

The sound of spoken words changes as time goes by. Some words may be uttered in their present-day form, and at the same time retain their ancient pronunciations. In other words, a word may have its ancient pronunciation as well as its contemporary one. For example, 婦 is pronounced Fúh nowadays. But it was uttered as Póuh in ancient times. Originally, 新婦 should be said Sànpóuh. Since the initial P of the second syllable is a bilabial — one has to use or to close one's lips in pronouncing it, the "n" of Sàn was assimilated by it and the whole word became Sàm. That is why 新婦 is currently pronounced Sàmpóuh. (Later, the two words of the expression were switched to another two, i.e. 心抱, whose pronunciations are exactly sàmpóuh.)

    Sometimes, phonetic assimilation may be imposed by the first syllable on the following one, e.g. Gàmyaht (today) → Gàmmaht, Sahpngh (fifteen) → Sahpm̀h.

Furthermore, the initial F and P are very easily mixed up by some people. You can see the example of 婦 above with P changed into F. The character 浮 (fàuh) will do so in the opposite way. Some people will pronounce it as Pòuh. Pòuhtàuh actually is "fàuhtàuh" meaning that after diving into the water, a man floats with his head coming out of the water.

語音是不斷隨時代而變化的，所以一個字有古音，也有今音。有時某個字同時保留了古音和今音，例如：

「婦」，古音是「抱」（Póuh），今音讀「夫」的陽上聲（Fúh）。

原本新婦應讀成「新抱」（Sànpóuh），但P是雙唇音，發聲時口唇先要閉上，於是影響前面的n變讀成m，結果這詞語讀成了Sàmpóuh。後來，人們索性用另外兩個同音字「心抱」來代替。

有時前面的字音也會影響後面的發音，例如：今日→今「物」；十五→十「ḿh」，以上所說的都是語音的同化現象*。

還有，語音裏聲母F與P很容易混淆，上面的「婦」聲母由P變F是例子。相反地，「浮」音Fàuh，但有人把它讀成「浦」Pòuh。所以「浦頭」其實是「浮頭」，指人潛進水底後浮上水面，露出頭來。

* 見葉蜚聲、徐通鏘著，p. 84；高華年著，p. 11；及劉涌泉、趙世開編，p. 28。

Séuipèih 水皮; ngàuhyāt 牛一

Séuipèih

SV   poor in knowledge or in skill, sloppy
沒有學問或本領

e.g.   Kéuihge Yìngmàhn hóu séuipèih.
佢嘅　英文　好　水皮。

(He is poor in English.)
（他的英語很差勁。）

Ngàuhyāt

N/FV   birthday
生日

e.g.   Gàmyaht haih ngóh ngàuhyāt.
今日　係　我　牛一。

(Today is my birthday.)
（今天是我的生辰。）

There are many Chinese characters which can be broken down* into two or three parts. For example, 波 can be deciphered as 氵(水) and 皮, 生 as 牛 and 一, 兵 as 丘 and 八. 牛一 (Ngàuhyāt) is another way of saying birthday while 丘八 (yàubaat) still means soldier.

As for 水皮 (Séuipèih), it was first mentioned by a famous politician Wòhng Ngòn Sehk who was born in the Sung dynasty (A.D. 1021–1086). In his dictionary, he split the character 波 (i.e. wave) and interpreted it as 皮 (skin) of 水 (water). His contemporary, Sōu Sīk, another famous man of letters, did not agree with him. He teased Wòhng Ngòn Sehk and said, "According to what you say, can the character 滑 (slippery) be viewed as 骨 (bone) of 水 (water)?" He considered Wòhng's etymology sloppy in this case.

有許多中國字，可以拆開成兩三個部分，例如：「波」可以拆成「氵」（水）及「皮」，「生」可拆成「牛」及「一」，「兵」可拆成「丘」及「八」。所以「牛一」即是「生」（生日），「丘八」即是「兵」。

　　至於「水皮」，是宋代的王安石（公元 1021-1086）創的。他在《字說》裏說：「波者，水之皮也。」（波是水的表皮。）但這解釋不妥當，蘇軾就嘲笑他：「波是水之皮，那麼『滑』是『水之骨』嗎？」唉！王安石是堂堂一個文學家，但把「波」字亂說胡解，蘇軾覺得他太「水皮」── 差勁了！

* See T. K. Ann, chap. 14.

Gùnjih Léuhnggo Háu 官字兩個口；
Sīk Jih Tàuhseuhng Yātbá Dōu 色字頭上一把刀

Gùnjih Léuhnggo Háu

I.E. the officials rely on their positions and become irrational
做官的仗官威，不講道理

e.g. Gùnjih léuhnggo háu, néih dím gau dī gùn ngaau ā?
官字　兩個　　口，你　點　夠　啲　官　拗　吖？

(As the saying goes, the officials all have got two mouths. How can you argue with them?)
（做官的有話事權，你怎辯得過他們？）

Sīk Jih Tàuhseuhng Yātbá Dōu

I.E. (lit.) the top of the character 色 is a knife

There is a game called "chaakjih". We break down the characters into several parts and try to get the meanings out of them. For example 官, the character for officials, appears to have two mouths 口 in it. Ordinary people just have one. Even though you are right, you are still not strong enough to defend yourself. The officials have two mouths. Surely they can speak much louder, and whether they are right or wrong, you have to listen to them.

Another example is 色 (i.e. colour, beautiful woman, sex). A knife 刀 is put on the 巴 (which can be taken as snake, serpent). It indicates the danger of being too fond of women or having too much sex.

But according to *Syut Màhn Gáai Jih*, an etymological dictionary of the Han dynasty, 色 is made up of 人 (man) and 卩 (control, a seal) but not of 刀 (knife) and 巴 (snake). The pattern and the meaning of it were distorted by ordinary people. The same thing happened to 官.

有一種遊戲叫「拆字」，就是把一個字拆成幾部分來解釋。例如「官」字，裏面有兩個「口」。普通人只有一個口，有理也說不清，但官有兩個「口」，他當然聲音大，不管有理沒理，你總要聽他的吩咐了。

　　又例如「色」字，字形由「巴」和「刀」合成。（「巴」可被視爲蛇。）而今在「巴」的上面安一把「刀」，可見好色的危險。但根據《說文解字》：「色，從人、卪」，並非由「刀」、「巴」組成。俗人把色字寫錯解錯了。官字亦然。

Sàanyàhn Jih Yáuh Miuhgai 山人自有妙計

Sàanyàhn Jih Yáuh Miuhgai

I.E. (I) have got a good idea
（我）有好主意

e.g. Daaihgā m̀sái gèng, sàanyàhn jih yáuh miuhgai.
大家 唔使 驚， 山人 自 有 妙計。
(Don't be afraid, I've got a good idea.)
（大家不用着慌，我有好主意。）

We all know the word for blackboard r̄ black + board.* There are many similar compounds in Chinese characters. Let me tell you a story first:

Once, there was a filial boy. He loved his mother and was willing to help the poor. One day, his mother fell sick. The doctor said that she could only be cured by the herb of immortality grown on the top of Mt. Kwàn Lèuhn. When he got to the foot of the mountain, he found that what lay before him were just high mountains and deep valleys where tigers and serpents abounded. Suddenly, there appeared an old man. He taught him how to overcome all difficulties and get the herb. When the boy was about to go home, he asked the old man who he was. The old man smiled without answering and left. The boy thought for a long time before he realized who the old man was.

The above story is just made up by me, but you will always find such familiar scenarios in Chinese folk tales. After all, who is that old man? He is 人 (yàhn: a man) + 山 (Sàan: mountain, in the mountain) = 仙 (i.e. immortal, fairy). So, to say 山人 is to say 仙 who, in Chinese myths, can develop superpower to help people overcome disasters. Moreover, 仙 is a compound ideograph, one of the six principles concerning the formation of Chinese characters.

英文"blackboard"「黑板」一詞，相信大家都認識是black + board = blackboard。中國字也常見這種情形。但我們不如先看一個故事：

　　從前有個孝子，他既孝順母親，又肯幫助窮苦人。一次，他母親病了，醫生說要吃崑崙山頂的靈芝草才能醫治。孝子去到崑崙山腳，只見山高谷深，又有猛虎和毒蛇。忽然有個老人出現，指點他巧妙地渡過難關，取得仙草。臨別時孝子問老人是誰，老人笑而不答，就走了。孝子想了好久才想出答案。

　　上面的故事是虛構的，但類似的情節常出現在中國民間故事裏。到底那老人是誰？原來是「山」旁邊的一個「人」，即是「仙」。神仙可以施法術，幫助人渡過難關。在中國文字構造中，「仙」算是一個會意字。

* a compound word in English morphology.

Chyun 串/寸

Chyun

SV   disgustingly bad attitude
　　　態度粗鄙得令人反感

e.g.　Wai, sailóu! M̀hóu gam chyun hóu boh!
　　　喂　細佬　唔好　咁　串　好　啵！

　　　(Hey, you guy! Don't be so cheeky.)
　　　（喂，兄弟！你對我的態度不要那麼差，好吧？）

Many Chinese characters are hieroglyphic (or pictographic). There is a close relationship between the meaning and the pattern. Let us take 串 as an example. It looks like a string stringing together two circles. It also looks like a chain. When a policeman catches a thief, he will 串 (handcuff him and take) him to the police station. When we report a case to the police, we would say "bouchyun" for "boungon". Unfortunately, some policeman were so rude that people disliked them very much. Gradually, "hóu Chyun" acquired a derogatory meaning.

　　　中國字有很多是象形文字，字的意義和它的形狀往往很有關係，例如「串」字，看來就像用一根繩子把兩個圈穿起來。還有，「串」又像鎖鏈。所以警察捉到賊，就「串」他回去。而「報串」就是報警。

　　　可惜以前的警察有些修養差，說話無禮，常常惹人反感。久而久之，「好串」就成了個貶義詞。

Chè Daaihpaau 車大炮/
Chètīn Chèdeih 車天車地

Chè Daaihpaau/Chètin Chèdeih

VO/PH boast, talk big; tell a lie
　　　　撒謊

e.g. Kéuih lyuhn chè daaihpaau, móuh geui jàn.
　　　佢　亂　車　大炮，　冇　句　真。

(He is just boasting. All that he says is not true.)
（他吹牛皮。）

There are many Cantonese words or expressions handed down from ancient times. But the characters used by the ancient people have become so rare that we have replaced them with frequently used homophones. Chè Daaihpaau is one of them. The meaning of the original Chè is "to boast" and Paau, according to the dictionary, is "to fool people with exaggeration". So you can easily get the meaning of the combination of Chè Daaihpaau, but now we replace those characters with the ones for "chariot" and "big cannon".

　　廣州話裏有很多字詞原來是古字，但因爲不常見，人們就以常見的同音字來代替它。例如「車大炮」，原本寫作「奢大奅」。奢，意思是「誇張」。奅，《正字通》說是「以大言冒人」（用誇大的話蒙騙人）。所以奢大奅就是撒謊、講大話。

Yāttàuh Mouhséui 一頭霧水

Yāttàuh Mouhséui

I.E. cannot understand; be puzzled, become lost (lit. head in the fog)
不明真相

e.g. Néihdeih jínggú jouhgwaai, gáaudou ngóh yāttàuh mouhséui.
你哋 整古 做怪， 攪到 我 一頭 霧水。
(You make me feel puzzled by making mystery of something.)
（你們諸多古怪，弄得我丈八金剛，摸不着頭腦。）

Chinese characters are monosyllabic with independent patterns. We can make use of this special feature to create couplets. A couplet is composed of two sentences or two groups of sentences, the first half is called "seuhnglyùhn" and the second half, "hahlyùhn". There is similarity in the number of words and in the symmetrical structure in both the seuhnglyùhn and hahlyùhn. Also, there is strong relationship between the meanings and the tones of the words of the two halves. A Cantonese poet named Hòh Daahm Yùh wrote this interesting couplet:

symmetrical structure

one	yāt	一	← NU →	四	sei	four
head	tàuh	頭	← M →	面	mihn	sides
fog	mouh	霧	← N →	雲	wàhn	cloud
water	séui	水	← N →	山	sàan	mountain
not	bāt	不	← A N →	誰	sèuih	which
know	jī	知	← FV →	作	jok	is
the direction	jùng	宗	← N →	主	jyú	the highest

hahlyùhn seuhnglyùhn
which ends with which ends with
a level* tone an oblique* tone

The meaning of the couplet is: Which is the highest of the cloudy mountains that surround me? I lost my way in the heavy fog.

From then on, Yāttàuh Mouhséui became an expression known to everybody.

中國字是單音節、獨立字形的。我們利用這種特性創出「對聯」來。對聯一定有兩句（或兩組句子），上句叫上聯，下句叫下聯。兩者必須字數相同，結構一樣，而意思及平仄聲也要相對。

　　廣東有位詩人叫何淡如的，寫了一副有趣的對聯：

　　四面雲山誰作主？（四面都是頂上罩着雲的山峯，哪一個是主峰？）（上聯）

　　一頭霧水不知宗。（我的頭迷在大霧裏，不知東南西北。）（下聯）

　　由此「一頭霧水」成了名句。

---

* The level tones (pìhngsing) are equal to the H.F., L.F. and H.L. tones of the Yale system while the oblique tones (jāksing) refer to the H.R., L.R., M.L., L.L. tones and those H.L. tones with p, t or k stopped finals.

Tòuh Gújéng 淘古井

Tòuh Gújéng

VO   try to take advantage of a widow
　　打寡婦的主意

e.g. Tòuh gújéng, chòihsīk gìmsàu.
　　　淘　古井，財色　兼收。

(He marries the widow, and has got the woman and her wealth.)

Maahng Gàau (A.D. 751-814), a poet in the Tang dynasty, wrote a poem about a virtuous and chaste woman:

> Lakka* trees will grow old together,
> A pair of mandarin ducks would rather die together too.
> A faithful woman is willing to do like the birds,
> She will be greatly respected if she dies (kills herself) after the death of her husband.
> Since my husband died, my heart is as calm as the water in the old well,
> No billows (I will not fall in love nor marry again).*

The Cantonese people use an old well (i.e. Gújéng) as a symbol for a widow and Tòuh means to get water (i.e. money) out of it.

唐代詩人孟郊（公元751-814）有首《烈女操》：

> 梧桐相待老，鴛鴦會雙死。
> 貞婦貴殉夫，捨生亦如此。
> 波瀾誓不起，妾心古井水。

　　大意說：梧桐樹上的鳳凰會相伴到老，雌雄鴛鴦鳥會選擇一同死去。貞節的婦人甘願像鳥一樣。自從丈夫去世後，我的心已像古井裏的水，不起波瀾。

　　廣東人用「古井」象徵寡婦，而淘古井就是想抽取井裏的水（錢）。

* See Witter Bynner, p. 102.

Sōujàusí 蘇州屎/Sáuméih 手尾

Sōujàusí/Sáuméih

N   troubles left behind/unfinished things [M: bāt, dūk/dī]
未辦完的事務

e.g.   Kéuih fātyìhn chìhjīk jáujó, làuhdài dī sáuméih béi ngóh.
佢　忽然　辭職　走咗，留低 啲　手尾　俾 我。

(He suddenly quit his job and left everything to me to finish.)
（他突然辭職走了，留下的事務要我替他完成。）

During the Tang dynasty, there was a poet called Làuh Yúh Sehk (A.D. 772–843). When he was a chisí (a rank quite equal to that of a provincial governor) at Sōujàu, he saw a beautiful girl at a banquet given by the sīhùng (minister of public works in the Tang dynasty) Léih Sàn. Her name was Douh Wáih Lèuhng, one of Léih's concubines. Besides being beautiful and fashionable, she was also good at singing. As the poet was unlikely ever to meet her again, so he wrote her this poem:

> She sets her cloudy hair in the most popular style,
> The songs which she sings are as soft as spring breezes.
> Minister Léih will take it as a very usual thing since he sees her very often,
> But I will miss her so much that I will become broken-hearted.

Finally she was gone and left the Sōujàu(chi)sí behind. Later, people substituted another character for Sí which means "excrement" to refer to troubles left behind.

唐代詩人劉禹錫（公元772-843）當蘇州刺史的時候，一次在司空李紳所設的宴會上遇見一個美女，她是李紳的歌姬，叫杜韋娘，樣子漂亮，打扮入時，唱的歌尤其好聽。只可惜以後難有機會再見面，劉禹錫於是寫了首詩送給她：

> 高髻雲鬟宮樣粧，春風一曲杜韋娘。
> 司空見慣渾閒事，斷盡蘇州刺史腸。

最後，杜韋娘離去，只留下一個蘇州（刺）史。後來「蘇州史」轉化讀作「蘇州屎」。

Yáuh Mòuh Yáuh Yihk 有毛有翼

Yáuh Mòuh Yáuh Yihk

PH   grown up children no more listen to their parents (lit. have feathers and wings)
比喻孩子長大便不聽父母的話

e.g. Néih go sèui jái, yìhgā yáuh mòuh yáuh yihk, juhng sái léih a
你 個 衰 仔 宜家 有 毛 有 翼，仲 使 理 阿
mā mè?
媽咩？

(You bad boy! Now that you have grown up like a bird with all its wings and feathers. You don't care about me any more, do you?)
（你這不肖子，今天翅膀硬了，還會關心媽媽嗎？）

Baahk Gèui Yih (A.D. 772–846) was a famous poet of the Tang dynasty. Once he heard a tragic story about an unfilial son who abandoned his parents. He was so saddened and agitated that he wrote a poem about it entitled *Swallow*. The meaning of the poem is as follows:

> A pair of swallows built a nest under the eaves,
> And the mother swallow bore four babies.
> The babies grew bigger day by day,
> They always demanded food as if they never got enough to eat.
> Although the two swallows were already very tired, they still tried their best to look for food for fear that the babies were still hungry.
> After a month, the babies grew bigger and bigger but the mother was getting thinner and thinner.
> She also taught them how to sing and fly.
> Once they got all their wings and feathers and were able to fly, they just flew away in the wind and never came back.

Baahk Gèui Yih wrote this poem in order to remind people to be filial to their parents.

白居易（公元772-846）是唐代的大詩人。他聽到一個不孝子離棄父母的悲慘故事後，很是感慨，就寫了首《燕詩》：

梁上有雙燕，翩翩雄與雌。銜泥兩椽間，一巢生四兒。
四兒日夜長，索食聲孜孜。青蟲不易捕，黃口〔指小燕〕無飽期。
嘴爪雖欲敝，心力不知疲。須臾〔幾分鐘〕十來往，猶恐巢中飢。
辛勤三十日，母瘦雛〔小燕〕漸肥。喃喃教言語，一一刷毛衣。
一旦羽翼長，引上庭樹枝。舉翅不回顧，隨風四散飛。

Syùngēungkíuh 酸薑蕎；
Màauhgānjūk 茅根竹

Syùngēungkíuh

N   an indirect way of saying "the head" [M: go]
      是「頭」的轉彎抹角的說法

e.g.   Kéuih dāpdài go syùngēungkíuh.
      佢　耷低　個　酸薑蕎。

      (He lowered his head.)
      （他垂下頭。）

Màauhgānjūk

FV/VO an indirect way of saying "to borrow money"
      是「借水（錢）」的轉彎抹角的說法

e.g.   Laahndóu Yí jáulàih wán ngóh, yùhnlòih haih séung màauhgānjūk.
      爛賭　二　走嚟　搵　我，原來　係　想　茅根竹。

      (The gambler A-Yí called on me. I found that he just came to borrow money.)

This time I would like you to solve a riddle first: "The friendship among gentlemen." The answer is the name of a town in Taiwan.

    Have you guessed it? The answer is Daahm Séui (lit. as calm and as tasteless as water), a small town near Taipei. As the saying goes, "The friendship among gentlemen is as calm and as tasteless as water."

    In Cantonese, there is one way of expressing oneself, similar to the above riddle. The part of the expression which contains the main thing that we really want to say is left out and the rest of it is revealed. We want other people to guess the missing word or words.

    Syùngēung is sour ginger and Kíuhtàuh, echalote. Màauhgān is sweet imperatae and Jūkjeséui, sugar cane soup. Cantonese people all know what they are. Once we say the first part of it, we know what follows after it. "Tàuh" means "head" and "Jeséui" is pronounced the same way as for "borrowing money". Thus Syùngēungkíuh → Tàuh, Màauhgānjūk → Jeséui.

今次先請你猜個謎語：「君子之交」。猜臺灣一個市鎮。

猜到嗎？答案是「淡水」（台北市附近的小鎮）。── 俗語說：「君子之交淡如水。」

廣東話有一種類似上述謎語的表達方式，就是把某個流行語句的一些部分省去，只說出其他部分，而由聽者自己猜出所省去的部分來。

因為「酸薑蕎頭」（一種小吃）和「茅根竹蔗水」（一種飲料）都是廣東人熟知的，所以說了前半截，大家就猜到後半截。「蔗水」諧音為「借水」，即借錢。所以：酸薑蕎 → 頭，茅根竹 → 蔗水。

Sihdaahn 是但；
Bunyeh Chèuhn(chàh) 半夜巡(茶)；
Gàmtùhng Yuhk(néuih) 金童玉(女)；
Pèitàuh Sáan(faat) 披頭散(髮)；
Yìngtòuh Síu(háu) 櫻桃小(口)

Sihdaahn

PH   anything will do
　　　隨便甚麼都可以，不拘

e.g. "Néih séung tái bīntou hei a?" "Sihdaahn lā."
　　　「你 想 睇 邊套 戲呀？」「是但 啦。」

　　　("What movie would you like to see?" "Anyone will do.")
　　　(「想看哪一齣電影？」答：「隨便哪一齣都可以。」)

In our language, there is one special way of expressing oneself. We will say the most part of a phrase omitting a word, but what we really want to say is the word that we omit. For example, in *The Book of Songs*, we can read two sentences: "yinyíh sànfàn" (i.e. just married and enjoy marital happiness) and "hìngdaih yáuhyù" (i.e. good friendship between brothers). Though we just say "yinyíh", actually we want to say "sànfàn" (just married) and "yáuhyù", "hìngdaih" (brothers). We can also find such kind of expressions among triad gangs. For example:

The original form and meaning of the saying	The meaning of the word left out
Bunyeh chèuhn (chàh)　A midnight inspection	chàh　Tea (which is pronounced the same as the word for "to inspect")
Gàmtùhng yuhk (néuih)　Golden Boy and Jade Girl	néuih　Girl, woman

Pèitàuh sáan (faat)	faat
Disheveled hair	Hair
Yìngtòuh síu (háu)	háu
Small mouth as lovely as a cherry	Mouth

Now we can also see the original words for Sihdaahn were coined in a set phrase si-mòuh-geih-daahn (i.e. without restraint of any kind). When we say the contracted form Sihdaahn, we mean "mòuhgeih": anything will do.

　　我們有一種很特別的表達方式，就是拿一句慣用語來拆開，只說出一部分，實際想表達的卻是未有說出的那部分的意思。例如《詩經》有「燕爾新婚」和「兄弟友于」的句子，於是說「燕爾」就等於說「新婚」，說「友于」就等於說「兄弟」。黑幫暗語也有類似的說法：

「半夜巡」是茶
「金童玉」是女
「櫻桃小」是口
「披頭散」是髮

　　廣東口語的「是但」，應寫作「肆……憚」。我們把成語「肆無忌憚」拆開，說「肆憚→是但」，意思其實就是「無忌」。無忌即不拘忌，甚麼也可以。

Lóuhyìhbāt 老而不#;
Wàih Lóuh Bātjyùn, Gaauwaaih Jísyùn
爲老不尊，教壞子孫

Lóuhyìhbāt

N   old bastard (a term of abuse to an old man while literally it means old but not yet dead) [M: go, tìuh]
言行失當的老年人（這是罵人的話）

Wàih Lóuh Bātjyùn, Gaauwaaih Jísyùn

I.E.   said of an old man who failed to set a good example for his descendants
身爲長輩而言行失當，是後輩的壞榜樣

Yùhn Yeuhng was a man who did not like to observe rites or proprieties. When his mother died, he sang happily. Once he had an appointment with Confucius, and was a little early. He disrespectfully squatted down to await Confucius. When Confucius came, he was annoyed by Yùhn Yeuhng's manner and criticized him. Confucius said, "You didn't listen to any teachings or admonitions of the elders when you were a child and you didn't have any achievements when you grew up. Now you are old but not yet dead (lóuh yìh bātséi). You are evil!"

The above story is from *The Analects*. Now the expression is quoted with the last word hidden.

    原壤這人不愛禮法，母親死了，他竟然高興地唱起歌來。一次，孔子約了他見面，原壤早到了，就很放肆地蹲踞着等候。孔子來到看見，就不客氣地批評他：「你這人小時不聽教誨，長大了又沒有成就，現在老而不死，是個賊！」

    這故事出自《論語》。

Lóuhsyú Làaigwāi → Móuhdehng Màaihsáu
老鼠拉龜→冇定(地)埋手

Lóuhsyú Làaigwāi→Móuhdehng Màaihsáu

HIT   don't know where or how to start
      意思是「無地入手」

e.g. Nīgihn sih kéuih séung jouh. Daahnhaih lóuhsyú làaigwāi,
      呢件 事 佢 想 做， 但係 老鼠 拉龜，

      móuhdehng màaihsáu.
      冇定 埋手。

      (He wants to do it, but doesn't know how to put his hand to it, just like a rat trying to pull a tortoise.)
      (這事他想幹，但不知從何入手。)

In the Chinese language, there is one particular figure of speech called Hithauhyúh, enigmatic parallelism* or tail-less pun[+]. It consists of two clauses and appears like a kind of word game. In one Hithauhyúh, the first half sometimes is a simile, similar to the verbal version of a riddle or a charade. The second half is quite like the answer of a riddle, having the words that a person really wants to say. Like in a riddle, one has to work out the solution by oneself by just reading or listening to the description. But for a Hithauhyúh, both the clauses are revealing, only that more emphasis is put on the latter one.

  Now close your eyes and imagine. A rat (i.e. Lóuhsyú) is hungry. It wants to bite the tortoise (i.e. gwāi) which is unable to fight with the rat. But the tortoise is clever enough to hide its head and feet inside its shell. Staring at the tortoise with anger, the rat can do nothing about it. This situation is illustrated by an enigmatic parallelism "Lóuhsyú Làaigwāi → Móuhdehng Màaihsáu". You can find that there are many such vivid metaphorical descriptions in Chinese.

中國話裏有一種特殊的表達方式，叫「歇後語」，它通常像謎語般有兩部分，前半似謎面，後半似謎底。謎語只提供謎面，由猜謎者猜出謎底來。歇後語則前半（謎面）與後半（謎底）都說出，而重點在後半。

　　讓我們閉上眼想一想：老鼠肚子餓了，想咬烏龜；烏龜當然打不過老鼠，但牠另有妙計，就是把龜頭和四肢都縮進龜殼裏。這下子，老鼠瞪着龜，氣得團團轉！

　　歇後語常常有類似的、極生動的說法。

---

* first initiated by Pearce, T. W. & Lockhart, J. H. Steward. John S. Rohsenow called them enigmatic folk similes in his book.

+ see *A Bibliography of Yue Dialect Studies* p. 55.

Nàih Pòuhsaat Gwogōng→Jihsàn Nàahnbóu
泥菩薩過江→自身難保

Nàih Pòuhsaat Gwogōng→Jihsàn Nàahnbóu

HIT   unable even to protect oneself
意思是「自身難保」

e.g. Néih giu kéuih bòng néih àh? Kéuih nàih pòuhsaat gwogōng,
你　叫　佢　幫　你　呀？佢　泥　菩薩　過江，

jihsàn nàahnbóu a!
自身　難保　呀！

(You ask him to help you? He cannot manage even to help himself, just like a clay god trying to cross the river.)
（你請他幫忙？他連自己也救不了哩。）

During the last years of the Northern Sung dynasty, China was seriously defeated by the invading army of Gàm. Even the emperor was captured. Luckily, one of the princes managed to run away from the concentration camp. He fled to the south until he arrived at the bank of the Yangtze River. He was caught between the devil and the deep blue sea because the enemy's army was after him and would soon reach him. Just in the nick of time, a horse suddenly appeared. It rushed out from nowhere. The prince rode on the horse and crossed the river (i.e. Gwogōng) to free himself from the enemy. After he reached the shore, he took a look at the horse which suddenly turned into clay and cracked. He then realized that it was the horse (or the clay god, i.e. Nàih Pòuhsaat) that saved him. Later, the prince became the emperor and established a new government in the southern part of the Yangtze River.

Chinese people believe that god will bless and protect those who are destined to be the real king. The above expression is also a Hithauhyúh. The first part of it originates from the above legendary story in Chinese history.

在北宋末年，金國的軍隊攻打中國，中國大敗，北宋的皇帝也給金兵捉去。這時有一個王子叫趙構的，他從俘虜營逃出來，向南方跑，跑到長江邊。前面是滔滔江水，後面有金國的追兵。正在危急的時候，不知從那裏跑來一匹馬。趙構就騎上馬背，涉水過江，脫了身。

　　上岸之後，看看那匹馬，忽然馬身變化成泥，裂開數段。趙構這才知道，救他的是隻泥馬（泥菩薩）。後來趙構在長江以南建立新政府，他做了皇帝。

　　中國人相信，「真命天子」一定有菩薩保祐的。

Sihyàuh Lòufaahn→Jíngsīk (Jíng) Séui
豉油撈飯→整色(整)水

Sihyàuh Lòufaahn→Jíngsik (Jíng)Séui

HIT put on airs; pretend it to be genuine and cheat people
(the lit. meaning of the first half is to add soy sauce to rice)
擺架子；作偽騙人

e.g. Néih m̀sái sihyàuh lòufaahn, jíng sīk jíngséui la,
你 唔使 豉油 撈飯， 整 色 整水 嘑，

ngóh māt dōu jìdousaai la.
我 乜 都 知道晒 嘑。

(You don't have to pretend any more. OR: You don't have to cheat me with this artificial thing, I know everything about it.)
(你不用裝模作樣了，我甚麼都知道了。)

The percentage of sterling silver in a silver coin is called Séui. There is a recognized standard percentage. Sometimes you have to put in more silver. People call it "tipséui". Sometimes you have to take away some and this is called "sànséui". Jíngsīk (Jíng) Séui is to adjust the percentage of sterling silver in a silver coin.

There is another interpretation. The value of jade is estimated according to Sīk (i.e. color) and Séui (i.e. transparency). A good piece of jade should be green, bright and as clear as water. A piece of jade which is excellent in both colour and transparency is very rare. So a cunning merchant will take one of poor quality and use some artificial way to make it green, bright, and as clear as water. When soy sauce is put on rice, it will change the colour of rice from white to brown. You will fool other people into thinking that you have delicious food to eat, not just rice. This illustration is used to describe the same thing that people would do to make jade look green.

銀兩的成色叫做「水」。意即銀兩中含銀的成分要達到某個公認的水平。有時要加銀，叫「貼水」；有時要減銀，叫「申水」。所以調整銀兩的成色叫「整色水」。

　　另一種說法：玉器的價值高低關乎它的「色」和「水」。色指色彩，要鮮明悅目。水指透明度，要看上去通透如水。但是兼有好色好水的玉不易得，於是奸商便用人工作僞的手法，拿劣玉來染色，使它表面看來似是好色水。同樣地，把「豉油」（醬油）加在白飯上，使飯變成棕色，人們便以爲你有美味菜汁的餸菜下飯，其實，你吃的祇是一碗「飯」。

Wòhng Daaih Sīn→Yáuh Kàuh Bīt Ying
黃大仙→有求必應

Wòhng Daaih Sīn→Yáuh Kàuh Bīt Ying

HIT   one will certainly promise you whatever you ask for
有求必應

e.g. Kaiyèh haih Wòhng Daaih Sīn, kàuh kéuih jechín, saht móuh tok
契爺 係 黃 大 仙，求 佢 借錢，實 冇 托

sáujàang ge.
手睜 嘅。

(Our foster father is as kind as Wòhng Daaih Sīn. If we ask him to lend us some money, he will not say no.)
（誼父是好好先生，求他借錢一定不會推搪。）

In Hong Kong, there is a temple called Wòhng Daaih Sīn. Wòhng Daaih Sīn was called Wòhng Chò Pìhng. When he was a child, he was a shepherd on Mt. Gàm Wàh in Jitgōng province. There he encountered an immortal who taught him how to practise Taoist rules. Later, he himself became an immortal. When his elder brother went to look for him in the mountain, he could see nothing but rocks everywhere. But when Wòhng Daaih Sīn shouted at the rocks, they all started to move and turned into sheep.

Now Wòhng Daaih Sīn Temple has become the most famous in Hong Kong. It is said that he will make your wish come true. You can always get whatever you pray for. So he is really the great immortal, the lit. meaning of Daaih Sīn.

    香港有一間「黃大仙廟」。黃大仙原名黃初平，童年時在中國浙江省的金華山裏牧羊過活。他遇到神仙教他修煉的方法，結果他也成了神仙。他哥哥去山裏找他，只見到處是石頭，但黃大仙一叱喝，忽然石頭都活動起來，變成一隻隻羊兒呢！

    香港最有名的廟宇就是「黃大仙廟」，據說黃大仙很靈驗，祈求的必定得到。

Dálaahn Sàpùhn Mahndou Dūk
打爛砂盤問(罅)到篤
Fuhngjí Sìhngfàn 奉子(旨)成婚
Sih Gāp Máh Hàahng Tìhn 事(士)急馬行田
Jáugāi 走雞(機)
Chìhntòuh Chíh Gám 前途似噉(錦)

Dálaahn Sàpùhn Mahndou Dūk

I.E. keep on asking until one completely understands what one wants to know
不斷追問，務求徹底明白

e.g. M̀gòi néih m̀hóu dálaahn sàpùhn mahndou dūk lā.
唔該 你 唔好 打爛 砂盤 問到 篤 啦。

(Please don't keep on asking me about it any more.)
（請你不要追問。）

In Chinese language, there are many words which are pronounced the same but are different in meaning. We like to use two such homophones to make a pun. This is called "sèunggwàan" in rhetoric. The original word for Mahn refers to a crack in pottery. It is pronounced the same as the word for "to ask". Superficially, this idiomatic expression describes the kind of "crack" which runs all the way to the bottom (i.e. Dūk) of the pot (i.e. Sàpùhn), but actually it means to repeatedly "ask" about one thing until one understands it completely.

中文裏有許多同音字，讀音同，但意思有異。我們利用同音字同時表達兩種意思，這在修辭學上稱爲「雙關」。

「罅」，原意指器皿破裂了，但仍未散碎。它與「問」同音。「打爛砂盤罅到篤」表面上說盤子裂了，一條裂痕直透到盤底，實際上指查問事情，問到最盡頭。

其他的例子如：

A few more examples:

Fuhngjí Sìhngfàn
奉子(旨)成婚

I.E. a shotgun wedding, a pregnant bride getting married because of the baby. Jí, the emperor's decree, is replaced by the word for "a child". The meaning of the original form of this expression is being ordered by the emperor to get married.
少女懷了孕而被迫結婚

Sih Gāp Máh Hàahng Tìhn
事(士)急馬行田

I.E. one need not follow the normal way of handling things in emergencies. Originally it was a rule in playing Chinese chess. Sih, a name for a chess, is replaced by that for "event".
事情危急時便要打破常規去解決問題

Jáugāi
走雞(機)

VO miss a chance. The original word for the object was "gèi", a chance.
錯失機會

Chìhntòuh Chíh Gám
前途似噉(錦)

I.E. (said in a negative sense) your future is like this. Originally it means "to have a promising future like brocade". A pun is made on the word "gám", while Chìhntòuh means "future".

Maaihyùhlóu Sáisàn→Móuhsaai Sènghei
賣魚佬洗身→無晒腥(聲)氣；
Fósìu Kèihgōn→Chèuhng Taan
火燒旗桿→長炭(嘆)；
Daahn'gālóu Dájiu→Móuh Tàahn
蛋家佬打醮→冇壇(彈)；
Sauchói Sáugān→Bàau syù
秀才手巾→包書(輸)

Maaihyùhlóu Sáisàn→Móuhsaai Sènghei

HIT not any sign of hope
      沒有回音、消息

e.g. Ngóh tok A-Gaap wán'gùng jouh, dímjì kéuih sātjó jūng.
      我 託 亞甲 搵 工 做，點知 佢 失咗 踪。

 Gàmchi dōuhaih maaihyùhlóu sáisàn, móuhsaai sènghei ge lo.
 今次 都係 賣魚佬 洗身， 無晒 聲氣 嘅咯。

(I entrusted A to look for a job for me. How was I supposed to know that he would disappear without a trace? I can see that it is hopeless to ask for his help.)
(我託人找工作，誰知他失了踪。這次是沒有希望了。)

Sènghei (i.e. hope) was first mentioned in *The Book of Changes*. It says, "People of the same Sèng(voice) and Hei (disposition) will get along well together." Both Sèng and Hei indicate the responses of colloquial interchange.

In spoken Cantonese, many people like to use two or several words of similar or identical pronunciation to refer to different things (i.e. to make puns). Let's take the above Hit as an example. Maaihyùhlóu is a fish monger. He will always be stained by the blood of the fish and smell fishy too. After he takes a bath (i.e. Maaihyùhlóu Sáisàn), the fishy smell would all go away (i.e. Móuhsaai Sènghei).

But Sènghei (fishy) sound the same as the two words for "news, hope". So we make a pun on them by switching the meaning of the above sènghei and by making them refer to "hope" but not "fishy" any more. Therefore, Maaihyùhlóu Sáisàn → Móuhsaai Sènghei is considered as a tail-less pun, one of the two categories of Hithauhyúh.

廣州話裏用諧音作相關語的例子很多。這句裏，賣魚的小販被魚血沾污了，滿身是魚腥氣味（諧音「聲氣」），到他回家洗個澡，身上的腥味除了，就是「無晒腥（聲）氣」。

「聲氣」一詞，出自《周易》：「同聲相應，同氣相求。」意思是：有相同的聲調和氣質，就會互相呼應。「聲氣」就是呼喚和回答的聲音。即指有回應，有希望。

Other examples of tail-less pun:
其他相關語的例子如：

Fósiu Kèihgōn → Chèuhng Taan
火燒旗桿 → 長炭（嘆）

the flag staff is burned → It becomes a long charcoal → one can enjoy oneself forever

Daahn'gālóu Dájiu → Móuh Tàahn
蛋家佬打醮 → 冇壇（彈）

when the boat people worship a god → they have not an altar → perfect; there should be no compaint about it

Sauchói Sáugān → Bàau syù
秀才手巾 → 包書（輸）

the handkerchief of a scholar → is used to wrap the books → surely you will lose in gambling

Jyūyihsíng 朱義盛

Jyūyihsíng

N   jewelry not made of real gold [M:dī]
      假的金飾

e.g. Nīdī jyūyihsíng, m̀jihkchín ge.
      呢啲 朱義盛， 唔值錢 嘅。

> (These pieces of jewelry are not made of real gold. They do not worth much money.)
> （這些假金飾不值錢。）

Some Cantonese colloquial expressions originate from things that happened in Canton. I would like to introduce some to you.

    About one hundred years ago, in Canton there was a goldsmith's shop called Jyū Yih Síng which specialized in making jewelry plated with gold and the jewelry was famous for not changing colour. The business was very good. But when Jyū Yih Síng, also the name of the founder of the shop, first started his business in Faht Sāan, the business was not that good. He sold his shop and moved to Canton and tried his best to develop his business again. He was successful this time and he opened six branch shops with nine thousand employees then. Although the jewelry which he made was not of real gold but just gold-plated, it was very popular because it glittered just like that made of real gold and the workmanship was good. People then called false things Jyūyihsíng.

    廣州話往往起源於廣州的事物，以下為你介紹幾則。

    在一百年前，廣州市有一間「朱義盛金飾店」，專門製賣鍍金首飾，以「永不變色」為號召，生意很好。最初創辦人朱義盛在佛山開店，業績欠佳而轉讓予人。他遷到廣州，大力發展，居然分店開至六間，有員工九千人。他出售的首飾不是真金製，只是鍍金，但色澤鮮明，手工不錯，所以大受歡迎。人們也就把假東西稱為「朱義盛」。

Paaktō 拍拖；Jáamlaahm 斬纜/Lātto 甩拖

Paaktō

VO (said of lovers) going out, dating
男女談戀愛或約會

Jáamlaahm/Lātto

VO (said of lovers) be over (Lātto also means to fail to appear at an appointment)
情侶感情出問題而分手；甩拖也指失約

e.g. Kéuihdeih paakjó géinìhn tō, séungm̀dou dōu wúih lātto.
　　　佢哋　拍咗　幾年 拖，想唔到　都　會　甩拖。

(They have been going steady for several years. We didn't expect that it is over now.)
（他倆戀愛了幾年，想不到仍要分手。）

The Pearl River is a large river that runs through the city of Canton. The river banks are widely separated and the traffic on the river is very busy. People used a special way to pull the boats that went through this river. They put two boats side by side first, and then tied them together with ropes. When one of them moved, the other would follow so that they could go together. This was called Paaktō, which later was borrowed to describe lovers when they went out hand in hand.

But when people wanted to separate the two boats, they would cut the ropes which were used to tie the boats. This was called Jáamlaahm/ Lātto which was also used as a metaphor for lovers when they no longer dated each other.

　　珠江是穿過廣州市的一條大河，河面寬闊，水路交通繁忙。駛經這處的船有時會採用一種較特別的拖拉方法，就是兩隻船並排靠攏，用繩纜縛緊，然後由甲船拖動乙船前進。這就是「拍拖」。後來用以形容男女把臂同行。

　　由拍拖引申，斬斷連繫的繩纜，令兩船分開，就是「斬纜」或「甩拖」，比喻情侶分手。

Hāau Jūkgong 敲竹杠

Hāau Jūkgong

    VO   to blackmail (money) (lit. tap the bamboo cane)
           敲詐勒索（金錢）

    e.g. Kéuih béi yàhn jūkjyuh tunggeuk hāau jūkgong.
          佢　俾　人　捉住　痛腳　敲　竹杠。

        (He was blackmailed for not making known something discreditable about him.)
        （他有把柄在人家手裏而被勒索金錢。）

Just before the Opium War broke out in 1840, Làhm Jāk Chèuih was ordered by the Ching government to go to Canton to prohibit the opium trade. He upheld the law very strictly. The opium sellers had to surrender all the opium they had. The price of opium on the black market was even more expensive than that of gold.

    Once, Làhm Jāk Chèuih went on board a merchant ship to make a search. It seemed that there was not any contraband. One of his confidential secretaries tapped a bamboo cane at the bulwark. It sounded a little strange. The secretary was a clever man. He immediately understood that the owner of the ship had hidden the opium inside the bamboo canes. He did not report it to Làhm Jāk Chèuih but intentionally tapped the bamboo cane two more times. The ship owner was also a clever man and immediately gave the secretary some money secretly. The hidden opium was not exposed.

公元1840年中英鴉片戰爭前夕，林則徐奉清廷命令到廣州查禁鴉片。當時他執法很嚴厲，販賣鴉片的人都須要自動繳出鴉片，而鴉片的黑市價格比黃金還貴。

　　一次，林則徐帶人上一艘商船上搜查，似乎沒有甚麼違禁品。林則徐手下一個「師爺」無意中敲了一下船舷邊的竹杠，竹杠所發出的聲音有點古怪。師爺是聰明人，他立刻猜到船主把鴉片藏在竹杠裏，但他沒有立即向林則徐報告，只是故意地再在竹杠上敲了兩下。那船主也是個聰明人，立即悄悄地給師爺塞了紅包（錢），於是偷藏的鴉片沒有被發現。

Sàinàahm Yih Baakfú 西南二伯父

Sàinàahm Yih Baakfú

N   a senior who spoils the youth intentionally [M: go, tìuh]
一個縱容頑劣青少年的老人

e.g. Ngóh nìhngyún jouh sàinàahm yih baakfú, dōu faisih gaaujèng kéuih.
我　寧願　做　西南　二　伯父，都費事　教精　佢。

(I'd rather let him do wrong. I don't want to give him any instructions or advice.)
（我寧願任由他變壞，也不想敎好他。）

Formerly when there was still apprenticeship, a young man had to find a master. He would follow him to learn a certain skill or trade before he could make a living. He would live in his master's shop and learn what his master taught him. The master, besides teaching the young man the skill, was also responsible for the discipline of his apprentice.

There was a shop which made different kinds of sauces in Sàinàahm town near Canton. The owner was called Yih Baakfú (lit. the second elder uncle). He would never advise nor scold his apprentice whenever his apprentice was lazy or learnt something bad. However, he would fire his apprentice and sent him away when his apprentice had become corrupted. No one else would then employ that apprentice.*

從前有「學徒制度」，一些少年人欲投身某行業，就要拜個師傅，住在師傅的店裏，跟師傅學藝。做師傅的，除了教某行業的技藝外，也有責任管着學徒的品行。

在廣州附近的西南鎮有個醬園，東主叫「二伯父」，他對學徒相當縱容，學徒偷懶他不會責罵，學徒學壞他也不會勸阻。直到一天學徒已經很不成才，他就突然把學徒解僱趕走，以後誰也不會再僱用那名學徒了。

* adapted from Kwan Kit Choi, p. 70.

Bòlòhgāi→Kaau Chì 波羅雞→靠黐

Bòlòhgāi→Kaau Chì

HIT look for someone to get a free meal
意即揩油水，佔他人的便宜

e.g. Gógo gùhòhn chòihjyú chìyám chìsihk, jingyāt bòlòhgāi.
嗰個 孤寒 財主 黐飲 黐食，正一 波羅雞。

(When it comes to eating and drinking, that miser always takes advantage of others.)
（那各嗇鬼揩油水，白吃白喝。）

There is a Bòlòh temple in the eastern suburb of Canton. People can worship the god of the South China Sea there. Being one of the scenic spots in Canton, many people visit the temple to worship the god. After that, most of them will buy a toy chicken from the hawkers at the temple. It is made of pieces of paper held together by glue. Therefore, we have the expression Bòlòhgāi → Kaau Chì (lit. all depends on the sticky glue). Note that the common usage of "Chì" suggests stickiness, similar to a human parasite.

When Western people go outside to eat, each person will pay for himself. Chinese people conduct themselves differently. There is always a generous person who will pay the bill for all. Since we have such a custom, some people will intentionally not pay to get a free meal.

廣州東郊有間「波羅廟」，是供奉南海神的。這處是廣州的名勝，遊人很多，他們參神後多數會跟廟前的小販買隻玩具紙雞。這紙雞用漿糊黏成。於是出現了「波羅雞 → 靠黐」這句歇後語。

西方人一起出外吃喝，多數各自付賬，但中國人不會這樣。總有一個慷慨的人付了全部人的賬。由於這種習慣，有人就故意「靠黐」（借機會揩油水），白吃一頓。

Maaih Jyūjái 賣豬仔

Maaih Jyūjái

VO   be sold out like a piggy (lit. to sell a piggy)
被當作小豬一樣出賣了

e.g.   Gógàan hohkhaauh jāplāp, jauh jèung dī hohksāang maaih jyūjái
嗰間　學校　執笠，就　將　啲　學生　賣　豬仔
béi lihng yātgàan.
俾　另　一間。

(That school closed down. They passed the students to another school like selling piggies.)
（那間學校停辦，就將學生「賣」給另一間學校。）

To raise pigs has always been the side job of a farmer. When piglets are born, some of them are reared by the farmer while some were sold to other farmers. Usually piglets are not worth much money.

    About one hundred years ago, people of the coastal area of Gwóngdùng province led a very hard life. There was no way for them to improve their livelihood. So they went overseas to look for better opportunities. It just happened that large quantities of cheap labour were needed at that time for the development of North America and latter Australia. Indentured labour or coolie agents devised all kinds of ways and means to recruit young and strong men along the coastal area of China and then shipped them to North America and other places where cheap labour was needed. People who were employed had to sign a contract of their own free will or under force. In return they got a small sum of money which they handed to their family. Separated from their families, they were then shipped to far away places to hard labour. It was very likely that they would never return home. People called this coolie trade operated by the slave brokers "the selling of piglets" as people were sold like piglets.

養豬一向是農村人的副業。母豬生下小豬，農人有時自己飼養，有時把小豬賣給他人。但是小豬通常不值錢。

　　在大約一百年前，那時廣東沿海地區的人，生活很苦，被迫到海外找尋機會。適值北美洲剛開發，需要大量廉價勞工，於是由中國沿海地區招募壯丁往美洲工作。應募的人簽了契約，拿到一筆安家費後，就拋妻棄子，漂洋過海，去到外地做苦工，很可能永遠不再回家。他們被稱為「豬仔」，給中間人出賣了。

Wūlēi Dàandōu 烏利單刀

Wūlēi Dàandōu

I.E.   muddled, chaotic
一塌糊塗

e.g.   Gógo sànjái m̀jì sáuméih, gáaudou wūlēi dàandōu.
嗰個 新仔唔知首尾， 搞到 烏利 單刀。

(The new employee doesn't know the procedures well. He gets everything mixed up.)
（那新來的人不曉方法，弄得一團糟。）

There is a folk-tale circulated among the people in a village near Swatow in Gwóngdùng province. It is said that during the Yuan dynasty, a Mongolian military officer called Wū Leih arrived. He was good at fighting with a short-hilted broadsword, Dàandōu, that weighed more than 70 catties. He killed people whenever he felt like it. The villagers all hated him.

    Once Wū Leih went out to sea and the boatman made the boat turn over. Wū Leih and his sword sank to the bottom of the sea and the commander of the Yuan army was very angry. He gave an order that every family had to put a tablet of Wū Leih on their door. Those who did not do it were held to be the murderers. After many years, Wū Leih's sword was found. It was put in the temple to be shown to the people who teased the Yuan army being so stupid. Thereafter, Wūlēi Dàandōu became a more popular expression than "wùhlēi wùhtòuh".

    You may find the above story very interesting. However, there is another interpretation of the expression. It was the mistaken form of Wùhlòih Dìndóu, which means to do something recklessly or to mix up the right with the wrong. If these words were sung in the language that people used when performing a Peking opera, they would sound identical with what we utter today.

在廣東潮州附近的周郡鄉，流傳着「烏利單刀」的民間故事。據說元朝時當地來了一個蒙古軍官叫烏利的，擅使一口七十多斤重的單刀，殺人不眨眼，周郡鄉的人都憎恨他。

一次，烏利乘船出海，船夫就故意弄翻了船，烏利和他的單刀就沉到水底。元兵的首領很憤怒，下令家家門口都要貼上烏利的神位，誰不貼的就是兇手！

多年之後，有人從海裏撈回烏利那口單刀，就放在廟裏示眾，譏笑元兵的糊塗。從此，「烏利單刀」就成了較「糊裏糊塗」流行的俗語。

上面的故事很有趣，不過我們有另一個猜想：「烏利單刀」是「胡來顛倒」的訛寫。胡來顛倒意思就是胡亂地幹，把是非顛倒了。如果以官話把「胡來顛倒」唱出，聲音就似「烏利單刀」。

Jeukhéi Lùhngpòuh Dōu M̀chíh Taaijí
著起龍袍都唔似太子；
Sihk Gáu Daaih Gwái 食九大簋

Jeukhéi Lùhngpòuh Dōu M̀chíh Taaijí

I.E. it's a waste for one to get well dressed because it doesn't match (lit. even if you put on a dragon robe, you don't look like a crown prince at all)
雖經刻意打扮，總不像樣

e.g. Tái néihgo sèui yéung, jeukhéi lùhngpòuh dōu m̀chíh taaijí lā!
睇你個衰樣，著起龍袍都唔似太子啦!
(How terrible you look, even with a nice dress on!)
（你相貌不好，打扮也沒用。）

Sihk Gáu Daaih Gwái

VO to have a very rich meal like that of a king
享用很豐富的一餐

e.g. Gàmmáahn sihk gáu daaih gwái.
今晚食九大簋。
(We're going to have a very rich meal to-night.)

There were some strict rules concerning dressing in ancient China. The ordinary people could only wear cotton clothes. The officials put on official dress while the king put on a "dragon robe" (i.e. Lùhngpòuh), an imperial dress which was embroidered with dragons. A crown prince could put on a dragon robe too, because he would become the king. He would look dignified with his dragon robe on.

There were also rules about the numbers of dishes at a meal. The emperor could have nine dishes. The feudal kings could have seven. A nobleman could have five, officials three, and ordinary people only two. Ancient Chinese people used a vessel called Gwái to hold food. Most of the Gwáis were made of wood. Some were made of bronze or bamboo. So you can learn how Chinese distinguish their social rank from the way they eat and dress.

古代中國人穿衣服是有規定的,不准亂穿。平民穿布衣,官員穿官服,皇帝穿龍袍。太子因為是未來的皇帝,所以也可以穿龍袍。龍袍穿在身上,當然很神氣。

　　不但穿衣有規定,吃飯吃多少簋菜也有限制。天子一頓最多可吃九簋菜,諸侯吃七簋,卿吃五簋,大夫吃三簋,平民吃兩簋。簋是用來盛載食物的器具,多用木做成,有些則用銅或竹來做。

　　中國人重視尊卑上下的區別,就表現在衣食和生活上。

Gwái, a container for food
簋,盛食物的器具

Ngàhyīn 牙煙

Ngàhyīn

SV dangerous
危險

e.g. Go jiupàaih béi daaihfùng chèuidou yìuhyìuhháh, táigin jauh ngàhyīn.
個 招牌 俾 大風 吹到 搖搖吓， 睇見 就 牙煙。

(Being blown by the strong wind, the signboard becomes dangerous as if it is going to fall.)

（那招牌被大風吹得搖來搖去，看來很危險。）

Ngàh (lit. teeth) can be used as a symbol of fighting. We can see that when a beast is ready to bite or to fight, it will open its mouth wide and show its fearful teeth. In ancient China, certain words related to military affairs were coined with Ngàh, such as "ngàhkèih" (i.e. military banners), "ngàhmùhn" (i.e. the entrance of a barracks) and "ngàhjeung" (i.e. military officer of middle rank).

Yīn means smoke. We have reason to believe that Ngàhyīn is the signal fire or smoke made by the soldiers for military communication. In ancient China, tall structures similar to that of a watch-tower were set up at intervals on a city wall or at a strategic place or at an important road. A troop would be stationed there to guard against the enemy and to detect the enemy's presence. Once there was any sign of invasion in the day time, the soldiers would let off some smoke by burning the excrement of the wolves, which would last for quite a long time, while fire would be raised at night by burning firewood and hay. There were regulations denoting the frequency of the smoke or the fire according to the number of enemies. Once a fire or smoke was seen, the soldiers at the neighbouring spot would do the same and the message would be relayed to the commander quickly.

On the other hand, if we try to interpret it on a phonological basis, we would find that the more accurate origin of it would be Yùhyīn, the combination of the words "fish" and "swallow". In ancient times, the word for "fish" (yùh) was pronounced very closely to Ngàh. In his *Handbook of the Ancient Pronunciation of Chinese Words*, the author successfully retrieves its original pronunciation and presents its hypothetical phonetic spelling as "ŋia". The written form of the expression under discussion was mistakenly changed to two different words of similar sounds over the centuries.

However, how did fish and swallow relate to "danger"? These two figures were adopted by the author of a well-known literary prose *A Letter to Chàhn Baak-jì* from Yàu Chìh (A.D. 464-508) whereby the sender warned his friend of the perilous circumstance the latter was in by using figurative descriptions which read:

ŋia (now "yùh") yàuh yù faih díng jìjùng
(lit. [you are like] fish swimming in boiling caldron)
Yin (now "yìn") chàauh yù fèimohk jì seuhng
(lit. swallow making nest on shaking tent)

The great danger was thus indicated.

「牙」是戰鬥的象徵；狗打鬥時總會露出牙齒示威、嚙咬。在古代漢語，由「牙」字組成的詞常與軍事有關：牙旗即軍旗；牙門即軍營的門；牙將是中級軍官。

牙煙，指軍士所燃放的烽煙，用以傳遞危急的訊息。在中國古代，爲了迅速傳遞消息，尤其是防禦敵人的侵襲，軍隊在要塞和交通孔道築有烽火臺，臺上駐有守兵，負責偵察敵情。烽火臺相隔若干里設一個。假若敵人入侵，烽火臺的守兵一發覺，在日間便燒狼糞放煙（狼煙頗能保持不散），夜間便燒柴草放火。煙火的數目有規定，按敵人的人數多寡而不同。旁近的烽火臺也會跟着點燃煙火，於是可以把消息很快傳達軍隊的司令部。

「牙煙」又或是一個記音詞，正確的寫法是「魚燕」，就是魚和燕子。「魚」字現在讀作「如」，但古音近似「牙」。郭錫良著的《漢字古音手冊》裏給「魚」字擬的上古音是"ŋia"，極近"ngàh"。「魚燕」在口耳相傳之後，誤記作「牙煙」。

但是「魚燕」和「危險」有甚麼關係呢？原來這詞出自一篇有名的古文 ── 丘遲（公元464-508）《與陳伯之書》，文中描寫陳伯之處境危險，好像「魚游於沸鼎之中，燕巢於飛幕之上」（魚兒在沸水鍋裏游，燕子在不穩固的營幕上築巢）。你說是不是非常危險？

Sihk Chāt Gam Sihk 食七咁食

Sihk Chāt Gam Sihk

I.E. eat and drink as much as possible
大吃大喝

e.g. Nīchāan yáuh fūkséui chénghaak, ngóhdeih yātyù sihk chāt gam sihk lo.
呢餐 有 福水 請客， 我地 一於 食 七 咁 食 咯

(We are being treated by a sucker for this meal. Let's eat and drink as much as possible.)
（這頓飯有冤大頭付鈔，我們正好大吃大喝哩。）

What will the number 7 make you think of? "Seven Up" or a lucky number? Note that a number is not only used to denote quantity, it also carries some cultural connotations.

It says in *The Book of Changes* that seven days make one cycle. It is quite the same as a week of seven days in the Western culture. Chinese people believe that seven days after the death of a man, his ghost will come back home to see his kinfolks. So on that day, ritual ceremonies would be held and a Buddhist or Taoist monk would be asked to recite sutras for him. It is called "jouh chāt". People do the same on the fourteenth, the twenty-first,... and so forth till the forty-ninth day. At the sixth or the seventh "chāt" (i.e. the forty-second or the forty-ninth day), all relatives and friends are invited to have a big vegetarian meal comprised of seven dishes. They can eat and drink as much as they can. They do not have to pay anything at all. That is Sihk Chāt Gam Sihk.

To some people in Hong Kong nowadays, it is still considered a taboo to have 7 dishes for a meal.

數字7令你想起甚麼？「七喜」抑或「幸運號碼」？我們要注意：數字不僅是數字，還有它背後的文化含義。

　　《周易》說：「七日來復」。這和西方人每星期有七日相似。中國人相信，人死之後第七日，他的靈魂會回家見親人，所以他們會在這天請和尚或道士來做法事，稱為「做七」。跟着是第十四天，第廿一天……一直至第四十九天，都會舉行法事。而在第四十二天那次，更會大設齋筵，請親友來吃喝一頓。這種齋筵有七個菜，被請的人只管盡情吃喝，分文也不必付出。這就是「食七咁食」。

　　在今天仍有人視七碟菜為禁忌。

Daaihmòuh Sīyeuhng 大模尸樣

Daaihmòuh Sīyeuhng

I.E. with full composure; proudly
大模大樣

e.g. Hauhsàangjái, m̀hóu daaihmòuh sīyeuhng, yiu hìmhèuidī.
後生仔，唔好 大模 尸樣，要 謙虛啲。

(You youngsters should be humble. You should not be proud.)
（年輕人不好大模大樣，要謙虛一點。）

In ancient China, it was a religious custom that during ceremonies of offering sacrifices, people had to worship a boy sitting on the altar. He was called Sī which means "lord". He was chosen to dress and act as a god and to be worshipped by other people. On usual days, the boy was very low in social status, but once he sat on the altar and acted as the god, even the monarch had to bow down to him and worship him.

A person is said to be Daaihmòuh Sīyeuhng if he is so proud and arrogant that no one is important in his eyes.

古代中國有一種宗教風俗，就是在大祭典時，選一個童子扮作神，坐在壇上，供其他人膜拜。這個童子叫做「尸」。尸是「主」的意思。平日這童子輩份很低，可一旦坐在「尸」的位置，連國君也要向他下拜。

有些人一副不可一世、視他人如無物的樣子，就是「大模尸樣」。

Jāplāp 執笠

Jāplāp

VO (said of business or factories) close down because of losing money
　　店鋪經營不善而倒閉

e.g. Gāaiháu gógàan jáulàuh jāpjó lāp.
　　　街口　嗰間　酒樓　執咗 笠。

(The restaurant at the corner of the street closed down.)
（街角那間酒樓關了門。）

In ancient times, the tribe of Yuht lived in the southern part of China. They were very virtuous people, frank and sincere. When they made friends with one another, they would build an altar and offer chicken or dogmeat as a sacrifice. They would swear and pray:

> One day when we meet,
> you will get down from your chariot
> 　　and greet me who wears just a bamboo hat.
> One day when we meet,
> I'll get down from my horse
> 　　and greet you who carries just an umbrella.

Once they made friends with each other, they would always be friends regardless of being high or low.

Lāp is a bamboo hat. Jāplāp means to pick up one's bamboo hat, ready to go on one's way. If the shop closed down, the owner of the shop could only pick up his hat and go.

　　古時居住在中國南方的越族，性情直率厚重，他們與人初結交，就會築個神壇，放置雞狗作祭品，祝禱說：「君乘車，我戴笠，他日相逢下車揖。君擔簦（傘子），我跨馬，他日相逢為君下。」大意謂不會因為貴賤而改變了友情。

　　執笠，執起笠子，準備上路。因為店鋪要「倒閉」，東主只好執起笠子離去。

Jouhdūng 做東

Jouhdūng

VO   play host
做主人招待客人

e.g. Gàmchāan Lóuh Wóng jouhdūng.
今餐　老　王　做東。

(Lóuh Wóng will pay the bill for this meal.)
（這一頓飯由老王付賬。）

Dūng is the short form for "dùngjyú" (lit. the host of the east). It originated from the story in *Jó Jyuhn*, a commentary on *The Spring and Autumn Annals*: The states of Chèuhn and Jeun were going to attack the state of Jehng. The king of Jehng sent an envoy to persuade the king of Chèuhn to withdraw his troops. The envoy said, "Actually you can't get any benefits if our country is eliminated. On the contrary, the territory of Jeun will become larger and it will be quite dangerous for Chèuhn in the future. Please stop invading Jehng. Then we will try to be your host to receive your envoys when they travel eastwards and you won't suffer any loss." As a result, the troops of Chèuhn withdrew, and so did the troops of Jeun.

    Thereafter, "Dùng(douh)jyú" became a daily expression and the arrangement of seats was that the host would sit on the east side while the guest would sit on the west. We can see in feasts nowadays that the seats are arranged according to the position of the guests.

(Note that A is the table for the host and his family and B is for the guests. 1 is for the most senior person while 8, the most junior.)

把「主人」稱作「東主」，出自《左傳》裏一段故事：

秦國和晉國聯合出兵攻打鄭國，鄭國派使者說秦退兵，他說：「滅了鄭國，對秦沒有好處，只會擴大了晉的領土，將來對秦不利。不如放過鄭國，那麼鄭國可以作東方道路上的主人，招待秦國的外交人員，秦亦沒有損失。」結果，秦國退兵，而晉國也退了兵。

自此以後，「東道主」成為常用語。而在座位的安排上，主人常居東，而客人常居西。假設現在請客，A是主家席，B是客人席，其座位安排按各人的地位編排如下（1最尊，8最卑）：

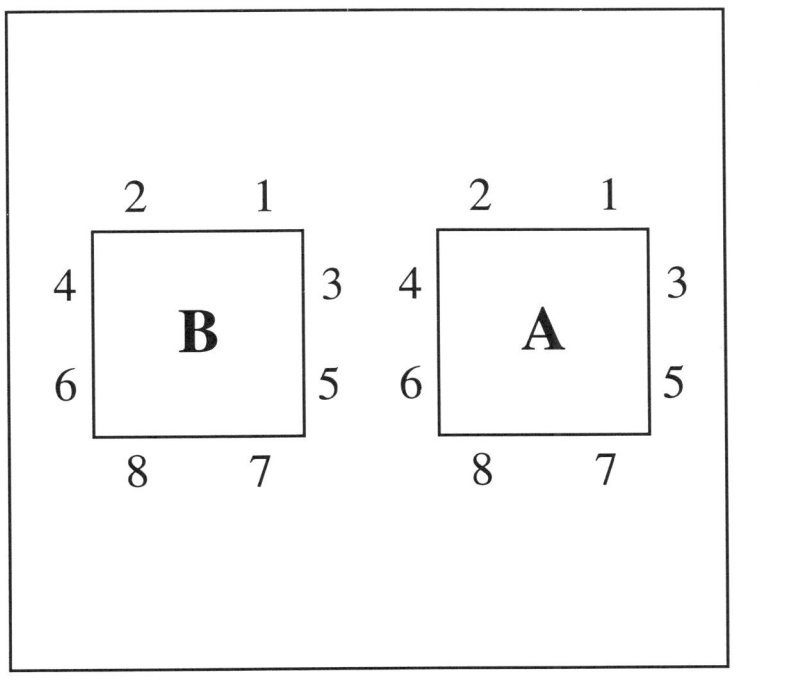

Tipcho Mùhnsàhn 貼錯門神

Tipcho Mùhnsàhn

I.E. something wrong between two lovers; even when they meet, they pay no attention to each other
是說一對男女鬧意見，互不瞅睬

e.g. Kéuih léuhnggo tipcho mùhnsàhn, m̀jì géisìh ji hóudākfàan.
佢　　兩個　　貼錯　　門神，唔知幾時至　好得番。

(The two of them don't even talk to each other. I don't know when things will be better again.)
（他倆鬧意見，不知甚麼時候才和好如初。）

The first ruler of the Tang dynasty, who reigned from A.D. 618 to 627, had three sons: Léih Gin Sìhng, Léih Sai Màhn and Léih Yùhn Gāt. The three brothers were not on good terms because all of them wanted to succeed their father. Later, two brothers were shot dead by the soldiers of Léih Sai Màhn at the north gate of the imperial city. It is recorded in history as "The Rebellion of Yùhn Móuh Gate".

After Léih Sai Màhn became emperor, he always had nightmares. He saw in his dreams his two brothers come to take revenge. He could not sleep well unless two of his famous generals kept watch at the door outside his bedroom. Later, he simply put the pictures of them on the door, and those are the two door-gods (i.e. Mùhnsàhn) that we put on the main door of our houses today. But one has to be careful to put them facing each other. They will look funny if we put them facing the wrong way.

唐高祖（公元618-627在位）有三個兒子：李建成、李世民、李元吉。但這三兄弟因為爭奪皇位的繼承權而不和，李世民就伏兵在皇城的北門，射殺了建成和元吉。歷史上稱為「玄武門之變」。

李世民當了皇帝，但他常常發惡夢，夢見建成和元吉來索命。世民休息時，要派兩名猛將守在寢室門外，這才睡得安寧。後來索性把他們的畫像掛在門上，漸漸成了今日的「門神」。張貼「門神」的時候，一定要兩人面對面，貼錯了就很好笑。

Jí Héui Jàugùn Fongfó, Bātjéun Baaksing Dímdāng 只許州官放火，不准百姓點燈

Jí Héui Jàugùn Fongfó, Bātjéun Baaksing Dímdāng

I.E.   ordinary people are not allowed to light a lamp while the officials can set fire as they like. In other words, the powerful people are privileged to be dictatorial. All the powerless people can do is just to tolerate the situation.
有權位的人可以很專橫，無權位的人只好忍受

Have you ever heard of "Gùnyām Pòuhsaat" (Bodhisattva or the Goddess of Mercy)? Legend has it that she will listen to the prayers of the suffering ones. She also will use her supernatural power to rescue them. Originally she was called "Gùn Sai Yām". People of the Tang dynasty abbreviated it to "Gùn Yām" in order to avoid mentioning "Sai", the name of the second emperor of the Tang dynasty who reigned from A.D. 627 to 649.

It's an old Chinese taboo to do so. People respect the emperor, their ancestors and their elders so much that they dare not call them by their names. There is a joke about this:

There was a provincial official (i.e. Jàugùn) called Tìhn Dāng in the Sung dynasty. He was so arbitrary that he did not allow people (i.e. Baaksing) to say "dāng" (i.e. lamp or lantern). People had to change it into "fó" (i.e. fire). It was a custom that every year people would hang lanterns to celebrate the Lantern Festival on the fifteenth day of the first lunar month. The secretary of Tìhn Dāng wrote a notice and posted it on the street. On it was written, "We'll observe the custom and celebrate the festival by setting a fire for three days." When people saw it, they whispered and just laughed in secret.

你聽過「觀音菩薩」嗎？傳說她能夠聽取受苦難的人的禱告，施法力去拯救他們。但是她原本叫「觀世音」，人們爲了避唐太宗李世民（公元627-649在位）諱而只稱她「觀音」。

　　甚麼叫「避諱」？就是出於對長輩的尊敬而不敢說及他的名字，也因此而生出一個笑話：

　　宋朝有個州官叫田登的，很專橫，不准百姓提及「登」字。百姓於是把「燈」改說成「火」。每年正月十五，習俗必張掛花燈慶祝，於是田登的祕書出告示貼在街上，寫作：「本州依例放火三日。」看到的人都掩着嘴笑。

Yātlàuh 一流；Gáulàuh 九流

Yātlàuh

PH the best
最高級的

Gáulàuh

PH very bad, very poor
很差的

e.g. Nīgihn sàijòng jātlíu yātlàuh/gáulàuh.
呢件 西裝 質料 一流／九流。

(The material of this Western suit is the best/very poor.)
（這件西服質料極好／很差。）

In China, from the Tang to the Ching dynasty, there were nine ranks of officials. The highest was called "yātbán", then followed "yihbán, sàambán,... etc., to the lowest, "gáubán". Usually the court ministers ranked the highest, the prime minister held the third rank and a county governor, the seventh.

The first rank was also called Yātlàuh and the ninth, Gáulàuh. As for those officers who were lower than the ninth rank, they were simply said to be "m̀yahplàuh" (excluded from all ranks).

　　由唐代至清代，中國的官員分為九個階級，最高的是「一品」，其次是「二品」、「三品」……最低級的是「九品」。通常居一品的是元老大臣；宰相是三品，縣官是七品。
　　一品又稱為「一流」，九品又稱為「九流」。至於那些連九品也攀不上的小吏，就被譏笑為「唔入流」（不入流）。

Sahpnìhn (Dōu) M̀fùhng Yātyeuhn
十年(都)唔逢一閏

Sahpnìhn (Dōu) M̀fùhng Yātyeuhn

I.E. very rare, once in a blue moon
罕見

e.g. Gùhòhn chòihjyú chénghaak, sahpnìhn (dōu) m̀fùhng yātyeuhn.
孤寒　財主　請客，　十年　（都）　唔逢　一閏。

(It's very rare for that miser to treat you to a meal.)
（守財奴花錢請客，難得一見。）

In Hong Kong, two different types of calendars are used simultaneously, the solar calendar and the lunar calendar. The solar calendar is made by following the movements of the earth, which revolves around the sun. There are approximately 365 days in one solar year. The lunar calendar on the other hand is made by following the movements of the moon which revolves around the earth. There are ten days fewer in one lunar year than in one solar year. Thus an extra month, "yeuhnyuht", will be inserted once in three years or twice in five years to make up for the difference between the solar and the lunar years.

Normally, there will be one intercalary month in two or three years, but Cantonese people made up an exaggeration from it: Sahpnìhn (Dōu) M̀fùhng Yātyeuhn which means something will only occur once in a blue moon, while literally it means not to have a leap year in ten years. Furthermore, Yeuhn has the meaning of "to enrich", "to benefit".

　　香港人同時使用兩種曆法：西曆和農曆。西曆主要以地球繞太陽去定曆法，每年大約有365日。農曆以月球繞地球去定曆法，農曆一年較西曆一年約少了十天，所以就用置閏月的方法去調節，每三年置一次閏月，五年置兩次閏月。

　　原本閏月是每隔兩三年就會出現的，但廣東人把情況誇張了，說成「十年唔逢一閏」，意即難得遇上。又「閏」有「潤澤」的意思，即給予恩惠和好處。

Lohksáu Dá Sàamgāang 落手打三更 /
Lohkbāt Dá Sàamgāang 落筆打三更

Lohksáu Dá Sàamgāang/Lohkbāt Dá Sàamgāang

I.E. make mistakes just when starting to work
事情一開始就犯了錯

e.g. Kéuih gàmjìu jìngsàhn fōngfāt, yāt hòigūng jauh lohkbāt dá sàamgāang
佢 今朝 精神 恍忽，一 開工 就 落筆 打 三更。

(He was not in high spirits this morning. So he made mistakes in his work when he just started to do it.)
（他今早精神恍惚，剛開始工作就出了錯。）

Formerly before clocks were invented, Chinese had dágāanglóu (i.e. a night watch-man) to tell people time throughout the night. He was also supposed to make rounds on the streets to see if there was any burglary or fire. Dágāang is to tell time by striking a gong and a rattle. In the past, the night was divided into five gāangs (i.e. periods of time or measure of time):

yātgāang:	around	7:00–9:00 p.m.
yihgāang:	around	9:00–11:00 p.m.
sàamgāang:	around	11:00–1:00 a.m.
seigāang:	around	1:00–3:00 a.m.
nǵhgāang:	around	3:00–5:00 a.m.

Although we had the clepsydra (i.e. water clock) in ancient times, the night watchman usually had no clock to look at. He struck the gong and the rattle according to his experience or by looking at the sky. Sometimes he would not be very accurate. At "yātgāang", he was supposed to strike the gong and the rattle once, and twice at "yihgāang"...and so forth until it was "nǵhgāang". But if he struck three times when it was just "yātgāang", then we say Lohksáu Dá Sàamgāang.

舊日有「打更佬」，負責在夜間打更，兼且巡視街道，防範小偷或失火。所謂「打更」，即是打鑼和敲梆子報時。人們把一夜分為五個「更」：大約晚上7-9時為一更，9-11時為二更，11-1時為三更，凌晨1-3時為四更，凌晨3-5時為五更。

　　「打更佬」多數沒有時鐘（古代叫「銅壺滴漏」），只憑經驗，看天色猜測着來打，所以不太準確。一更時他會敲一下梆子，敲一下鑼。二更時敲兩下，如此至五更。如果一更時分敲了三下鑼，就是「落手打三更」了。

Néih Jouh Chòyāt, Ngóh Jouh Sahpnǵh
你做初一，我做十五

Néih Jouh Chòyāt, Ngóh Jouh Sahpnǵh

I.E. tit for tat, blow for blow
意思等如「以牙還牙」

e.g. Néih hóu ngóh hóu, m̀haih jauh néih jouh chòyāt, ngóh jouh
你 好 我 好，唔係 就 你 做 初一，我 做

sahpnǵh.
十五。

(Let's be fair with each other. Otherwise, it is each one for himself.)
（你對我好，我自然也對你好。你要是對我不客氣，我也當然對你不客氣。）

There were once a large number of walled villages in the New Territories of Hong Kong. A shrine of the earth god was placed at the entrance of the village. It is believed that actually two gods were being venerated: The god and the goddess of the land. They were an old couple. They were the guardians of the land and of the people who believed that they would protect them against evil spirits. Whenever the inhabitants of the village had any anxieties, they would reveal them to the god and goddess of the land and at the same time pray for their blessings and divine help to ward off disasters. It was a custom that the people of those villages had to worship the gods solemnly on the first and on the fifteenth day of the month.

They had to take turns to do it. For example, if family A took the turn on Chòyāt (i.e. the first day of the lunar month), then family B would do it on Sahpnǵh (i.e. the fifteenth day) and family C on the first day of the next month..., etc. Thus, originated the expression Néih Jouh Chòyāt, Ngóh Jouh Sahpnǵh, which now, with the meaning changed, is used as a warning expressing anger or hostility.

香港新界有許多圍村,村前總會安放土地神位,又叫社神。土地神傳說是一對老人,土地公公又叫伯公,土地婆婆又叫伯婆。他們是這塊土地的守護神,保護這處的居民。鄉民有心事會向土地神傾訴,當然也祈求他們保祐,消災賜福。

　　鄉民有例逢農曆的初一及十五日,都要隆重地拜祭土地神。鄉民採用輪更的制度,例如二月初一由甲家拜,二月十五由乙家拜,三月初一由丙家拜……。於是產生「你做(拜神)初一,我做十五」這句話。

　　不過現在說這句話時常常表示憤怒、敵意。

Bīuchēng 標青；Gèngchēng 驚青；Kàhmchēng (Kàhmkàhmchēng) (Kàhmkámchēng) 噙青

Bīuchēng

SV outstanding, distinguished
    指人才出眾

e.g. Kéuih nīchi háausíh hóu bīuchēng.
     佢 呢次 考試 好 標青。

> (He did very well in the examination./He did much better than the others in the examination.)
> （他這次考試，成績超卓。）

Gèngchēng

SV frightened, afraid
    驚慌

e.g. Néih dihngdī làih, m̀sái gam gèngchēng.
     你 定啲 嚟 唔使 咁 驚青。

> (Please be calm. You don't have to be so frightened.)
> （你鎮定一點，不用驚怕。）

Kàhmchēng (Kàhmkàhmchēng) (Kàhmkámchēng)

SV in a hurry, impatient
    急躁的樣子

e.g. Maahnmáan làih, m̀sái gam kàhmchēng.
     慢慢 嚟，唔使咁 噙青。

> (Take your time. You don't have to be in such a hurry.)
> （慢慢來幹，不用那麼急。）

The lion dance is a very popular way of celebrating the Chinese New Year and other festive occasions. Businessmen believe that a visit of a lion will bring them prosperity in their business. In order to draw the attention of the lion, they place a Chēng high up on a bamboo cane. A Chēng (lit. green) is made from a stalk of green vegetable, usually lettuce, bound together with a red packet containing lucky money. This is the origin of Bīuchēng.

While dancing to the beat of drums and gongs, the dancers use any means to get the Chēng. Two men will play in good cooperation in the lion dance. Sometimes the Chēng is hung so high that one man has to stand on the shoulders of the other. People will be afraid that they will fall. This situation has generated the expression Gèngchēng. It is very common for two lions to compete for one Chēng (i.e. Chéungchēng). Each of them try to snatch the Chēng and swallow it first. This is why we say Kàhmchēng.

　　廣東人在新年時盛行舞獅子的玩意，商戶會準備「青」來吸引獅子。用青菜一把，連同利市紮好，叫做「青」。「青」多數用竹竿高高舉起，所以說「標青」。舞獅子的人要舞動獅子，設法把「青」吞入獅口裏。可是有時「青」標得太高，舞獅子的人用人疊人的方式爬上去，驚險百出，就是「驚青」。有時兩隻獅子碰頭，爭採一個「青」，就會互相推碰，叫「搶青」。假如甲獅子快一步搶「青」在手，他怕乙獅子來爭，就急急忙忙把「青」噙（吞）下，這就是「噙青」了。

Wán Kaausàan 搵靠山

Wán Kaausàan

VO to look for a powerful man to back you up
找有勢力的人在背後支持自己

e.g. Kéuih yáuh/wándóu kaausàan, móuh yàhn gám hā kéuih.
佢　有/　搵到　　靠山，冇　人　敢　蝦　佢。

(He has a powerful man to rely on. So nobody dares offend him.)
（他有人撐腰，誰也不敢得罪他。）

Chinese people are very particular about geomancy. When they choose a house, they prefer one that faces water (i.e. sea, river, lake..., etc.) and with a hill or mountain at the back. As we know, China is in the northern hemisphere. In winter, it is very cold when there is a north wind. Therefore, most of our houses face south.

People will try their best to build their houses on the southern slope of a hill which will appear like a screen to keep off the north wind. Furthermore, people will feel much safer, if they have something to protect them, with the hill at the back of their houses. They can also grow fruit trees on the hill slope and use twigs and leaves as fuel. A hill at your back! How nice! So by extension, a powerful person that backs you up is your Kaausàan.

中國人講究風水，選擇居處時，最理想是背山面水的地方。因為中國在北半球，冬天吹北風，非常寒冷，所以我們的房屋大多背北朝南，房子都盡量選建在山的南坡，利用後面的山擋住北風。而且背後有山，似乎就有了倚靠，有了安全感。在山坡種些果樹，不但有水果吃，也有樹枝樹葉作燃料。靠山，好得很！

由此引申，一個在背後支持你的人，就是你的靠山。

Séui Wàih Chòih 水爲財

Séui Wàih Chòih

PH   to use water to stand for money (lit. water is wealth)
以「水」作爲金錢的代詞

e.g.   Séui wàih chòih, móuh séui dím gwodāk yaht ā?
水 爲 財, 無 水 點 過得 日 吖?

(Water is money. How can one live without water?)
(「水」就是錢,沒錢怎行?)

Cantonese people always say "water" for money. "Dohkséui" means to borrow money. If a man is in need of money and he goes everywhere to raise money, then we would say that he is "dashing out for water" (pokséui). Once a fireman threatened an owner of a factory. He said, "Pass the water (money) and we'll let the water go." They would use bribery before putting out the fire.

The usage of "water" for money originates from a common saying in Chinese geomancy. It says, "A mountain can bring you descendants while water can bring you wealth." The specialists in geomancy will tell you that if there is a hill near your house, then you'll have a lot of sons and grandsons. If there is a stream, a river, a lake or the sea near your house, then you'll become rich. It holds true in China since water is used for cultivation. One can get one's own riches from rich soil. Did you see the movie *Yellow Earth*? That poor family had to go ten miles just for two buckets of water. So believe it or not, they would not be that poor if they had water near their house.

    廣東人常常把錢說作「水」,借錢叫「度水」,有急需而四處張羅叫「撲水」。曾經有消防員要挾失火工廠的東主:「『過水』就放水。」意思是東主付了黑錢,消防員才開水喉救火。

    把錢叫「水」,源於風水學上的一句慣用語:「山管人丁水管財。」風水先生認爲,住宅附近的山可以幫助屋主人丁興旺,而水(溪、河、湖、海)可以帶來錢財。看看電影「黃土地」裏那戶窮人家,要走十里路去挑一擔水,窮得家徒四壁,那麼,水爲財,不由你不信。

Mahnbūi 問杯

Mahnbūi

VO one way of foretelling fate
一種占卜的方法

e.g. Nīchi mahnbūi, hóuchói jaahkdóu singbūi.
呢次　問杯，好彩　擲到　勝杯。

(This time in casting the "Būi", the result is a good one.)
（這次卜問，得到吉兆。）

Let us have a game of Mahnbūi. You need an oyster shell split into two halves. After that, you hold the two halves together and bring it back to its original form. Pray to the sky and say what you want to know, for example, "Can I do well in the coming examination?" Then you release your hands and let the two halves of the shell fall. Take a look at them and see how they lie on the ground. It is "yāmbūi" if the back of them is facing up and "yèuhngbūi" if the back is touching the ground. You can try again if you get the latter one. But if you get the former one, it means that you are not that lucky and you have to take care. Everything will turn out to be fine soon if you get a "singbūi" with the two halves of the shell lying differently on the ground. Note that nowadays people use a substitute made of wood similar to the shape of a shell.

　　讓我們玩一次「問杯」遊戲。你需要一個蚌殼（左右兩半可以分開的）。首先把蚌殼的左右兩半合起來，像蚌殼天然的樣子，用兩手捧着。你這時可以向天禱告，問一個問題或祈求一件事，例如：「我這次考試會否得到好成績？」接着，你放開手，讓蚌殼跌下，看看蚌殼放置的樣子。假如兩半蚌殼都是凹下的一邊向上，這叫「陽杯」，你可以撿起蚌殼，重複先前的動作，再擲一次。假如擲出兩半蚌殼都是凸起的一邊向上，這叫「陰杯」，對不起，你的運氣似乎不大好，你做事要小心一點。假如擲出的蚌殼一半凹一半凸，就叫「勝杯」，恭喜你，你卜問的事多數有好消息。

Jouh Galéung 做架樑

Jouh Galéung

VO   be the mediator on behalf of someone
代人出頭談判

e.g.   Nīgihn sih m̀gwāan néih sih, m̀sái néih jouh galéung.
呢件事唔關你事唔使你做架樑。

(It's none of your business! We don't want you to interfere.)
（這事與你無干，不必你強代出頭。）

In China, an old style house is built with a pillar and beam structure. People put up pillars and beams to make the frame of the house. Then they built up walls and cover the house with a roof. In between the roof and the main beam, there was one more beam, Galéung, which shared the pressure from the roof to the main beam.

If A comes to pick on B and C wants to stop him, then C is said to be Jouh Galéung.

中國的舊式房屋，多數採用「樑柱式」結構，即是以柱子和橫樑構成屋的骨架，再砌外牆和蓋屋頂。在主樑和屋頂之間，有些架樑，它替主樑承受了上面的壓力。

假如某甲要找某乙的晦氣，而某丙插身中間，替乙擋駕，他就是「做架樑」。

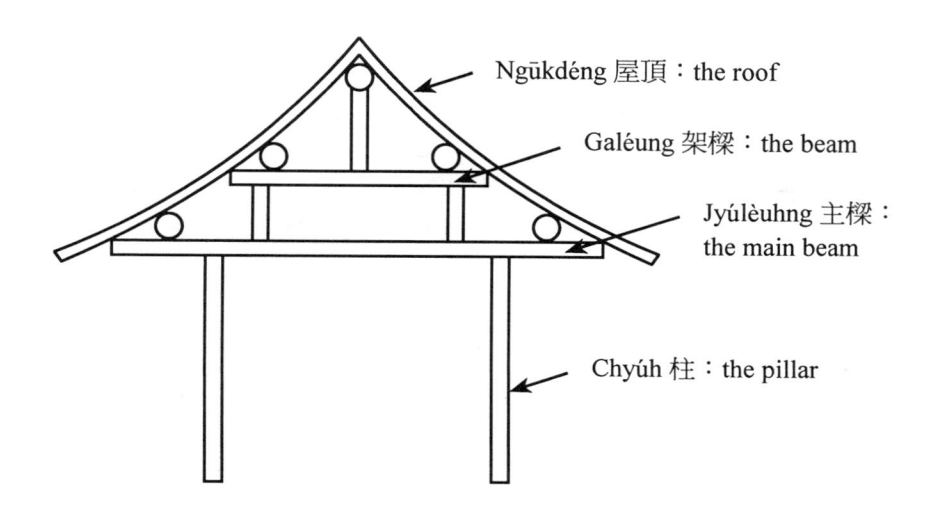

Ngūkdéng 屋頂：the roof

Galéung 架樑：the beam

Jyúlèuhng 主樑：the main beam

Chyúh 柱：the pillar

Giuh Chèuhnggeuk 撬牆腳

Giuh Chèuhnggeuk

- VO carry off somebody's (wife or) girl friend
  搶走人家的（妻子或）女友
- e.g. Giuh yàhn chèuhnggeuk, dái béi yàhn dá.
  撬　人　　牆腳，　抵俾人打！
  (He carried off somebody's lover. He deserved to get a beating.)
  （搶走人家的女友，該打！）

Chinese people knew how to build a wall with bricks in early times. They protected themselves by building a wall around their house. During a war, if the defender build up a wall, it would be hard for the other side to attack. Of course, there are many ways to invade a walled city. Soldiers can use a scaling ladder and climb up to the top of the wall. But it is too obvious because they can be seen very easily. There is one good way to do it. Soldiers can make a hole by secretly taking away (i.e. Giuh) bricks at Chèuhnggeuk (i.e. the foot of the wall). Then they can creep in and give the enemy a surprise attack. In Chinese, a home not only means the house, but also refers to one's wife. If one carries off the wife of another, one also ruins his house/home.

　　中國人很早就發明用磚築牆，並且用牆把居室圍起來保護自己。打仗時守的一方築好城牆，攻的一方就不易取勝。當然攻城有許多方法，例如爬雲梯上城頭，但目標太明顯了。有一種攻城法就是偷偷撬走城牆腳的磚，挖出一個洞來，再鑽進去偷襲。

　　中文裏，「家室」不只是房屋，也可解爲「妻子」；撬了人家的牆腳，就是毀了他的「家室」。

Jèung (PN) Gwàn 將(某人)軍；
Dàudūk Jèunggwān 兜篤將軍

Jèung (PN) Gwàn

VO to cause someone perplexity
使某人窘迫難受

e.g. Ngóh heung lóuhsai jèung kéuih gwàn, kéuih gàmchi séigáng la.
我　向　老細　將　佢　軍，佢　今次　死梗　嘑。
(I spoke ill of him to our boss. He'll be in great trouble this time.)
（我向老闆告他一狀，他這回受罪了。）

Dàudūk Jèunggwān

I.E. to go to the rear of the enemy and attack them while they are not aware
乘敵人不防備，繞到敵人背後施襲

e.g. Gíngfòng yātjìu dàudūk jèunggwàn, gùngpo chaakchàauh.
警方　一招「兜篤　將軍」，攻破　　賊巢。
(The police go to the back of the den and succeed in destroying it.)
（警方在賊人的背後進攻，搗破賊巢。）

Have you ever played Chinese chess? When you want to show you've made a winning move, you must say to your opponent, "Jèunggwàn!" (check!*) So it is a call to indicate checkmate. Jèunggwàn originally is the general in the army, and is also used to address powerful people. If we say Jèunggwàn in playing chess, we mean "sir" to warn our opponent. It will also cause him difficulty. Sometimes you will win if you attack your enemy from behind, instead of from the front.

你玩過中國象棋嗎？如果你走某一着，想吃掉對手的「帥」，你必須向對手說：「將軍！」

　　將軍，原本指軍隊的指揮，古代常用以稱呼掌大權的人。下棋時說「將軍」，等於說「先生」，是稱呼對手一聲，請他留意。但這句話常常帶來窘迫，令那被「將軍」的人很難受。

　　下象棋時不作正面進攻，「兜篤將軍」往往可以取勝哩。

* See Lee Wai-mun, p. 17.

Haapchou 呷醋

Haapchou

VO   be jealous (lit. take a sip of vinegar)
     妒忌

e.g. Néih jihnghaih máaih wuhngeuih béi go jái, go néui haapchou la.
     你　淨係　　買　　玩具　俾個仔個女　　呷醋　喇。

(You only buy toys for your son, your daughter is jealous of him.)
（你只是買玩具給兒子，女兒不開心啦。）

Once there was an emperor. He wanted to give one of his female attendants as concubine to a minister who achieved distinction. It was not unusual for a monarch to do this in ancient China. But the minister dared not accept his kindness because his wife was a jealous woman. The emperor called the woman to his court and asked her, "I'm going to give your husband a concubine. Will you say yes or no?" "No, Your Majesty," said she. "I would rather die if you do so." The emperor said, "Well then, I'll give you a cup of poison." He told the attendants to bring her some poison. The woman took it and drank it up without hesitation. Do you think that she would die? No, because what she drank was just vinegar, not poison. The emperor just wanted to play a prank on her.

　　話說從前有個皇帝，見某大臣立了大功，便打算給大臣賜個宮女作妾（這在中國古代是平常事）。不料大臣不敢接受，原來他的妻子是妒婦。皇帝傳大臣之妻上朝，對她說：「朕打算給你丈夫賜個妾，你答應嗎？」那女人答：「若是這樣，我寧願死去。」皇帝說：「好，朕就賜你一碗毒藥。」皇帝叫人端來毒藥，那女人想也不想，接過來就一口喝光。

　　結果怎樣？大臣的妻子沒有死，因為皇帝只是跟她開玩笑，她喝下的是 —— 醋。

Gànhùhng Díngbaahk 跟紅頂白

Gànhùhng Díngbaahk

I.E. flatter those in power and injure those already in great difficulty (lit. follow the red and boycott the white)
討好當權得勢的人，但對不幸的人就落井下石

e.g. Kéuih nīgo yàhn gànhùhng díngbaahk, saileih dou séi.
　　 佢　呢個人　　跟紅　　頂白，勢利　到　死。

(He is a snobbish man. He flatters those in good luck and boycotts those in bad luck. How disgusting he is!)
（他爲人趨炎附勢，好討厭！）

Western people think that purple is a romantic colour and blue, a sad colour. Chinese people think of red as a colour for happiness, while white is associated with bad things. Therefore, a bride has to put on a red gown on her wedding day and the bridegroom has to distribute lucky money in red packets. A happy occasion is also called a "hùhngsih" (lit. red event). Those lucky people who are in power are called "hùhngyàhn" (lit. red people). When someone dies, it is said to be a "baahksih" (lit. white event). The mourning dress is made of white hemp material.

Gànhùhng Díngbaahk was first used among gamblers. They like to follow those who are winning in betting, or they will bet on the race on which the losers are not betting.

　　西方人說紫色是浪漫，藍色是憂鬱。中國人卻把紅色代表喜慶，白色代表不吉利。所以新娘子出嫁要穿紅衣袍，新郎要大派紅封包（利市），喜事又叫「紅事」。那些走運當權的是「紅人」。至於喪事稱爲「白事」，喪服用白麻布縫製。

　　「跟紅頂白」，原本指賭徒賭博時，跟着走運贏錢的人下注，或者投注在運氣差的人不下注的地方。

Wòhng Máh'kwá 黃馬褂；
Baahk Beihgō 白鼻哥

Wòhng Máh'kwá

N   the relative(s) of the boss [M: go] (lit. yellow jacket)
老闆的親戚

e.g.   Kéuih haih wòhng máh'kwá, m̀sái jouhyéh, baahkjì sànséui.
       佢　係　黃　馬褂，唔使　做嘢，　白支　薪水。

(He is the relative of the boss. He can get a salary without doing anything.)
（他是老闆的親戚，不用工作，白領薪水。）

Baahk Beihgō

N   a cunning person, a wicked person [M: go] (lit. white nose)
奸人，壞人

In the Ching dynasty, Máh'kwá was the jacket worn by the Manchurians when they went horse riding. Usually it was blue or black, but the emperors would sometimes bestow a yellow jacket on imperial relatives or on officials who showed merit. Therefore, Wòhng Máh'Kwá represented those people who won the favour of the emperor.

In Chinese opera, there is something special in the make up of actors playing the parts of a playboy or a cunning official, for instance. They have to put some white on their nose. When the audience sees them, they will immediately understand that they are playing bad men.

馬褂是清朝滿洲人騎馬時常穿的一種短外衣，一般是藍、黑色。清朝皇帝對一些立了大功的官員或者皇族子弟，有時會賞賜一件黃色的馬褂，所以黃馬褂代表得寵的人。

粵劇裏有些扮演花花公子、奸官之類的小角色，他的扮相有個特點，就是鼻尖塗上白色，觀眾一看就知道他是壞人。

Sá Fàchēung 耍花槍

Sá Fàchēung

VO slight dispute of a young couple for fun
年輕夫婦的小爭吵

e.g. Kéuihdeih léuhng gùngpó sáháh fàchēung jē, yātjahn'gāan jauh móuh
     佢哋   兩   公婆   耍吓   花槍   啫，一陣間   就   無
sih ga lā.
事 㗎啦。

(The couple is just having a slight dispute. They will be all right again very soon.)
（他們兩小口鬧意見，一會兒就沒事的了。）

Sá Fàchēung is a jargon used in Cantonese opera. For instance, when the heroine leads some soldiers to the battle, she meets the hero who is the general of the enemy. So they fight with each other. But Chinese opera emphasizes the art of playing. The fighting of the hero and the heroine is just symbolic, not real, the implication of Sá. They won't hurt each other at all. Meanwhile, the audience can enjoy the fancy ways (fà) of their fighting when they thrust and resist with their chēung, the spear. But no one is going to win. Finally, a happy ending will usually result in the marriage of the hero and the heroine.

「耍花槍」是粵劇的術語。比如劇裏的女主角帶兵上陣，遇上扮演敵方將領的男主角，於是雙方大打出手。但是粵劇講究表演藝術，男女主角的打鬥，並非拼死命，而是象徵式的，兩人在舞台上持槍攻刺招架，花樣百出，最後打個平手。而結局時，男女主角結成夫婦。

Hahpsaai Hòhchē 合晒合尺；
Lèihpóu 離譜；Johngbáan 撞板

Hahpsaai Hòhchē

I.E.   meet one's need, be one's cup of tea (lit. sing every note right)
       很配合，很滿意

e.g.   Nīdàan yéh, hahpsaai kéuih hòhchē lā.
       呢單　嘢，合晒　佢　合尺　啦。

       (This is just what he wants.)
       （這事很合他心意。）

Lèihpóu

SV/VO   irresponsible, illogical
        不合理

e.g.   Kéuih yahtyaht chìhdou, lèihsaai daaihpóu.
       佢　日日　遲到，離晒　大譜。

       (He comes late everyday. He is really irresponsible.)
       （他天天遲到，很不守規則。）

Johngbáan

VO   run into trouble; make mistakes; sing in the wrong beat
     做錯事，碰釘子；(唱歌)走板

e.g.   M̀nám chìngchó jauh jouh, johng jing daaihbáan.
       唔諗　清楚　就　做，撞　正　大板。

       (He made mistakes because he didn't think before he acted.)
       （未想清楚就幹，闖了禍。）

The above expressions have something to do with Chinese music. The most frequently sung notes in the Cantonese operatic songs and their counterparts in Western music are scored as follows:

5̣	6̣	7̣	1	2	3	4	5
合	士	乙	上	尺	工	反	六
hòh	sih	yih	saang	che	guhng	faan	liu

The two notes 合 and 尺* are picked to represent songs. Hahpsaai means all are right. If one sings every note right and if there is good cooperation between the singers and the musicians, then they would say Hahpsaai Hòhchē. Otherwise, if the singer sings without following the melody, he will be said to be Lèihpóu (lit. deviate from the melody). The timing of the Cantonese operatic songs is called Báan. If one sings in the wrong beat, one surely makes a mistake, i.e. Johngbáan.

　　今次談的三個詞，都和音樂有關。西洋音樂裏的 5̇4̇321765̣ 在粵曲譜子裏寫作「六反工尺上乙士合」。從七音裏抽出「合尺」[+]，代表樂曲。「合晒」意思是全對了。如果唱粵曲的人把所有的音調都唱對了，和拍和音樂師合作無間，就叫「合晒合尺」。相反，唱的人亂唱，違反了曲譜的規定，就是「離譜」。還有，曲的拍子叫「板」，亂唱自然「撞板」了。

---

* 合 and 尺 are pronounced differently from their normal ways.
[+]「合尺」讀作「荷車」。

Dohkkíu 度喬

Dohkkíu

VO try to think of a way/a solution
想辦法／計策

e.g. Gàmchi m̀dihm la, faaidī dohkháh yáuh mātyéh hóu kíu lā.
今次 唔掂 嘿 快啲 度吓 有 乜嘢 好 喬啦。
(We are in great trouble this time. Try to find a solution fast.)
（這回不妙，快想個好辦法。）

Kíu was opera jargon in former times. It referred to those funny plays full of comic actions. Dohk literally means to measure or to consider. Dohkkíu means to work out a scenario of a play, and now it means to think of a way or to find a solution, by extension.

    Fifty or sixty years ago, Cantonese opera was very popular in Canton and Hong Kong. New scripts were in great demand and the playwrights had to produce a new play in a very short time. The actors also had not enough time for rehearsal. However, people in that line of business found a good way to handle the difficulty. They broke apart the old scripts which were well learned by the actors into many episodes called "pàaihchéung". There were definite roles, scenarios, actions, songs, dialogues and music in each one of the episodes. Then the playwrights could manage to make up a new play by rearranging the various episodes in a new sequence. This is how Dohkkíu has come into being.

「喬」是個古代戲劇術語，指以滑稽動作引人發笑的胡鬧戲劇*。「度喬」就是「度戲」——構思戲劇的情節，引申為想辦法。

　　大概在五、六十年前，廣州和香港粵劇很流行，新劇本的需求很大，編劇人往往要在短時間內編出新劇，而演員的排練時間也不多。但戲班中人有一個巧妙的做法，就是把演員早已熟習的舊劇本分拆成許多個片段，叫做「排場」，每個排場裏有既定的角色、情節、動作、曲牌、說白和音樂。編劇人再把多個排場設法串連起來，就編成新劇。這就是「度喬」。

* 見《中國戲曲曲藝詞典》「喬」字條。

M̀sái Mahn A-Gwai 唔使問阿貴

M̀sái Mahn A-Gwai

PH   no need to ask about it because it's a known secret
大家（心知肚明）心照不宣，不必再問

e.g.   M̀sái mahn a-gwai, gánghaih kéuih tàujó dī heiséui yám lā.
唔使 問 阿貴， 梗係 佢 偷咗啲 汽水 飲 啦。

(No need to inquire, it must be he who stole and drank the soft drinks.)
（用不着問，一定是他偷喝了汽水。）

It is said that A-Gwai is the given name of Paak Gwai, who was the governor of Gwóngdùng province during the last years of the Ching dynasty. There were two ranking officials inside the city of Canton then. One was Paak Gwai, and the other was the governor of Gwóngdùng and Gwóngsài province. He was superior to A-Gwai. Whenever the inferiors needed to ask for instruction, they would all go straight to the governor of the two provinces. No one would go to ask A-Gwai. They all understood that there was no need to ask him.

There is another story about this. Some say A-Gwai is Gwai Jaat who was a noble of the state of Nǹgh during the period of the Spring and Autumn Annals. Once, while he was on the way to another state as an ambassador, he passed the state of Chèuih. He made good friends with the king there. The king liked the sword that Gwai Jaat was carrying, but he didn't say so. Gwai Jaat understood him very well but he had to go on his way to accomplish his mission. He planned to give his sword to the king when he returned. Unfortunately before he came back, the king died. He hung his sword on the tree in front of the king's tomb and then left.

So when something is understood and there is no need to ask about it, we would also say M̀sái Mahn A-Gwai.

阿貴，有人說是清末廣東巡撫柏貴。當時廣州城內有兩位大官，一個是柏貴，另一個是官階更高的兩廣總督。低級官吏有公事要請示上司，都直接問兩廣總督，沒有人去問柏貴。所以說：「唔使問阿貴。」*

　　另一說：阿貴是指季札（季、貴同音）。季札是春秋時代吳國的貴族。一次他出使，經過徐國，和徐君談話很投契。徐君很欣賞季札的佩劍，但沒有說出口。季札知道，但因有使命未完成，打算歸國時才把劍相贈。怎料季札再經過徐國時，徐君已去世，季札就把佩劍掛在徐君墓前的樹上而離去。

　　有時大家有了默契，不必說出口，也是「唔使問阿貴」。

*改寫自丘學強《妙語方言》，頁12。

Yahpmàaih (PN) Sou 入埋(某人)數

Yahpmàaih (PN) Sou

PH   credit it to somebody's account; lay the blame on others; impute the guilt to somebody else
記入某人的帳內，由某人負責；又指把罪過歸咎於他人

e.g.   Chàailóu jèung géidàan baausit ngon yahpmàaih ngóh sou, wāt ngóh yihngsaai.
差佬　將　幾單　爆竊　案　入埋　我　數，屈　我 認晒。

(The police had me booked for several cases of burglary and forced me to admit them.)
(警方將幾宗盜竊案都算在我頭上，逼我認罪。)

Legend has it that the last ruler of the Shang dynasty was a very cruel man. He had his people pay heavy taxes. He made lakes of wine and forests of meat. He enjoyed himself day and night. He had a concubine called Táan Géi whom he loved very much. He killed his loyal uncle Béi Gōn, who frequently gave him remonstrance. As a result, his people rebelled against him and he burned himself to death.

Jí Gung, one of the disciples of Confucius, criticized him and said in *The Analects*, "Actually the evil deeds that he had done are not as many as the legend says. Therefore, a gentleman doesn't want to be a mean person lest people accuse him of other evil deeds."

傳說商代的紂王殘暴不仁，他抽重稅，造酒池肉林，日夜享樂，又寵信美人妲己，殺忠心勸諫的叔父比干，最後人民反叛，紂王自焚而死。

孔子的學生子貢就評論說：紂王所做的壞事，不像傳說那麼多。所以君子不願意做下流人，免得大家把壞事都歸到自己頭上。(出自《論語》)

Yáuh Fànsou 有分數/Yáuh Fànchyun 有分寸

Yáuh Fànsou/Yáuh Fànchyun

PH/SV   know what to do and how to do it
      心中有數；知道應該怎樣做

e.g.   Nīgihn sih, ngóh yáuh fànsou ge la.
      呢件 事，我 有 分數 嘅 嘑。

    (I know how to manage it.)
    （我自有主意。）

Duke Wùhn of the state of Chàih (?–643 B.C.) was studying one day. Wheelwright Bín* asked him, "What are you reading, Your Majesty?" "The instructions of the saints," answered Duke Wùhn. "Are the saints still alive?" Wheelwright Bín asked again. "No," said Duke Wùhn, "they are already dead." Wheelwright Bín said, "Then what you are reading is the rubbish of the dead." Duke Wùhn was very angry and said, "Explain immediately what you mean. I will kill you if you don't give me a satisfactory explanation."

    Wheelwright Bin then said, "I'm a wheel-maker and I'll take this as an example. When I'm making a wheel, I know it will not be any good if I do it too fast or too slow. I understand how to do it well by myself. As for the art (i.e. Fànsou/Fànchyun) of wheel-making, I've got it all in my mind, but I just can't explain it. It's hard for me to tell or to teach other people. They would not understand it even if they hear about it. It's the same with the so-called instructions of the saints. It's of no use to study them."

    齊桓公（公元前？–643）在讀書。輪扁問：「大王讀的是甚麼？」答道：「是聖人的訓言。」輪扁又問「聖人還活着嗎？」答道：「已經死了。」輪扁說：「那麼大王所讀的，不過是死人遺下的垃圾！」桓公大怒，說：「快快解釋！解釋得不好就殺了你！」輪扁說：「我是做打車輪的，就拿這事說吧。打輪的時候，打得太快不好，太慢也不好。我說不出來，但是心裏有分數。這分數不能講授給他人，他人即使聽了也不明白。可見讀書，讀那些所謂『聖人的訓言』，一點用也沒有！」

* See Vincent Yu-chung Shih, p. 305.

Jouhdou Jek Kehk Gám 做到隻屐噉

Jouhdou Jek Kehk Gám

PH   (said of an employee) work very hard
工作得很苦

e.g.   Jouhdou jek kehk gám, lóuhbáan dōu m̀gà yàhngùng.
做到 隻 屐 噉，老闆 都 唔加 人工。

(Our boss doesn't increase my salary even though I work very hard.)
（工作得那麼苦，東主也不加點薪。）

During the time of the Spring and Autumn Annals, there was civil disorder in the state of Chàih. A prince called Chùhng Yíh was exiled to another state. He had a very loyal servant called Gaai Jì Tèui who accompanied him. They always suffered from hunger while travelling. Once, they asked a farmer for some food. The farmer not only didn't give them any, but also laughed at them. The prince wanted to kill him, but Gaai Jì Tèui stopped him. A while later, he brought the prince a bowl of meat soup. The prince took it and ate. Later he found out that the meat soup was made from a piece of flesh cut from Gaai Jì Tèui's leg.

More than ten years later, the prince returned to his own place and became king. The servants who had followed him during his exile all got rewards, except Gaai Jì Tèui. He hid in a hill. The king ordered someone to set fire to the hill so that he would come out. But unfortunately, Gaai Jì Tèui was burnt to death. The king was very sad. He made a pair of slippers from the tree where Gaai Jì Tèui lay dead. He wore that pair of wooden slippers (i.e. Kehk) in memory of his good servant who loved him and worked so devotedly for him.

春秋時代，齊國內亂，公子重耳流亡到外國。他有個僕人叫介之推的，非常忠心。他們在路上常常捱餓，有一次，他們向一個農夫討食物，農夫不但不肯給，還嘲笑他們。重耳想殺掉農夫，但給介之推勸止了。過了一會，介之推端來一碗肉湯，重耳接過來便吃下。他實在太餓了！後來他才發覺，那是介之推割下自己腿上的肉而造的肉湯！

　　十幾年後，重耳回到齊國，做了國君。追隨他流亡在外的僕人都得了厚賞。只是介之推沒有受賞，躲到深山裏。重耳派人放火燒山，想把介之推逼出來，結果把他燒死了。重耳很傷心，就把介之推屍體旁邊的一棵大樹，用來造木屐，穿在腳上，以紀念這個好僕人。

　　「做到隻屐噉」，意即工作得像介之推一樣苦，到頭來，祇變了兩隻屐。

M̀jìcháu 唔知醜

M̀jìcháu

PH shameless; not knowing the weak point of oneself (lit. not knowing that one is ugly) (a phrase for scolding people)
不自量或不知羞恥（這是句罵人的話）

e.g. Mōk gwòngjyū béi yàhn yíngséung, néih jànhaih m̀jìcháu!
剝　光豬　俾人　映相，你　眞係　唔知醜！
(You let somebody take naked pictures of you. How shameless of you!)
（讓人家拍裸照，你眞是不知羞恥！）

Once, there was a man called Jàu Geih. Tall and handsome, he always compared himself with another handsome man in the same city called Mr. Chèuih. He asked his wife, "Who is more handsome, me or Mr. Chèuih?" His wife answered, "Mr. Chèuih is not as handsome as you." Then he asked his concubine. She gave him the same answer as his wife did.

One day, a man came to visit him, and Jàu Geih asked him the same question. The guest said, "You are extremely handsome. How can Mr. Chèuih be compared with you?" Jàu Geih was very happy on hearing that.

After a few days, Mr. Chèuih came to visit Jàu Geih. He had something to discuss with him. As soon as Jàu Geih saw Mr. Chèuih, he immediately saw that he was not as handsome as Mr. Chèuih. He took a mirror and looked at himself. The more he looked, the more he felt that he was less handsome than Mr. Chèuih. "But why did my wife, my concubine and my guest all say that I am more handsome than Mr. Chèuih?" He was wondering. "Oh, I see! My wife loves me. My concubine is afraid of me. The guest came to ask for my help. They did not say what they meant."*

從前有個叫鄒忌的人，相貌堂堂，他常常拿城裏一個著名的美男子徐公和自己相比，問他的妻子說：「徐公跟我比，哪個英俊？」妻子答：「徐公不及你英俊。」鄒忌問他的妾，她同樣答：「徐公不及你英俊哩。」

　　一天，有客人來，鄒忌又用同樣的問題問他。客人說：「你英俊極了，徐公哪裏及得你？」鄒忌聽了就很高興。

　　過了幾天，那位徐公有事來訪，鄒忌一見他面，就知道自己不及他英俊；再拿面鏡子照照，更覺得自己遠遠不及。「爲甚麼我的妻、妾和客人都說我比徐公英俊？」鄒忌心裏想：「呀！是這樣：妻子愛我，妾怕我，客人來有求於我，他們說的都不是眞心的話啊！」

* adapted from *Anecdotes of the Warring States*.

Yāt Bātjouh, Yih Bātyàu 一不做，二不休

Yāt Bātjouh, Yih Bātyàu

ADV.PH to do something by hook or by crook; not to stop half way once a thing is started
除非不做，一動手就做到底

e.g. Wàahngdihm saatjó yàhn, yāt bātjouh yih bāt yàu, fongfó jèung gàan
橫掂　　殺咗　人，一　不做　二　不　休，放火　將　　間

ngūk dōu sìumàaih bálà.
屋　都　燒埋　把啦。

(Since we killed, we might as well just go on and set fire to the house to burn it.)
（反正殺了人，一不做二不休，放把火把房子也燒掉罷。）

During the Warring States Period, King Wài of the state of Chàih did not care about state affairs. He drank and enjoyed himself day and night. The state of Chàih became weaker and weaker and was in a critical situation. King Wài liked to solve riddles. A man called Sèuhn Yù Kwān gave him a riddle to solve. He said, "A big bird has been staying in your imperial courtyard for three years and yet it doesn't even try to fly or sing. Do you know what kind of bird it is?" King Wài answered, "Sure. Nothing special when it stays there and is quiet. But once it starts to fly, it will fly high up into the sky. Once it starts to sing, it will sing so well that everybody will be surprised."

From then on King Wài tried his best to work on the state affairs and Chàih became a powerful state. Yāt Bātjouh, Yih Bātyàu was originated from the above story. But what a pity that the expression was used to refer to doing something evil, later.

戰國時代，齊威王喜歡猜謎語，日夜飲酒玩樂，不理政事，齊國國勢岌岌可危。淳于髡給威王出了一個謎語，說：「有一隻大鳥，停在大王的庭院裏，足足有三年，既不飛走，又不鳴叫。大王您知道這是甚麼鳥嗎？」威王回答說：「我知道，牠不飛就沒甚麼，但一飛便沖破天空；牠不叫就沒甚麼，但一叫便令人人吃驚。」

　　從此之後，威王勵精圖治，齊國聲威遠播。「一不做，二不休」這句話出自以上的故事，可惜後來卻被用來指做壞事方面去。

Lìhngse 零舍；Lìhngse M̀tùhng 零舍唔同

Lìhngse

A   especially, particularly
特別的，與眾不同的

Lìhngse M̀tùhng

PH   look different, be unique
特別的，與眾不同的

e.g.   Dábaahnháh, go yéung lìhngse leng ga!
打扮吓，個樣零舍靚㗎！

(Put on a little make-up and you'll look more beautiful.)
（打扮一下，樣子特別好看。）

Prince Maahng Sèuhng was a nobleman during the Warring States Period. He liked to invite talented people to his house to be his retainers, or guests on the payroll*, and provide them with food and lodging. A poor man called Fùhng Hyūn also went to seek refuge with him. As he looked like an ordinary man, he was put in the lower lodging. There the food was poor. After a few days, Fùhng Hyūn hit his sword and sang, "Let me go! There's no fish to eat here." Prince Maahng Sèuhng heard about it and moved him to the middle lodging where fish was available. But after a few days, Fùhng Hyūn hit his sword and sang again, "Let me go! Here there's no carriage to ride on." Prince Maahng Sèuhng heard about it and moved him to the higher lodging where carriages were available. Seeing that Prince Maahng Sèuhng was so nice to him, Fùhng Hyūn exerted his talent to help him later and Prince Maahng Sèuhng became the prime minister of the state of Chàih.

    Lìhngse actually was "lihngse" which means to be arranged to stay in another better lodging. Now it means "particularly, especially" by extension.

戰國時有個貴族叫孟嘗君，他喜歡招攬人才，家裏養了三千個食客。有個窮人叫馮驩的，走去投靠孟嘗君，孟嘗君見他外表平凡，就隨便把他安置在最低級的客舍裏。這處的食物粗劣，過了幾天，馮驩敲着佩劍唱歌說：「離去吧！這裏吃不到魚。」孟嘗君聽見，就把馮驩遷到中級的客舍裏，常有魚供應了。可是過了幾天，馮驩又敲着劍唱歌說：「離去吧！出入沒有車子。」孟嘗君聽見，又把馮驩遷到高級的客舍裏，出入有車子了。馮驩見孟嘗君對自己好，就用盡才智為孟嘗君做事，令孟嘗君當上齊國的宰相。

　　「零舍」，其實是「另舍」，即安置在另一類特別好的客舍裏，引申為「特別」。

* See Ch'en Shou-yi, p. 107.

Dáiséi 抵死；Dái (PN) Séi 抵(某人)死

Dáiséi

PH/SV   you deserve it (a term of abuse); very bad; go too far in doing or saying something
該死，行爲過份

Dái (PN) Séi

PH   you deserve it (a term of abuse)
該死

e.g.   Kéuih m̀jouh gùngfo béi sìnsàang faht, dái (kéuih) séi!
佢 唔做 功課 俾 先生 罰，抵(佢)死！

(He didn't do his homework and was punished by the teacher. He deserved it!)
（他不做功課被老師責罰，活該！）

    The First Emperor of Chin who reigned from 221 to 210 B.C. made many strict laws and imposed severe punishments, particularly to oppress those who resisted his tyranny. As soon as he died, Làuh Bòng and Hohng Yúh rose in rebellion against the sovereignty of Chin and succeeded in overthrowing the Chin dynasty. After Làuh Bòng and his army conquered Hàahm Yèuhng, the capital of Chin, he gave an order to abolish all the harsh laws of Chin. New and very simple laws were made by Làuh Bòng saying that those who killed would be sentenced to death and those who hurt others or stole would be punished according to the seriousness of the crime. People of that city were all very happy about that. Later, Làuh Bòng became the first emperor of the Han dynasty.

    Dáiséi originally meant that anyone committing a major crime deserved to be put to death, but now it has come to mean "rejoicing in the misfortune of others". It also means to go too far in doing or saying something.

秦始皇（公元前221-210在位）爲了對付反抗他的暴政的人，特別制訂了種種嚴刑峻法。可是，秦始皇一死，劉邦和項羽就起來推翻秦的統治。劉邦帶兵攻下秦國首都咸陽，就下令把舊有的苛刻法令全部廢除。新訂的法令很簡單，就是：「殺人者死，傷人及盜抵罪。」（打傷他人或者盜劫財物的，按情況的輕重適當地處罰。）咸陽的人民都很高興，後來劉邦當了漢朝第一任皇帝。

　　「抵死」，原意說某人所犯的罪很大，值得判死刑；現在用來表示幸災樂禍，又指說話或行爲太過份。

Jítìn Dūkdeih 指天篤地/
Yātméi Kaau Jí 一味靠指

Jítìn Dūkdeih/Yātméi Kaau Jí

I.E. talk nonsense and fool other people
用說話欺騙人

e.g. Dī sàhn'gwan jítìn dūkdeih/yātméi kaau jí, chìnkèih m̀hóu
哋 神 棍 指天 篤地/ 一味 靠 指，千祈 唔好

séuhngdong a.
上當 呀。

(The fake priests just talk nonsense. Be sure not to be fooled by them.)
(那些神棍騙人，不好上當。)

Legend has it that when the Buddha was born, he had one of his hands pointing towards the sky (i.e. Jítìn) and the other, towards the ground (i.e. Dūkdeih). He said, "I'm the supreme one in heaven and on earth." When people swear, they also act like this, using one hand to point to the sky or to the ground, but what they say may not be true.

It is recorded in *The Historical Records* that war broke out between Hohng Yúh and Làuh Bòng, the first emperor of the Han dynasty. Both of them wanted to be the ruler of China. In the last battle, the army of Hohng Yúh was surrounded by the Han army. One night, Hohng Yúh led 800 soldiers to make a breakthrough in the dark. Làuh Bòng didn't find out until daybreak. He sent 5,000 soldiers to chase Hohng Yúh. Hohng Yúh got lost on his way. He came across a farmer and asked him for directions. The farmer said, "Left." So he took the path on the left and went straight on. But it turned out that there was a big marsh ahead. He could not do anything but return and the Han army caught him. Hohng Yúh then realized that the farmer intentionally showed him the wrong way to go.

傳說佛祖釋迦出生時，一手指天，一手指地，說：「天上天下，惟我獨尊。」有些人發誓時往往也指天指地，但是所說的話未必可信。

　　另外在《史記》裏記載：項羽和劉邦爭天下，最後一役，項羽的軍隊被包圍，他便帶八百人趁黑夜突圍逃走。劉邦至天亮才發覺，派五千兵去追。項羽逃到一處，迷了路，就問遇上的一個農夫。農夫說：「左！」項羽走左邊的小路，一直走，原來前頭是大沼澤，被迫折回來，而劉邦的軍隊就追上了。這時項羽才知道那農夫是故意引他走絕路，但也沒奈何了。

Jadai 詐帝

Jadai

FV   pretend
假裝

e.g.   Néih m̀hóu jadai la, ngóh m̀wúih séuhngdong ge.
你 唔好詐帝噓，我 唔會 上當 嘅。

(Don't pretend. I won't be cheated.)
（你不必裝模作樣，我不會受騙。）

We can read a story in *The Historical Records* written by Sìmáh Chìn. During the last years of the Chin dynasty (around 211 B.C.), people suffered from severe punishment and paying heavy taxes to the tyrannical government. Hohng Yúh, a great warrior, rose in rebellion against the emperor. In the beginning, he only had a few thousands of men. In order to get more people to join him, he made a noble of the old state of Chó as king. The army of Hohng Yúh got stronger and stronger. The government tried to put them down but its army was defeated by Hohng Yúh. Unfortunately the noble, bearing the title of a king, became the thorn in the flesh of Hohng Yúh. Hohng Yúh further hailed him as emperor but had him drowned by sinking his ship while he was crossing a river.

    Dai (lit. an emperor) in the phrase "Jadai" is a verb: to put someone on a throne. But actually, Hohng Yúh just did it deceitfully (i.e. Ja). So, Jadai implies "cunning → to pretend".

    故事出於《史記》。在秦朝末年（約公元前211），酷刑重稅，人民生活痛苦。項羽帶領幾千人起來造反。初時他們勢力薄弱，為了號召更多人加入革命軍，項羽立了一個楚國的舊貴族為楚王。項羽的勢力愈來愈大，秦皇派來鎮壓的大軍也被他擊破。那個楚王名義上是項羽的君主，實際上已經是項羽的眼中釘。於是項羽派人尊楚王為帝（帝比王高一級），但乘楚帝渡江時，暗中把船弄沉，讓楚帝淹死。

    詐帝的「帝」，是動詞，即尊某人為帝。項羽表面尊人為帝，實在要害人。現在用來表示「作偽」的意思。

Gīgī Gahtgaht 嘰嘰吃吃/
Háu Gahtgaht 口吃吃

Gīgī Gahtgaht/Háu Gahtgaht

PH   stammer, stutter
說話不順利的毛病

e.g.   Kéuih gīgī gahtgaht, m̀jì góng māt.
佢 嘰嘰 吃吃 唔知講 乜！

(He has difficulty in speaking. I can't understand what he says.)
（他口吃，不知說些甚麼。）

In *The History of the Han Dynasty*, there is a story about a man called Jàu Chēung who suffered from stammering.

    The first emperor of the Han dynasty (reigned: 206-194 B.C.) had already made the son of Queen Léuih the crown prince. But he loved Lady Chīk, one of his concubines, so much that he wanted to change his mind and make her son the crown prince. Jàu Chēung, an old official, was a very upright man. He remonstrated with the emperor saying, "I can't talk very well, but as far as I know, it would be ve...very wrong to elect a new crown prince. I'm ve...very unwilling to do what you say."

    He wanted to say "gihk" (i.e. very, extremely). But it became "gī...gī" and he was laughed at by other people.

    口吃，廣東人唸成「口跂」háugaht。《漢書》裏有個口吃人周昌的小故事：

    漢高祖（公元前206-194在位）原本立了呂皇后的兒子做太子，但他寵愛妃子戚氏，想改立戚氏的兒子。老臣周昌為人梗直，出言勸諫。他說：「我不懂說話，但改立太子的事，我『期期』知它不對，我『期期』不肯照你旨意辦。」

    他原來想說「極」（非常的意思），但有口吃的毛病，就說成「期期」（音姬）而成了大家取笑的話柄。

Báauséi 飽死/
Báauséi Hòhlāan Dáu 飽死荷蘭豆

Báauséi/Báauséi Hòhlāan Dáu

PH/I.E. feel disgusted because somebody is very proud
因爲別人太驕傲而覺得討厭

e.g. Kéuih gam sàchàhn, táigin kéuih go yéung jauh báauséi.
佢 咁 沙塵 睇見 佢 個 樣 就 飽死。

(I just feel disgusted when I see him talking/behaving so proudly.)
（他那麼囂張，我看見他那副「尊容」就討厭。）

We want food when we are hungry. However, when we have more than enough, we lose interest in it. We even get tired of it. This is what we mean by Báauséi. Hòhlāan Dáu (lit. Holland peas) is a climbing plant whose pods can be eaten as a fresh vegetable. When the pod is ripe, its appearance of being stuffed with peas is like a person who has overeaten. This is how the metaphor Báauséi Hòhlāan Dáu originated.

A story in *The History of the Han Dynasty* tells of a man Dùng Fòng Sok (about 161-86 B.C.) who planned to play a joke on the emperor because he was not satisfied with his salary. He told the favourite dwarfs of the emperor, "His Majesty wants to kill you because you are too short and too weak to do farm work. Your salary is wasteful." The dwarfs were so frightened that they cried. Then Dùng Fòng Sok taught them to go to the emperor and beg him not to kill them. Being disturbed by them, the emperor wanted to know what was going on. Dùng Fòng Sok, who was famous for his sense of humour, said to the emperor, "The dwarfs are just three feet tall, Your Majesty, yet they have a salary of two hundred and forty coins. I am nine feet tall but I have the same salary as they do. The dwarfs have enough to eat themselves to death (the lit. meaning of Báauséi) but I'm starving to death. Please let me go back to my home town lest you will waste your money on my salary." The emperor smiled and increased his salary.

我們肚餓的時候很想得到食物,但一旦吃飽了就對食物失去興趣,甚至討厭它。這就是「飽死」。至於「荷蘭豆」是一種豆莢,可以當蔬菜。豆莢裏塞滿了豆,就像人吃飽東西,所以說「飽死荷蘭豆」。

　　《漢書》裏有一則故事:東方朔嫌自己的俸錢太少,就給皇帝開了個玩笑。他對皇帝寵愛的侏儒說:「皇上嫌你們身體太矮,耕田又不夠氣力,只是白白浪費米飯,所以打算殺了你們。」侏儒害怕得大哭,於是東方朔教他們求皇帝赦免。胡鬧了半天之後,皇帝查問原委,幽默的東方朔答道:「侏儒身高三尺,有俸錢二百四十;臣高九尺,也是俸錢二百四十。侏儒飽得要死,而臣餓得要死。皇上不如放我回鄉,省得浪費。」皇帝一笑,就給他加了俸錢。

Jengdáu 正斗

Jengdáu

SV　excellent; genuine
　　貨色好

e.g.　Nīdī jengdáu fo, gachìhn gánghaih gwai lā.
　　　呢啲 正斗 貨，價錢 梗係 貴 啦！
　　　(These are excellent goods. No wonder they are so expensive.)
　　　（這是好貨色，價錢當然昂貴了。）

In the past, most of the provisions shops were famous for giving the exact weight of the things you bought and being honest even to children and the aged. Jengdáu meant to give the exact weight measured by the "dáu", a dipper (see picture). If you take an empty bottle to the provisions shop to buy some oil, the shopkeeper will fill the "dáu" full first, and then pour it into your bottle. He certainly will not give you less than what you want.

Since we have Jengdáu, we also have m̀jengdáu. In Chapter 17 of *The Romance of the Three Kingdoms*, Chòuh Chōu (A.D. 155–220) led the army of a hundred and seventy thousand soldiers to attack Yùhn Seuht. He fought for a long time and yet he could not defeat Yùhn Seuht. The food supplies for the army were getting less and less. Chòuh Chōu told the officer who was in charge of the food to give the soldiers food with a smaller "dáu". The soldiers complained about it. Chòuh Chōu caught the officer and beheaded him without letting him say a word about it. The poor officer was charged with stealing food from the army.

Now Jengdáu, originally meaning the exactness of quantity, has come to mean the excellence of quality. Some people will leave out "dáu" and just say "jeng".

從前糧油店多數以「斤兩十足，童叟無欺」為號召，「斤兩十足」就是「正斗」。比方說，你拿個空瓶子去買油，店小二（伙記）用小量斗盛得滿滿的，再倒在你的瓶子裏，果然絕不少給。

　　有「正斗」，當然就有「唔正斗」。《三國演義》第十七回說，曹操（公元155-220）帶十七萬大軍攻打袁術，但久攻不下，糧食不足。曹操叫糧官用較小的斗發軍糧，軍士怨讟，曹操抓來糧官，不由分說便把他斬了，罪名是「盜竊官糧」。

　　「正斗」由「量」的合標準，引申為「質」的美好。有些人會略去「斗」，祇說「正」。

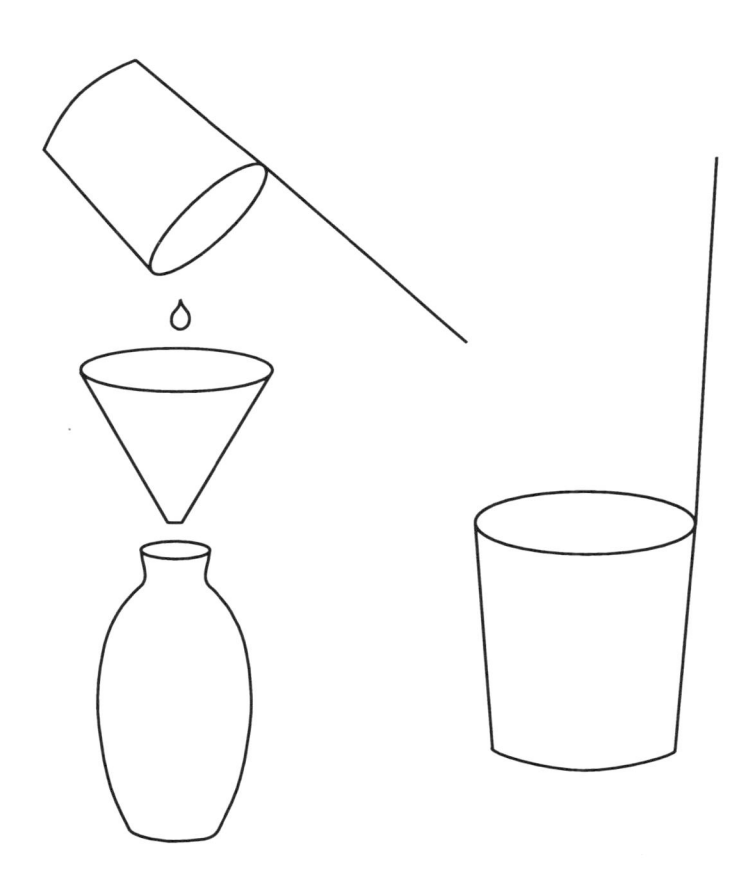

Dáu, a container used for measuring oil
斗，糧油的工具

Sīk Yìnghùhng Juhng Yìnghùhng
識英雄重英雄

Sīk Yìnghùhng Juhng Yìnghùhng

I.E.　mutual appreciation between heroes; to think highly of each other
英雄人物之間的互相賞識和器重

e.g.　Nàahndāk néih sīk yìnghùhng juhng yìnghùhng.
難得　你　識　英雄　重　英雄。

Néih ging ngóh yātchek, ngóh ging néih yātjeuhng.
你　敬　我　一尺，我　敬　你　一丈。

(It's very kind of you to appreciate me so much. I will surely repay your kindness since you are so nice to me.)
（難得你的賞識和器重，我一定盡力回報。）

　　During the last years of the Han dynasty, there were periods of great disorder in China. Chòuh Chōu, Làuh Béi, Yùhn Siuh and Léuih Bou all arose as warlords and attacked one another in a struggle for supremacy. Once, when Chòuh Chōu and Làuh Béi were having a drink and were talking and discussing the heroes of that time, Chòuh Chōu said to Làuh Béi, "Now only you and I are heroes (i.e. Yìnghùhng). Yùhn Siuh and the others cannot be regarded as heroes yet." When Làuh Béi heard this, he was so shocked that he dropped his chopsticks on the ground. He was afraid that Chòuh Chōu would be jealous of him and kill him. It just so happened that it was thundering when he dropped his chopsticks, so Làuh Béi pretended that he was startled by the thunder and, therefore, was not seen through by Chòuh Chōu.*

　　One day, Chòuh Chōu was accompanied by Làuh Béi and Gwāan Yúh to go hunting. Gwāan Yúh wanted to take this chance to kill Chòuh Chōu. Appreciated that Chòuh Chōu had respected him as a hero, Làuh Béi stopped Gwāan Yúh from doing so.

漢朝末年，天下大亂，曹操、劉備、袁紹、呂布等各自起兵，互相攻伐，爭佔地盤。一次，曹操與劉備在酒席上評論天下英雄人物，曹操說：「天下英雄，唯有你和我。袁紹之流，還算不上。」劉備聽了，大吃一驚，連手持的筷箸也跌在地下（劉備怕曹操妒才而殺自己）。剛巧這時有雷響，劉備假裝被雷嚇着，掩飾過去。

　　又一次，劉備、關羽陪曹操去打獵，關羽想趁機會殺曹操，但劉備因爲曹操曾把自己當是英雄，所以阻止了他。

* See *San Kuo* by Brewitt-Taylor

Jouh Chēungsáu 做槍手；Chéngchēung 請槍

Jouh Chēungsáu

VO   to pretend to be somebody else and do the examination or write an article for him
冒認他人身分參加考試或代人寫文章

Chéngchēung

FV   ask someone to do the examination or write an article for oneself
找他人代自己作文章或參加考試

e.g.   Ngóh m̀sīk jouh gùngfo, wàihyáuh chéngchēung.
       我 唔識 做 功課， 唯有 請槍。

(I don't know how to do the homework, so I ask somebody else to do it for me.)
（我不會做功課，只好找人代做。）

Chéngchēung might come from the story of "jūkdōu" (lit. holding a sword). We can read in *The New Social Anecdotes*, a famous literary work in the South and North dynasties, that during the Three Kingdoms Period, Chòuh Chōu once had to receive an envoy from Hùng Lòuh (i.e. the Hun). But having an ugly face, he was afraid that he was not dignified enough to make the envoy respect him. So he got an imposing man Chèui Yìhm to take his place. When Chèui Yìhm was receiving the envoy, Chòuh Chōu, disguised as a guard, just stood behind Chèui Yìhm with a sword in his hand.

Later, Chòuh Chōu sent a spy to learn how the envoy felt. The envoy said, "The one who was holding a sword is the real hero." When Chòuh Chōu learned about this, he immediately sent somebody to kill the envoy.

One who does something for somebody else without letting other people know is called "jūkdōuyàhn", which was changed to Chēungsáu later.

However, very few people are aware that the expression might have come from Chéngchōng, which means "to ask (Jāu) Chōng to hold the executioner's sword (for Gwāangūng*)". In the frequently seen portrait of Gwāangūng, you can very easily find Jāu Chōng standing behind him gripping a huge sword in his hand.

請槍，或者由「捉刀」的故事演變而來。《世說新語》說：曹操要接見匈奴使者，但自覺相貌醜陋，怕不能令對方敬服，於是找來相貌堂堂的崔琰冒充自己。崔琰接見匈奴使者時，曹操假扮衛士，捉刀站在崔琰背後。事後，曹操派人探匈奴使者的口風，使者答：「捉刀的那個才是英雄。」曹操聽見，立刻派人殺了匈奴使者。

　　隱藏身分而做事的，稱為「捉刀人」，後來演變為「槍手」。

　　但是很少人知道，請槍可能是「請倉」，即請周倉代關公捉刀。請看一張民間常見的關公畫像就會明白。圖中關公坐在前面，後面那個提刀而立的就是周倉。

* also born in the Three Kingdoms Period. Temples dedicated to him were erected after he was canonized as the God of War.

Kèh Làuhwòhngmáh 騎劉皇馬

Kèh Làuhwòhngmáh

VO/KIT borrow money from someone and then run away
借了人家的錢後一去不回

e.g. Yáuh sàammaahn ngàhn gùngsou, béi kéuih kèhjó làuhwòhngmáh.
      有   三萬   銀   公數，俾 佢   騎咗   劉皇馬。
      (He took thirty thousand dollars in public funds and ran away.)
      （有三萬元公家的錢，被他偷走了。）

Kèhmáh means to ride a horse. In Chapter 34 of *The Romance of the Three Kingdoms*, it is said that Làuh Béi (A.D. 162-223) was also called Làuh Wòhng Sūk. He had a very good horse named Dīk Lòuh which was offered to him by his men. They got it from a battle. Làuh Béi was in Gìngjàu then, working as a subordinate of Làuh Bíu. Choi Mouh, another subordinate of Làuh Bíu, was jealous of Làuh Béi. One day, Choi Mouh invited Làuh Béi to his feast and then tried to capture him. But someone told Làuh Béi about this. Pretending that he had to go to the toilet, Làuh Béi got on Dīk Lòuh, the good horse, and fled. The soldiers of Choi Mouh chased him. Làuh Béi came to a stream and there was no other way to go. All he could do was to urge the horse to cross the stream. The water was deep and running swiftly and it seemed that he could not succeed in crossing the stream. Suddenly the horse made a tremendous leap across the stream and Làuh Béi was free then.

Kèh Làuhwòhngmáh is also a Hithauhyúh → je séui deuhn (i.e. to flee by water). Actually it means to borrow water (i.e. money) and run away.

在《三國演義》第三十四回裏說：劉備（劉皇叔）（公元162-223）的手下在打仗時奪來一匹好馬，名叫「的盧」，就獻給劉備作坐騎。當時劉備在荊州依附劉表，而劉表的部將蔡瑁嫉忌他。一天，蔡瑁設酒宴請劉備來，打算在那時捉住他，沒想到有人把消息通知劉備，他藉口上廁，騎上的盧便逃跑。蔡瑁的軍士在後面追趕。劉備跑到一條溪水邊，無路可逃，唯有趕馬涉溪。溪水又深又急，眼看過不了，忽然的盧飛身一躍，躍上對岸，劉備於是脫險。
　　「騎劉皇馬」也是句歇後語，意即「借水遁」。指借了人家的水〔錢〕逃走了。

Yātgo Yuhn Dá, Yātgo Yuhn Ngàaih
一個願打，一個願捱

Yātgo Yuhn Dá, Yātgo Yuhn Ngàaih

I.E. an event involving two persons, in which one takes all the advantage without feeling sorry, while the other one is willing to suffer loss
一宗涉及兩人的事，一方佔盡便宜，但毫無內咎；另一方吃盡苦頭，但又甘心情願

e.g. Yàhndeih léuhng gùngpó, yātgo yuhn dá, yātgo yuhn ngàaih,
人哋　兩　公婆　一個 願 打 一個 願　捱，

ngoihyàhn m̀léihdāk gam dò ge la.
外人　唔理得 咁 多嘅嘑。

(We can't interfere in the affairs of a husband and wife. One likes to hurt and the other is glad to suffer.)
（別人夫婦家裏頭的事，旁人管不來。）

In Chapter 46 of *The Romance of the Three Kingdoms*, Chòuh Chōu led a great concentration of troops to attack Jàu Yùh in the southern part of China. Chòuh Chōu's soldiers were afraid of becoming sea-sick, so they linked up the battleships with iron chains. When Jàu Yùh saw that, he got a good idea. He summoned all his generals and told them to prepare food that could last for three months because they were going to attack Chòuh Chōu. Wòhng Koi, one of his generals, disagreed with him at once and said, "Even if we have thirty months' military provisions, we might not defeat Chòuh Chōu." Jàu Yùh became very angry on hearing that. He charged Wòhng Koi with harassment of the morale of the army and Wòhng Koi was given fifty lashes.

Then Wòhng Koi secretly sent someone to give a message to Chòuh Chōu, saying that he would come to surrender. Chòuh Chōu learnt from the spies that Wòhng Koi had been beaten by Jàu Yùh and then he received his letter. Chòuh Chōu believed that Wòhng Koi would really come to surrender, so he was not as cautious as before. One day, Wòhng Koi took a boat which sailed very fast to the chained battleships of Chòuh Chōu. As soon as he got close, he suddenly set fire to his boat and let it dash towards the chained battleships, which eventually were completely burnt up. This was the very famous "Battle of Chek Bīk" in Chinese history and it turned out that Jàu Yùh and Wòhng Koi were performing "fúyuhk gai" (a trick of securing the trust of another by suffering bodily injuries).

　　《三國演義》第四十六回裏說，曹操帶領大軍南下攻打周瑜，因爲曹兵怕「暈船浪」，便把戰船一艘艘用鐵鏈連起來。周瑜見了，便心生一計。他召集眾將，吩咐準備三個月軍糧，要攻打曹操。部將黃蓋即時反駁說：「就算有三十個月軍糧，也不一定能打敗曹操。」周瑜聽了大怒，就以「擾亂軍心」罪名，打了黃蓋五十棍。

　　黃蓋暗中派人送信給曹操，說要投降。曹操從密探處知道周瑜打黃蓋的事，又收到信，就以爲黃蓋眞的來降，鬆懈了戒備心。黃蓋這日乘快船駛向曹軍的連環船，待接近時，突然舉火，把快船燒着，乘勢衝前，把曹軍的船全部燒光。這就是有名的「赤壁之戰」。原來周瑜、黃蓋用的是「苦肉計」。

Lātsōu 甩鬚/Dìugá 丢架

Lātsōu/Dìugá

VO lose face
丢臉，失威

e.g. Daaih chyùhsī gíngyìhn jyúnūng faahn, jànhaih dìugá/lātsōu la.
大　廚師　竟然　煮燶　飯，眞係 丢架/甩鬚 嘑。

(An experienced cook burnt the rice. What a shame!)
（大廚師竟燒焦了飯，眞丢臉！）

In Chapter 58 of *The Romance of the Three Kingdoms*, we can read that once when Chòuh Chōu was defeated by Máh Chīu and was chased by him, one soldier in Máh Chīu's army cried loudly, "The one in a red robe is Chòuh Chōu." On hearing that, Chòuh Chōu took off his red robe at once. Then another soldier cried, "The one with the long beard is Chòuh Chōu." Chòuh Chōu immediately cut his beard with his sword. Finally he pulled down the tatters of the flag to wrap his head and ran away with his defeated army.

There is another interpretation of Lātsōu. It refers to the sudden dropping (i.e. Lāt) of the artificial beard (i.e. Sōu) worn on an actor's face; while Dìugá is to forget the action that the actor should play. Whether Dìugá or Lātsòu, all the actor will get is the catcalls of the audience. What a shame!

　　《三國演義》第五十八回裏說：馬超出兵攻打曹操，曹操落敗逃走，馬超一直緊追在後。馬超的軍士裏有人大叫：「穿紅袍的是曹操！」曹操聽了，連忙脫掉紅袍。又有人大叫：「長鬚的是曹操！」曹操急忙用劍割去長鬚，最後扯來旗角一塊破布包着頭，混在亂軍中逃脫了。

　　另一個說法，「甩鬚」是指演粵劇的時候，演員臉上掛的假鬚意外地掉了下來。而「丢架」，則指演戲時忘了「架式」（規定的動作）。

　　無論丢架或甩鬚，都會惹來觀眾的喝倒彩，多麼丢臉！

Āauwū/Ngāauwū 丫烏

Āauwū/Ngāauwū

N   a legendary devil [M: jek, go]
    傳說中的惡鬼

e.g. Faaidī dábaahnháh lā! Ngāauwū gám ge yéung, bīn'go nàahmjái
      快啲　　打扮吓　啦　　丫烏　　咁　嘅　　樣，　邊個　　男仔

      wúih jèui néih ā!
      會　　追　你　吖！

      (Go and put on some make-up. How will boys be interested in you if you look like an ugly devil?)
      （快打扮一下吧！夜叉似的模樣，誰會追求你？）

Legend has it that during the South and North dynasties, there was a military officer named Màh Wùh. He was a wicked and fierce man. People were all afraid of him. When a child cried, adults would threaten, "Stop crying. Màh Wùh is coming." This kind of threatening was usually very effective.

There was a similar legend in Jitgōng province that there was a devil named Màh Wùh in Wuih Kāi. It liked to capture children and eat their brains. Actually, Màh Wùh is the nickname of a northern barbarian (i.e. Wùh) in ancient China. He was very ugly and fierce, with pock-marks (i.e. Màh) on his face. The term "Màh Wùh" was phonetically changed to Ngāauwū when it came to Gwóngdùng. Even now, we threaten small children saying, "Be good, otherwise we will drive you out of the door and let Ngāauwū take you away."

    傳說在南北朝時，有個軍官叫「麻胡」的，為人兇險惡毒，百姓很怕他。小孩子啼哭時，大人就嚇他說：「快別哭！麻胡來了！」小孩就急急止了眼淚。

    浙江會稽地方上也有類似的傳說：會稽有惡鬼叫「麻胡」的，喜好捉去小孩，吃小孩的腦髓。

    「麻胡」是個渾號，大概他是個胡人，滿臉麻子，樣貌極醜陋而兇惡。「麻胡」傳到廣東，音變為「丫烏」。現在我們嚇小孩說：「你不聽話就趕你出門外，讓丫烏捉了你！」

Tok Daaihgeuk 托大腳/Chaathàaih 擦鞋

Tok Daaihgeuk/Chaathàaih

VO   flatter (the superior)/flatter (lit. shine the shoes [of others])
      拍馬屁；吹捧奉承，以取媚他人

e.g.   Kéuih jeui sīk tok daaihgeuk/chaathàaih, tam bōsí hòisàm.
      佢　最　識　托　大腳/　擦鞋，　氹　波士　開心。

      (He knows well how to please his boss and make him feel happy.)
      （他最會拍馬屁，討上司歡心。）

In the Tang dynasty, there was an empress called Móuh Jāk Tìn (A.D. 625–705). She had a favourite "lover" called Sit Wàaih Yih. Jèung Kāp, a low ranking official, always followed Sit Wàaih Yih wherever he went and was willing to be his attendant. When Sit was ready to mount his horse, Jèung Kāp immediately prostrated himself on the ground as a stepping stone for Sit. He was teased by the gentlemen for what he did. This may be the origin of Tok Daaihgeuk (lit. to carry on one's shoulder a pair of big feet).

    In Hong Kong, people who shine shoes for a living are called "chaathàaihjái". When a customer comes, the "chaathàaihjái" will make him sit first, then lift up the foot of the customer, put it on a small wooden box and start shining the shoe. So Chaathàaih can mean the same as Tok Daaihgeuk but one would do the latter to one's superior.

    唐代有個女皇帝武則天（公元625-705），她有個面首（男人）叫薛懷義，相當得寵。有個小官員叫張岌的，常跟着薛懷義出入，做他的「跟班」（隨從僕役）。薛懷義要上馬，張岌就趕快伏在地下，讓薛踩住他的背來上馬。張岌這種所爲，常受到正人君子的譏笑。「托大腳」這詞語近來在香港有所變化。香港有些以替人擦亮皮鞋爲生的人，俗稱「擦鞋仔」。客人來光顧，擦鞋仔請客人坐下，先托起客人的腳擱在小木箱上，然後開始擦鞋。所以說「擦鞋」等於說「托大腳」，祇是後者的對象多是身分地位比你高的人。

＊取自石人著，頁45。

Jáu Hauhmún 走後門

Jáu Hauhmún

I.E. to attain one's goal by means of improper ways or personal connection (lit. to enter by the back door)
用人事關係或不正當手段達到目的

e.g. Kéuih sìhngjīk chà, daahnhaih yauh séung yahp mìhnghaauh
佢　成績　差，　但係　又　想　入　名校

duhksyù, wàihyāt ge baahnfaat jauh haih jáu hauhmún.
讀書，　唯一　嘅　辦法　就　係　走　後門。

(His school records are poor but wants to get into a famous school. The only way is to use improper means.)
（他成績差劣，但又想入讀名校，唯有利用人事關係才成。）

Choi Gìng was a prime minister of the Sung dynasty. He discriminated against the officials of the Yùhn Yauh period (A.D. 1086-1092) as much as he could. Even the words "Yùhn Yauh" could not be mentioned among his officials. Once, when the governor of a county was conducting office work, a Buddhist monk came to ask him for permission to leave the city. When the governor saw that his identity paper was issued in the Yùhn Yauh period, he compelled the monk to cast away his identity as a monk and return to secular life. Then a Taoist monk came to ask him for the renewal of his identity paper because he lost it. When the governor realized that he became a monk in the Yùhn Yauh period, he told someone to take off the monk's robe and drove him away. While the governor was very infuriated, one of his subordinates came to him and asked him in a low voice, "Your Excellency, one thousand strings of copper coins were sent from the imperial treasury for our salary, should we take it or not?" The governor rebuked him, "How could we not take it?" "The coins are all minted with 'Yùhn Yauh' on them," the subordinate told him. After hesitating for a while, the governor ordered him in a low voice, "Get them in by the back door."

話說宋朝時，蔡京為宰相，對以前「元祐」時期（公元1086-1092）的舊臣拼命排斥，官場上甚至連「元祐」兩個字也視為禁忌，誰也不敢提。

　　有一次，某縣官審理公事，有個和尚請求離城外遊，縣官一看他的戒牒是「元祐」時發的，就強迫那和尚還俗。這時，又有個道士遺失度牒請求補發，縣官一問，又是「元祐」時出家的，就叫人剝下他的道士袍，並把他趕走。縣官正火氣上頭，他的屬員上前低聲問：「大人，國庫剛發下來一千貫俸錢，不知好不好收？」縣官反問：「怎麼不收？」屬員答：「錢上有『元祐』的鑄文。」縣官想了一想，悄聲吩咐：「那就走後門搬進來吧。」

Louhchēut Máhgeuk 露出馬腳

Louhchēut Máhgeuk

PH/VO incautiously reveal one's secret or fault; to belie (lit. to expose Máh's feet)
不留意而暴露了弱點或過失

e.g. Kéuih ngāak lóuhpòh wah heui hòiwúi, dímjì sāamléhng seuhngbihn ge
佢 呃 老婆 話 去 開會 點知 衫領 上邊 嘅

sèuhngòu yan louhchēutjó máhgeuk.
唇膏 印 露出咗 馬腳。

(He told his wife that he had a meeting. How could he know that his secret was revealed by the lipstick on his collar.)
（他騙太太說去開會，誰知衣領上的唇膏印洩露了祕密。）

If you go to Cat Street in the central district of Hong Kong Island, you will quite easily find very small shoes in the antique shops. If you ask the shopkeepers about them, they will tell you that those shoes were worn by the women who had their feet bound in the former times. The custom of binding feet started from the Sung dynasty. All the women born in the families of the officials or of the rich had to have their feet bound with long pieces of cloth from childhood so that their feet would not grow large. They all would feel proud of their small feet. On the other hand, maid servants or farm women or those who had to do menial work would not bind their feet. The heroine of Louhchēut Máhgeuk was the queen of the first emperor of the Ming dynasty (A.D. 1328-1399). She was surnamed Máh. Once, she was riding a sedan chair in the street. Suddenly, the curtain of the sedan chair was blown aside by a strong wind. People on the street could see that the queen did not have her feet bound. One man made a drawing of her feet for fun, but the emperor was angry with him and had him killed.

你到香港中環的摩囉街走走,在古董店不難發現一些小鞋子,問一下店員,原來它是以前纏小腳女人所穿的。這種纏足的風氣,宋朝以後就有,凡是富貴人家的女子,從小就用布纏足,令雙腳不能發育,以此為貴。相反,婢女農婦和要幹粗活的,便不會纏足。

　　「露出馬腳」的主人原來是明太祖(公元1328-1399)的馬皇后。一次,馬皇后坐轎子走在街上,忽然一陣大風掀起了轎的簾子,大家看見皇后原來沒有纏足,有雙大腳。有個人拿這事畫了幅畫開玩笑,誰知惹怒了明太祖,把他殺掉。

Chóh Láahngbáandang 坐冷板櫈

Chóh Láahngbáandang

VO have a cold reception (lit. sitting on a cool bench)
    受人冷落

e.g. Kéuih sìhngmáahn sihk lìhngmūng, bīkjyuh yiu chóh láahngbáandang.
     佢　成晚　食　檸檬，迫住　要　坐　冷板櫈。
     (No girls liked to dance with him [in the party]. All he could do was just sat there alone.)
     （〔在派對中〕沒有女孩子願意跟他跳舞，他只好呆坐一旁。）

The story of Chóh Láahngbáandang took place in Confucius' residence in Kūk Fauh county of Sàandūng province. Because many emperors of different dynasties honored Confucius, his house was converted into a grand mansion and his eldest descendants were installed as high officials. During the Ming dynasty, one of the girl decendants of Confucius married the emperor and became the queen. The influence of the family of Confucius' decendants became very strong. During that time, the prime minister Yìhm Sūng committed a crime and expected to be punished. So he went to Confucius mansion to see the queen's father. He wanted to bribe him, hoping that the queen would speak well of him. But the queen's father despised him and gave him the cold shoulder and left him sitting on a wooden bench alone for hours. This is the origin of Chóh Láahngbáandang.

「坐冷板櫈」的故事發生在山東省曲阜縣的孔府。由於歷代皇帝都很尊崇孔子，於是把孔子的府第擴修得極宏偉，而孔子的嫡子嫡孫都被封為大官。在明朝孔府有一位女兒嫁入皇宮做了皇后，孔家的影響力很大。那時，宰相嚴嵩犯了事，可能受到懲處，他便跑到孔府來求見皇后的父親，送些賄賂，希望將來皇后替他說些好話。但是皇后的父親看不起嚴嵩，故意冷落他，就讓他一個人坐在一條板櫈上，坐上幾小時。從此「坐冷板櫈」成了典故。

Wahtdaht 核突

Wahtdaht

SV   ugly, awful appearance
樣子難看

e.g.   Néihdī jih sédāk hóu wahtdaht.
你啲 字 寫得 好 核突。

(Your handwriting is terrible!)
（你的字體很劣。）

There is one delicious dim sum called "wàhn tān". It is made of mush-rooms, lean pork and shrimp wrapped in a piece of thin dough, and cooked in soup.

Originally wàhn tān was called Wahtdaht or "wahn deuhn". Legend has it that the youngest son of the emperor in heaven was called Wahn Deuhn. From birth he was very stupid. He had no eyes, ears, mouth or nose on his face and was extremely ugly. Sūk and Fāt, two friends of Wahn Deuhn, felt sorry for him. They decided to dig some holes in his face so that he could have the five organs. It took them seven days to finish. After Wahn Deuhn got the face of a human being, he also became clever. Unfortunately he suddenly died.

    有種好吃的東西叫「雲吞」——拿塊薄粉皮包着冬菇、豬肉和蝦肉，放進湯裏灼熟就可以吃。

    但是「雲吞」原本叫「核突」或者「渾沌」。

    傳說天帝有個小兒子叫「渾沌」，天生蠢鈍，他臉上沒有眼、耳、口、鼻，樣子難看極了。他的朋友儵和忽很可憐他，就決定給他在臉上開孔鑿出眼、耳、口、鼻來。儵和忽花了七日，鑿成了，「渾沌」有了人的樣子，也聰明起來，可惜他突然死了！

Baingai 蔽翳

Baingai

SV upset
    心境不開朗

e.g. Kéuih nīpáai sātyihp móuh chín, hóu baingai.
      佢　呢排　失業　無　錢，好　蔽翳。

(He has been unemployed recently. He has no money and is very upset.)
（他近日失業窮困，好苦。）

Baingai originally describes that the light is being shaded, but now it is used to mean "upset". Also legend has it that the dragon-king had nine sons. They all looked different and were interested in different things. The eldest son was called Beih Héi, which is now pronounced as Bai Ngai. He looked like a tortoise. He liked to carry a very heavy stone tablet on his back. The second son who was named Chì Máhn looked like a fish. He liked to stand on the ridge of the roof and watch. The third son Pòuh Lòuh had a sonorous voice. You could find him sitting on a bronze bell. Baih Ngohn, the fourth son, appeared as a watchman above a jail door. The fifth son was called Tòu Tip and enjoyed eating. The design on the huge tripod is an image of him. The sixth son Bà Hah is shown squatting on the railing of a bridge. Ngàaih Chì, the seventh son, is carved on the handle of a sword because he liked to kill people. The eighth son Syùn Ngàih liked to sit on the lid of a sandlewood burner. Jìu Tòuh, the youngest son of the dragon-king, can be easily found on doors, holding a ring in his mouth.

Carrying a heavy stone tablet on the back is a difficult and tiring job. That is why the creature becomes Baingai.

「蔽翳」是光線被遮蓋而昏暗，用來形容人心境不開朗。但有人說「蔽翳」原來寫作「贔屭」（音備喜）。

　　傳說龍王生了九個兒子，一個個模樣不同，喜好也異。大兒子贔屭樣子似龜，喜好背負重的石碑；二兒子叫螭吻（音痴吻），樣子似魚，喜愛站在屋脊上守望；三兒子叫蒲牢，聲音洪亮，常坐在銅鐘頂；四兒子叫狴犴（音幣岸），愛守獄門；五兒子叫饕餮（音滔帖），很貪吃，鼎上的圖形就是他；六兒子叫趴蝮（音蚆夏），就是橋欄上的石獅子；七兒子叫睚眦（音涯疵），好殺人，常作刀柄；八兒子叫狻猊（音酸倪），喜歡看守香爐；九兒子叫椒圖，喜歡銜着門環守門口。

　　贔屭背石碑很費力氣，怪不得牠「蔽翳」了。

Taaiseui Tàuhseuhng Duhng Tóu 太歲頭上動土/Lóuhfú Tàuhseuhng Dèng Sātná 老虎頭上釘虱乸

Taaiseui Tàuhseuhng Duhng Tóu/ Lóuhfú Tàuhseuhng Dèng Sātná

I.E.　daring to offend the bad or powerful people
　　　激怒惡人或有權勢的人，好大的膽子

e.g.　Kéuih lìhn gíngmouh chyúhjéung ge chè dōu séung tàu, jànhaih
　　　佢　連　警務　　署長　　嘅車都　想　偷，眞係

　　　taaiseui tàuhseuhng duhng tóu /lóuhfú tàuhseuhng dèng sātná la.
　　　太歲　頭上　　動　土/老虎　　頭上　　釘 虱乸 喇!

(He even wants to steal the car of the Police Commissioner. How daring he is!)
（他連警察局長的汽車也想偷走，好大膽子。）

　　Legend has it that Taaiseui was an imaginary god and takes charge of our land. But he is an evil deity. He travels in a path in opposite direction to that of Jupiter, and takes him twelve years to finish one celestial journey. When he moves to any place, people there should be very careful and especially not dig the land (i.e. Duhngtóu).

　　It is said that a long time ago, there was a flood. Many houses collapsed. A craftsman Póu Ngōn pleaded for the help of a Taoist god, Taaiseuhng Lóuhgwān. He taught him to build a kiln to make bricks and then build a house with those bricks. When Taaiseui came back, he was angry because the people had dug around to get mud for the bricks. Luckily, Taaiseuhng Lóuhgwān calmed him and soothed his anger.

　　People in the northern part of China like to say Taaiseui Tàuhseuhng Duhng Tóu while Cantonese people say Lóuhfú Tàuhseuhng Dèng Sātná (lit. spike lice on a tiger's head*). Isn't it a more vivid description?

傳說「太歲」是主管土地的神，是個凶神。他在與歲星（即木星）相反的方向雲遊四方，每十二年巡迴一周。每當他照臨某地，那塊地上的人就要小心行事，尤其不可亂動土壤。

　　話說許久之前，洪水泛濫，把平原上人民的土房子都沖塌了。工匠普安向太上老君求救，老君就敎普安建窯燒磚，再用磚建屋。太歲雲遊回來，發覺人們亂挖泥土（用來造磚），就大發脾氣。最後太上老君勸服了他。

　　北方人常說「太歲頭上動土」，但廣東人改成「老虎頭上釘虱乸」，不是更形象生動嗎？

* See Kwan Kit Choi, p. 75.

Chésin 扯線

Chésin

FV/VO be a matchmaker or broker (lit. pull thread)
　　　 替男女撮合姻緣或作中間人

e.g.　Kéuih jùngyi gógo néuihjái, séung ngóh tùhng kéuih chésin.
　　　佢　鍾意 嗰個　女仔，想　　我　　同　　佢　扯線。

(He loves that girl, and he wants me to be his matchmaker.)
（他愛上那女人，想我給他作媒撮合。）

In Western myths, Cupid is a lovely child. When he shoots his arrow of love into a boy and a girl, they will soon fall in love with each other. In China, the god of love is called "Yuht Lóuh" (lit. the old man in the moon). He does not have any arrows, but red threads.

Once, there was an educated young man called Wáih Gu. One day as he was travelling, he passed through the Sung city. There he met an old man who was carrying a bag. The old man took out a book from his bag and tried to read it under the moonlight. Wáih Gu asked him what book he was reading. The old man told him that it was a book recording the names of couples, and from studying the book, he could tell which man would marry which woman.* Wáih Gu also saw that there were red threads in the bag. He then asked what they were used for. The old man said that he would tie the red threads around the feet of a boy and a girl. They would then fall in love with each other and get married. Wáih Gu, upon reading the old man's book, also found the name of the girl whom he would later marry.

　　西方的愛神丘比特是個小孩，他拿愛的弓箭一射，就把一對男女的心串連起來。中國的愛神叫「月老」，沒有箭，卻有繩子。從前有個讀書人叫韋固的，旅途中經過宋城，遇見一個背着書囊的老人。老人從囊中取出書來在月光下翻看，韋固問是甚麼書，老人答是《鴛鴦譜》，裏面記載了將會結爲夫婦的每一對男女的名字。韋固見囊裏有紅色的繩子，又問有甚麼用。老人說用來把一對男女的腳繫連起來，他們就會愛上對方，而結爲夫婦。韋固從老人的書裏查出將來妻子的名字，後來果然娶了她。

* See Wolfram Eberhard, p. 193

Ngàaihdou Gàmjìng Fó'ngáahn
捱到金睛火眼

Ngàaihdou Gàmjìng Fó'ngáahn

I.E. work very hard
工作得很辛苦

e.g. Gógo néuihyán séijó lóuhgùng, yauh yiu yéuhng nghgo jáinéui,
嗰個 女人 死咗 老公， 又 要 養 五個 仔女，

jànhaih ngàaihdou gàmjìng fó'ngáahn.
眞係 捱到 金睛 火 眼。

(After the death of her husband, that woman had to work very hard to raise her five children.)
(那女人死了丈夫，要養活五個子女，眞給生活折磨得苦極了。)

It says in Chapter 7 of *The Journey to the West* that after the Monkey God, Chàih Tìn Daaih Sing, started an uprising in the palace of the emperor in heaven, he was caught by a Taoist god, Taaiseuhng Lóuhgwān, who pushed him into a furnace with the shape of the eight trigrams and let him be burnt with fierce fire. The Monkey God found a ventilation hole in the corner of the furnace and crouched over there because there was no fire, just wind. However, its eyes became red from the smoke.

After the furnace had been burning for many days, Taaiseuhng Lóuhgwān thought that the Monkey God must surely have been burnt to ashes, but when he opened the furnace, to his great surprise, not only had the Monkey God not been hurt at all, but he had been "refined" to have Gàmjìng Fó'ngáahn (lit. gold pupils and fiery eyes).

《西遊記》第七回說：齊天大聖（石猴精）大鬧天宮之後，被太上老君捉住，推入八卦爐中，用猛火來燒。齊天大聖躱到爐裏一角，那裏是通風位，有風無火。只是煙把他一雙眼睛燻紅了。燒了許多天之後，太上老君以爲齊天大聖已化了灰，便打開八卦爐，誰知他不但分毫不損，還煉成了「金睛火眼」。

Fèimchēut Ngóh Sáujíla 飛唔出我手指罅

Fèimchēut Ngóh Sáujíla

PH   no matter how you try, you can't get away from my control
      無論怎樣也逃不出我的控制

e.g.   Jauhsyun néih sīk fèi, dōu fèimchēut ngóh sáujíla.
       就算 你 識 飛 都 飛唔出 我 手指罅！

(Even if you can fly, you can't fly out of my hand.)
（即使你會飛，也逃不出我掌心。）

We can read in Chapter 7 of *The Journey to the West* that one day, the Buddha made a bet with the Monkey God, Chàih Tìn Daaih Sing, saying, "Can you get out of my right palm with just one somersault? If you win, then I'll ask the Jade Emperor (the emperor in heaven) to give his palace to you. But if you fail, you have to be demoted to the human world and be a goblin there." Thinking that he could get as far as 108,000 miles by just one somersault, the Monkey God agreed to the bet. Then he went to the centre of the Buddha's palm and made many somersaults until he got to the end of the sky. There he saw five pillars, and wrote on the middle one that Chàih Tìn Daaih Sing had been there. He pissed there and then went back to see the Buddha by somersaults. The Buddha stretched out his hand. To Monkey God's great surprise, he saw the words that he wrote on the pillar on the middle finger of the Buddha. He could also smell his own urine. The Buddha then turned over his hand. The five fingers of his hand turned into five big mountains and the Monkey God was trapped under the mountains.

　　《西遊記》第七回裏說：如來佛祖跟齊天大聖（石猴精）打賭，說：「你若有本事，一觔斗打出我這右手掌中，算你贏，就請玉帝把天宮讓你；若不能打出手掌，你便要下界為妖。」齊天大聖自恃一個觔斗可翻十萬八千里，便答應賭賽。於是他站到佛祖的掌心，跟着大打觔斗，一直翻到天的盡頭，在那處五根柱子的中間，寫上「齊天大聖到此一遊」八個字，又撒了泡猴尿，才又翻觔斗回來見佛祖。誰知佛祖把手掌一伸，中指上就寫着「齊天大聖」的字，還有他的尿的氣味。佛祖隨手一翻，五指分成五座山，就把齊天大聖壓在山下。

Chìhnsai 前世/Chìhnsai M̀sàu 前世唔修

Chìhnsai/Chìhnsai M̀sàu

PH/I.E.   be suffering very pitifully
　　　　指某人正受苦，很可憐

e.g.   Kéuih lóuhgùng sèhngyaht dá kéuih, jànhaih chìhnsai m̀sàu lo!
　　　　佢　老公　　成日　打　佢，眞係　　前世　唔修咯！

(Her husband always beats her. How pitiful she is!)
（丈夫常常打她，眞可憐。）

Buddhism has always been one of the three major philosophies that has great influence on Chinese people. The Buddhists believe that man has many lives. When we enter a Buddhist temple, we can see three statues of Buddha. The Buddha in the middle takes charge of our life. The one on the right is the Buddha who takes charge of our previous life, and the one on the left, our next life.

The Buddhists also believe in retribution. If we did evil deeds in our previous life, we will suffer in this life. We will enjoy happiness in our next life if we do good deeds in this life. Therefore, if a man is suffering now, he must have committed evil deeds during his previous life. This situation generated the expression Chìhnsai (lit. previous life) M̀sàu (lit. not do good deeds).

Sometimes we'll hear the Buddhists mumbling in prayer, "Nàahmmòh òlèih tòhfaht". They say this so that the Buddha who takes charge of our next life will save them.

　　佛教對中國人的影響很深，佛教徒相信，人有前世、今世與來世。走進佛殿，我們可能看到並排的三個佛像：在我們右方的是藥師琉璃光佛，主管人的前世；在正中的是釋迦牟尼佛，主管今世；而在左方的是阿彌陀佛，主管來世。

　　他們相信，前世作了孽，今世會有報應（受苦）；今世行了善，來世也有報應（享福）。所以一個人現在受折磨，必是他前世未有修種善因 —— 亦即「前世唔修」。

　　有時我們聽見佛教徒唸「喃嘸阿彌陀佛」，意思是祈求主管來世的阿彌陀佛施予解救。

Gwojó Hói Jauh Haih Sàhnsīn
過咗海就係神仙

Gwojó Hói Jauh Haih Sàhnsīn

I.E. No matter what devious way one uses, it would be all right to get the thing done
不管手段怎樣,把事情辦妥就行

e.g. Gwojó hói jauh haih sàhnsīn, néih léihdāk kéuih dím jouh ā!
過咗 海 就 係 神仙, 你 理得 佢 點 做 吖!

(It's none of your business as to how he got it done. Anyway, it's finished now.)
(事情已經做好,手段怎樣,你管不了。)

There is one Hithauhyúh: The eight immortals cross the sea → everyone tries his best. Legend has it that once the eight immortals were going to the birthday feast of the Queen Mother of the West on Mt. Kwān Lèuhn. They came to the seaside. They had to cross the sea (i.e. Gwohói) but there was no boat. As they were worrying about it, Léuih Duhng Bān suggested that each of them should use their supernatural powers to cross the sea. So the crippled Tit Gwáai Léih went surfing by stepping on his iron stick. Hon Jùng Lèih sat on his palm leaf fan and sailed like a boat. Jèung Gwó Lóuh unfolded his paper ass and turned it into a real one. He rode sitting backward on the ass, and the sea water just came up to its hoofs. Léuih Duhng Bān turned his sword into a dragon. Hòhn Sèung Jí turned his jade flute into a snake. They got on the dragon and the snake which carried them across the sea. Likewise, the rest of them made good use of their treasure, i.e. Chòuh Gwok Káuh with his pair of jade castanets, Làahm Chói Wòh a bamboo basket, Hòh Sīn Gū a lotus flower, and finally they all succeeded in crossing the sea.

Gwojó Hói Jauh Haih Sàhnsīn was generated from the above legendary story.

有句歇後語說：「八仙過海→各顯神通。」話說八仙一起參加西王母的蟠桃會（生日宴會），中途遇上大海。怎樣渡過去呢？呂洞賓倡議八仙各顯本領。於是鐵拐李踏着拐杖破浪而渡；漢鍾離把芭蕉扇當船，安坐而渡；張果老把紙驢變作活驢，倒騎着牠走過去，海水只沒到驢蹄；呂洞賓變寶劍為龍，韓湘子變玉笛做蛇，各自騎龍騎蛇渡了海；其餘的曹國舅、藍采和、何仙姑都憑自己的法寶（玉版、竹籃、荷花座）順利渡了海。

　　由此衍生出「過咗海就係神仙」。

Chídeih Mòuh Ngàhn Sàambaak Léung
此地無銀三百兩

Chídeih Mòuh Ngàhn Sàambaak Léung

I.E. let one's secret out foolishly (lit. this place does not have 300 taels of silver)
愚蠢地揭露自己的秘密

e.g. Múhnsàn jáuhei ge jeuhngfù hóu yeh fàan ngūkkéi. Kéuih juhng deui
滿身 酒氣 嘅 丈夫，好 夜 返 屋企，佢 仲 對

taaitáai wah, "Ngóh móuh heui yámjáu a." Taaitáai jauh naauh kéuih,
太太 話：「我 冇 去 飲酒呀！」太太 就 鬧 佢：

"Chídeih mòuh ngàhn sàambaak léung."
「此地 無 銀 三百 兩。」

(A drunk husband came home late at night and said to his wife, "I have not gone to drinking." She rebuked him, "Your denial reveals what you have done.")
滿身酒氣的丈夫很晚才回家，還對太太說：「我沒有去喝酒啊！」太太罵他說：「此地無銀三百兩。」

Once there was a poor man called Jèung Sàam. One day, he got a small sum of money, 300 silver coins, and put them under his bed. But he was worried that a thief might come and steal them. He thought it would be best for him to hide them in the ground at the back of his house. So he got up at mid-night, took a spade and stealthily buried the money. But afterwards, he was still worried about it. So he wrote a note and put it on the place where the money was hidden. His movement awakened his neighbour Wòhng Yih. He was curious and tried to find out what had happened while Jèung Sàam was asleep. He saw the note: "There's no 300 silver coins here." "How funny it is!" He thought. So he dug out the money and took it home.

But the story was not yet finished. Wòhng Yih was afraid that Jèung Sàam would find out that he was the thief. He also wrote a note and put it on the place where the money was stolen, just like Jèung Sàam had done: "Wòhng Yih didn't steal Jèung Sàam's money."

從前有個窮漢叫張三的，某日發了筆小財，有三百兩銀子。他把銀子藏在床下，但擔心有賊來偷去。他想，不如把銀子埋在屋後的土裏。於是他半夜起床，拿鏟子悄悄地到屋後埋好銀子。可是，他還不放心，又寫了一張字條，貼在埋銀子的地方。

　　張三鬼鬼祟祟的行動吵醒了鄰家的王二。他趁張三入了夢，便偷偷去看看。原來字條上寫着：「此地無銀三百兩。」王二心裏好笑，便動手掘出銀子，偷了回家。

　　不過故事還沒有完——

　　王二怕張三知道自己偷了銀子，也寫了張字條貼在原處，字條說：「隔壁王二不曾偷。」

Séuigwái Sìng Sìhng'wòhng 水鬼升城隍

Séuigwái Sìng Sìhng'wòhng

I.E. be promoted (said with jealousy)
職位提升了（這是句帶有妒意的嘲諷話）

e.g. Séuigwái sìng sìhng'wòhng, kaau tok daaihgeuk jìmáh!
水鬼 升 城隍， 靠 托 大腳 之馬！
(He got a promotion just by flattering the boss.)
（他的升職，不過靠吹拍逢迎所賜。）

Legend has it that after a man has drowned, he will become a water ghost (i.e. Séuigwái). The ghost cannot be reborn as a man unless it finds a substitute at the place where it drowned. There is a story in *Strange Stories from a Chinese Studio*: The fisherman Lóuh Héui and the water ghost Wòhng Luhk-lòhng were very good friends. They always got together and drank. One night Luhk-lòhng said to Lóuh Héui, "Someone will come and be my substitute. You can come and see tomorrow at noon." The next day, when Lóuh Héui went there, he saw a woman crossing the river by the bridge. She was carrying a baby. She fell into the water and struggled for a while. There was nobody to save her. Suddenly she was afloat as if she was supported by something under the water. She swam to the riverside. She and her baby went away in safety.

That night when Lóuh Héui saw Luhk-lòhng again, he asked about the woman. Luhk-lòhng said, "I cannot be so cruel as to kill two people."

Because Luhk-lòhng was so kind, he could not find a substitute for a long time. The Jade Emperor (i.e. the emperor in heaven) knew about it and canonized him as a city god (i.e. Sìhng'wòhng) which is a deity of lower rank.

傳說人被淹死會變水鬼；水鬼不可以轉世再做人,除非他找到「替死鬼」。《聊齋志異》裏有個故事：

　　漁夫老許和水鬼王六郎都是朋友,他們常常一起喝酒。一晚,六郎對老許說：「快有人來代替我了,你明天中午來河邊看看吧。」老許依時去看,見有個手抱嬰兒的婦人過橋,失足掉進河裏。她掙扎了一會,但沒有人救她。忽然,不知水裏有甚麼東西托她起來,她游回岸邊,就抱着嬰兒走了。那晚上,老許又見到六郎,問及婦人的事,六郎答：「我不忍心害了兩條命。」

　　六郎心地太好,許久都沒找到替死鬼。這事後來給玉帝知道了,就讓六郎當了土地(土地和城隍都是低職級的神)。

Mōkgwòng Jyū/Mōk Gwòngjyū 剝光豬

Mōkgwòng Jyū/Mōk Gwòngjyū

VO   take off all clothings; lose all in a game of chess
脫光衣服；也指下棋時吃光棋子

e.g. Kéuihdī kéi taai sí, béi ngóh mōk kéuih gwòngjyū.
佢啲 棋 太 屎 俾 我 剝 佢 光豬。

(He's too poor in playing chess. He lost all to me.)
（他的棋技太低，被我吃光他的棋子。）

Mōkgwòng already means to take off all one's clothes. What has that to do with Jyū (lit. a pig)? It turns out that the word originates from the history of Sung during the South and North dynasties.

The fifth emperor of the Sung didn't like his uncle, the younger brother of his father, who was called Yūk. Yūk was a very fat man and was nicknamed Jyūwòhng (lit. king of the pigs). The emperor told someone to dig a hole in the ground and put a trough of rice in it. The emperor would make Jyūwòhng take off all his clothes and eat the rice like a pig. He enjoyed himself very much by insulting his uncle.

Once, the emperor was infuriated by Jyūwòhng. He ordered his men to take off all his clothes. They tied up his hands and feet and use a bamboo cane to carry him away, intending to kill him. Luckily, people at the court advised the emperor not to do so. Jyūwòhng had a near escape from death. Later, Jyūwòhng usurped the throne and became the emperor of the country.

「剝光」就是脫光衣服，跟「豬」有甚麼關係？原來出自南北朝劉宋時一段歷史：

劉宋的第五任皇帝子業，很討厭他的叔父彧。彧身體肥胖，外號「豬王」。帝叫人在地坑裏用木槽盛飯，剝光「豬王」的衣服，逼他像豬一樣吃飯，以此為樂。一次，「豬王」氣惱了皇帝，皇帝下令人把他的衣服脫去，縛住手腳，用竹杖穿上，準備挑去「屠豬」。幸好左右勸說，「豬王」才逃過大難。後來「豬王」奪了皇帝的座位。

Waihsihkmāau 為食貓；
Sihk Séimāau 食死貓；Laaimāau 賴貓

Waihsihkmāau

N　　a man as greedy as a cat [M: jek, go]
　　　像貓一樣饞嘴的人

e.g.　Bīnjek waihsihkmāau tàujó ngóhge syutgōu sihk nē?
　　　邊隻　　為食貓　偷咗　我嘅　雪糕　食　呢？

　　　(Who is so greedy as to steal my ice-cream?)
　　　（哪個貪吃鬼偷吃了我的冰淇淋？）

Sihk Séimāau

VO　　suffer wrong, being accused falsely [M: jek] (lit. eat dead cat)
　　　被人冤枉做了錯事

e.g.　Ngóh béi yàhn wāt, sihk jek séimāau.
　　　我　俾人　屈，食隻　死貓。

　　　(I was accused falsely and had to take all the blame.)
　　　（我被冤枉而要背黑鍋。）

Laaimāau

FV/SV　to deny mistakes; shirk responsibilities
　　　　抵賴，推搪責任

e.g.　Kéuih séung laaimāau m̀béichín.
　　　佢　想　賴貓　唔俾錢。

　　　(He intends to avoid paying.)
　　　（他企圖抵賴而不付錢。）

A man bought a fish and put it in the kitchen. After a while, the fish was missing. He suspected that the cat stole and ate it. In fact, cats are notorious for their greediness. How could a cat just look at the fish and not eat it? As it is said, "A cat always steals (fish to eat), and nothing can make it change." So we call a greedy person Waihsihkmāau. After the fish was missing, the cat was reviled, "You steal my fish, go to hell!" But it couldn't answer back, even if it was innocent, it had to take the blame. This is called Sihk Séimāau.

It turned out that somebody else stole the fish. But he was so cunning that he imputed the blame to the cat. This is called Laaimāau. The original word for Laai means to slander.

Sihk Séimāau may have originated from an interesting scenario in a famous Chinese opera *Steal Away the Prince with a Dead Cat*:

It is said that the Emperor Jàn of the Sung dynasty had two concubines, Léih and Làuh. By coincidence both of them were going to give birth to a baby on the same day. Concubine Làuh had a lovely and healthy boy who later became the crown prince. But concubine Léih gave birth only to a "dead cat"! The emperor was very angry with her and had her removed to "the cold palace", a place for women who had lost the favour of the emperor. A short while later, Léih was supposed to have been killed in a fire.

After many years, the prince came to the throne and became Emperor Yàhn. At one time, the mayor of the capital city, Bāau Chíng (also known as Bāau Chìng Tīn), who was an upright official, came to Chàhnjàu for the relief of the people who were suffering from starvation. A woman came and submitted a case to him. She declared she was the concubine Léih of the late emperor. She told him about Làuh's plot which she had kept secret for so many years. It turned out that Làuh just pretended to be pregnant. She had bribed the midwife, asking her to steal Léih's baby and put a dead cat in its place. She took the stolen baby as her own child. She was also guilty of setting fire to "the cold palace". Luckily, a court lady saved Léih and got her out of the capital city.

Finally, after the investigation of Bāau Chíng, concubine Léih was vindicated for what she had suffered.

有人買了尾魚放在廚房裏，一會兒，魚失了，他懷疑是貓偷了去吃。實在，貓是出名饞嘴的，見了魚怎會光看不咬呢？俗語說：「偷食貓兒，死性不改。」於是我們把貪吃鬼稱作「為食貓」。一旦魚失了，那人就指着貓叱罵：「死貓偷食！」貓不懂辯駁，即使牠沒有偷魚吃，仍不免背上罪名。這就是「食死貓」。

　　事實是有個狡猾的人偷走了魚，卻把罪名推在貓的身上，這就是「賴貓」。「賴」是「讕」的轉音，意思是誣衊。

　　「食死貓」有另一個故事：

　　話說在宋朝，眞宗皇帝有兩個妃子 —— 李妃和劉妃 —— 同時懷孕，幾乎在同一日裏分娩，劉妃生的嬰兒很俊美，後來就立為太子；而李妃生下的不是嬰兒，竟然是隻死了的狸貓！眞宗皇帝很憤怒，就把李妃打入冷宮。過了不多久，冷宮失火，李妃說是給燒死了。許多年後，太子登上皇位，就是仁宗。那時有名正直的官包拯（包青天），到陳州賑濟災荒，半路遇上一個婦人告狀，查問之下，原來她是以前眞宗皇帝的李妃。李妃向包拯揭出一段宮闈祕密：劉妃知道李妃懷了孕，就假裝同樣懷孕，又買通接生婆，把李妃剛生下的嬰兒偷走，換上一隻死狸貓。接生婆把那嬰兒交給劉妃，劉妃就當成是自己生的兒子，以博取皇帝的寵愛。劉妃又暗中派人放火燒冷宮，想殺人滅口，幸好宮女救出了李妃。最後，經過包拯的追查，眞相大白，李妃所受的冤屈得到洗雪。以上就是中國著名劇曲「狸貓換太子」的劇情。

Chēutmāau 出貓

Chēutmāau

VO   do the examination by unfair means (lit. out the cat)
考試作弊

e.g.   Néihdeih háausíh yiu sáu kwàijāk, m̀jéun chēutmāau.
你哋　考試　要　守　規則，唔准　出貓。

(You must follow the regulations when doing the examination. You must not use tricks.)
（你們要守考試規則，不好作弊。）

In China, there are twelve years in one zodiac cycle. Each year is associated with one animal. Chinese people use twelve animals to represent the cycle in the order: rat, cow, tiger, rabbit, dragon, snake, horse, sheep, monkey, rooster, dog, boar. 1996 is the year of the Rat, 1997 the year of the Cow, and so on. It's a very interesting way of denoting the year.

    Legend has it that originally the emperor in heaven wanted to choose thirteen animals to represent the year. The cat was one of them. The emperor in heaven told the animals to compete in a race in his palace on a certain morning. Whichever animal ran the fastest would be put in the first place of the zodiac cycle. The cat and the rat were good friends. They agreed that they would go to the race together. But the cat realized that it liked to sleep very much and was afraid that it would get up late, so it asked the rat to wake it up in the morning. The rat promised it immediately. But on the day of the race, the rat did not wake up the cat. It just went alone. When the cat woke up, it was too late to go to the race.

    The rat used this trick to get the cat out of the race. Furthermore, it also won the first place. The cow was the fastest among the twelve creatures but the rat was so cunning that it jumped on the back of the cow and let the cow carry it during the race. Just before the cow came to the finishing line, the rat jumped forward and became the winner.

    Now you know why the cat chases the rat whenever it sees it and wants to bite it.

中國人有一種很有趣的紀年方法，叫「十二生肖紀年」，即是用十二種動物，每種動物代表一年，輪換下去，十二年一個循環。例如：

1996 年是鼠年（Rat；syú）
1997　　牛年（Cow；ngàuh）
1998　　虎年（Tiger；fú）
1999　　兔年（Rabbit；tou）
2000　　龍年（Dragon；lùhng）
2001　　蛇年（Snake；sèh）
2002　　馬年（Horse；máh）
2003　　羊年（Sheep；yèuhng）
2004　　猴年（Monkey；hàuh）
2005　　雞年（Rooster；gāi）
2006　　狗年（Dog；gáu）
2007　　豬年（Boar；jyū）

　　傳說最初天帝選了十三種動物來代表年，除了上述的十二種外，貓也是一分子。天帝吩咐牠們某朝到天宮賽跑，跑得快的就排在前面。貓和鼠原本是好朋友，牠們約好一起去參賽。可是貓知道自己有個貪睡遲起床的毛病，牠就叫老鼠在早上喚醒牠。老鼠滿口答應了。可是到了比賽那天，老鼠沒有喚醒貓，自己去了，貓睡醒時已經趕不及參賽。
　　老鼠施詭計令貓出了局，更跑了個第一。原來老牛是十二種動物裏跑得最快的，老鼠一跳跳到牛背上，讓牛背着牠跑。將到終點的時候，老鼠踩着牛頭向前一竄，就搶到個冠軍！
　　現在你知道貓為甚麼一見老鼠就要追咬牠了！

Ngàuh Séi Sung Ngàuh Sōng 牛死送牛喪

Ngàuh Séi Sung Ngàuh Sōng

I.E.   compensation results in greater loss (lit. the cow dies, hold a funeral for it)
想補償損失，結果損失更大

e.g.   Ngàuh séi sung ngàuh sōng, m̀jouh hóugwo jouh.
牛 死 送 牛 喪，唔做 好過 做。

(We'll lose more. It's better not to do it.)
（賠錢送賊，不必幹。）

The king of the state of Chó owned a horse which he loved very much. He gave it a good stable and good food to eat. How could he have known that the horse died of overeating and lack of exercise. The king loved it so much that he wanted to hold a funeral ceremony like that for an official in the horse's honour. Yàu Maahng, one of the king's musicians, even suggested that the king should hold a funeral service like that of a king for it. So what could be done about it? He said that the king should order the soldiers to build a large imperial tomb, and they should use jade to make a coffin for it. Furthermore, the king should invite other kings of the neighbouring states to come to the funeral.

    The king realized that Maahng was teasing him. So he asked him for another suggestion. The musician then said, "Well, let's do it in this way. We can apply some spices on its body, put it in a large caldron and cook it on the stove. Finally, it would be buried inside our stomachs."

    But now we have a cow (i.e. Ngàuh) instead of a horse.

    楚王有隻愛馬，住好吃好，誰知運動少，胖死了。楚王想用大夫之禮來葬牠。楚王的音樂師叫優孟的，勸王不如用國君之禮來葬牠。怎樣葬？動員士兵築座大陵墓，用玉造棺材，還要請鄰國的國君來參加喪禮。

    楚王知道優孟在開玩笑諷刺自己，於是請優孟另提建議。優孟說：「這樣吧！給馬身塗些香料，放進大鍋裏，擱到灶上去燒，最後葬牠在人的腸胃裏吧！」

    現在「馬」則變成了「牛」。

Gagāi Chèuih Gāi, Gagáu Chèuih Gáu
嫁雞隨雞，嫁狗隨狗

Gagāi Chèuih Gāi, Gagáu Chèuih Gáu

I.E. Follow the man you marry, no matter what he is
無論嫁了怎樣糟的丈夫，也甘願跟着他生活

e.g. Yìhgā dī néuihyán gadāk m̀hóu jauh lèihfàn, móuh yàhn joi góng gagāi
宜家 啲 女人 嫁得 唔好 就 離婚，冇 人 再 講 嫁雞
chèuih gāi, gagáu chèuih gáu ga la.
隨 雞 嫁狗 隨 狗 㗎喇。

(Nowadays, a woman will very easily divorce her husband. No woman will care about "gagāi chèuih gāi, gagáu chèuih gáu" any more.)
（今日的婦女對丈夫不滿意便鬧離婚，沒有人再信「嫁雞隨雞」的廢話了。）

Formerly, women had no social status. They were supposed to have three obediences and four virtues. The four virtues are fidelity, physical charm, propriety in speech and efficiency in needlework and housework. The three obediences are as follows: Before her marriage, a girl ought to obey her father and be a good daughter. During her marriage, she ought to obey her husband and be a good wife and if her husband died, she ought to follow her son. In a word, women always had to depend on men. They could not live on their own.

So you can see that Gagāi Chèuih Gāi, Gagáu Chèuih Gáu was generated from one of the three obediences*. Chèuih means to follow. Gāi (i.e. a cock) and Gáu (i.e. a dog) both refer to lousy men.

　　從前女子沒有地位，男人要求婦女做到「三從四德」。「四德」指婦人要貞潔、溫婉、懂應對和會做家務。「三從」指女子未嫁從父（順從父親的話做個乖女兒），既嫁從夫（順從丈夫的話做個好妻子），夫死從子（丈夫去世後，便聽從兒子的話）。總之，女人永遠依靠男人，沒有獨立的生活。

　　由「既嫁從夫」演變出「嫁雞隨雞，嫁狗隨狗」這俗語來。雞或狗，比喻很糟的男人。

* adapted from *A Dictionary of Cantonese Colloquialisms in English*.

Yātyàhn Dākdouh, Gài'hyún Gàai Sìng
一人得道，雞犬皆升

Yātyàhn Dākdouh, Gài'hyún Gàai Sìng

I.E. one's family or friends also receive benefit when one encounters good chance/ fortune
某人走了運，連帶他的家人朋友都得了好處

e.g. Kéuih lóuhdauh sìngjó jouh júng gìngléih, kéuih maih sìngjouh
佢 老豆 升咗 做 總 經理，佢 咪 升做

jyúyahm lō. Nīdī jauh giujouh "yātyàhn dākdouh, gài'hyún gàai sìng"
主任 囉,呢啲就 叫做 「一人 得道， 雞犬 皆 升」

ā máh.
吖 馬。

(Since his father has been promoted to the general manager, he is also promoted to the head of a division. This is how the saying goes, "yātyàhn dākdouh, gàihyún gàai sìng.")
（父親升爲總經理，他也升職主任，這就是「一人得道，雞犬皆升」了。）

Làuh Ngōn (died 122 B.C.), the Prince of Wàaih Nàahm during the early years of the Han dynasty, was very fond of practising Taoist cults in the hope that one day he would become immortal. One day, eight old men came to see him. The watchman said to them, "Our master won't receive you if you don't have the magic of immortality." When the eight old men heard this, they turned themselves into eight children. Làuh Ngōn then received them and talked with them very happily. He requested them to stay in his house.

The eight old men then taught Làuh Ngōn how to refine cinnabar. When the refinement was almost finished, someone spoke ill of him to the emperor. The emperor was going to question him. The eight old men said to Làuh Ngōn, "It's time to leave the mortal world." They brought him to the mountain and gave him the cinnabar to eat. After Làuh Ngōn swallowed the cinnabar, he slowly flew to the sky and became immortal. Having licked the remains of the cinnabar in the crucible, the hens and dogs of Làuh Ngōn's house also flew to the sky and crowed or barked in the clouds.

漢代初年，淮南王劉安（公元前？-122）喜好神仙之術。一天，有八個老人來求見，守門人說：「你們沒有不衰老的法術，我主人不會見你們。」老人聽了，立即變成八個小童。劉安接見他們，談得很高興，就留他們住下來。

　　八個老人教劉安煉丹藥的方法。丹藥差不多煉成的時候，有人在皇帝面前說劉安的壞話，皇帝準備要責問他。八老說：「是離開人世的時候了。」就帶劉安到山上，吃了丹藥，徐徐飛到天上去，做了神仙。劉安家裏的雞和狗，舐過爐裏丹藥的渣滓，也飛到天上，在雲裏吠叫。

Sihk Mòuhchìhnggāi 食無情雞；
Cháau Yàuhyú 炒魷魚

Sihk Mòuhchìhnggāi

VO   an alternative way of saying "to be fired" (lit. eat feelingless chicken)
     是「解僱」的代詞

Cháau Yàuhyú

VO   to fire, to dismiss (lit. cuttlefish sauté)
     解僱

e.g. Kéuih sìhsìh jouhcho yéh, yauh sìhsìh chìhdou,
     佢　時時　做錯　嘢，又　時時　遲到，

   sóyíh lóuhsai cháau kéuih yàuhyú/béi lóuhsai cháau yàuhyú.
   所以 老細　炒　佢　魷魚／俾　老細　炒　　魷魚。

   (He always made mistakes in his work and came to office late. So, our boss fired him/he was sacked by our boss.)
   (他在工作上常常犯錯誤，又常常遲上班，所以老闆解僱了他／他被老闆解僱了。)

During the 1950s–1960s, several hundred thousand refugees fled to Hong Kong from Mainland China. It was hard to find a job at that time. A shopkeeper would provide food and lodging for his employees. It was a custom that every year on the second day of the Chinese New Year, a shopkeeper would invite his employees to have a Hòi Nìhn (lit. the beginning of the year) meal. If an employee was given a chicken's head by his boss, then he would understand that he was to be fired. He had to remove all his things from the store. Usually, he would roll up his own bed sheet and mat and then tie them up before he left. The rolled bed sheet or mat looked like a curled up cuttlefish which had just been fried. (People would carve crisscross patterns on one side of the cuttlefish before they fry it. When fried, the carvings on the curled up side resemble the weaving patterns of a mat.)

Nowadays in Hong Kong, there is no such thing as Sihk Mòuhchìhnggāi or Cháau Yàuhyú any more, but the boss still can fire his employees. If an employee quits his job because he cannot get along well with his boss, he can proudly say, "Ngóh cháau lóuhbáan yàuhyú."

1950至60年代，有數十萬難民由中國大陸湧來香港。當時找工作很不易，那些在商店裏打工的人，吃和住都由店東供給。每年農曆正月初二，店東有例請員工吃「開年飯」，如果店東用箸夾一件雞頭給某職員，他就知道自己被解僱。被解僱的店員總要收拾私人物品離去，最常見的就是把自用的簾和被捲起來，綑好帶走。那捲曲的簾好像剛炒熟的魷魚。

　　今日香港已經沒有真正「食無情雞」和「炒魷魚」的事了，當然東主解僱職員還是有的。相反，要是僱員跟僱主關係不愉快，決定辭職不幹了，他大可以說：「我炒老闆魷魚。」

Chèuigūk 催谷；Tìhnngáap 塡鴨

Chèuigūk

FV   to quickly strengthen a man's or an animal's capacity to work or to race
在短時間內令人（或動物）的工作或競賽能力冒升

Tìhnngáap

N   Peking duck [M: jek]; students who are compelled to study a lot
北京烤鴨；被迫讀很多書的學生

e.g.   Sìnsàang jèung dī hohksāang dongjouh tìhnngáap, gālíu chèuigūk,
先生　將　啲　學生　　當做　　塡鴨，　加料　催谷，

hèimohng kéuihdeih háaudóu hóu sìhngjīk.
希望　　佢哋　　考到　好　成績。

(The teacher treats his students like Peking ducks. He pressures them to study a lot more than they need to, hoping that they will do well in the examination.)
（老師把學生看做塡鴨，大力催逼，希望他們考取好成績。）

In *The Book of Songs*, there is a song about mandarin ducks. It says in times of peace, the king's horses in the stable are fed with grass, but in times of war, in order to ready the horses for the battle, they are given Gūk (grain) to stimulate (Chèui) their energy in a short time.

    As for Tìhnngáap, people put the ducks in a small cage so that they cannot move around. They also feed the ducks by putting the food through a small tube put inside the mouths of the ducks. They give the ducks as much food as they can until the ducks can no longer eat. So the ducks grow big and fat. The famous Chinese dish Peking duck is one of these kinds of ducks roasted, and the kind of education that tortures the students in Hong Kong is criticized as "education of Tìhnngaap style" (spoon-fed education).

《詩經・鴛鴦》說：「乘馬在廄，摧之秣之。」摧是草，秣是穀。詩句意思是：國君的馬在馬廄裏，平日無事便餵牠吃草，遇有事要用牠時便餵牠吃穀。

　　催谷，就是餵馬吃穀（谷），催促牠在短時間內體能冒升。

　　至於「塡鴨」，是養鴨的時候，把鴨囚在小籠子裏，令牠不能自由活動，又用小管塞進鴨口，把飼料通過小管強餵給鴨吃，餵得牠很飽很飽，於是養出很肥大的鴨來。著名的中國菜「北京烤鴨」，烤的就是塡鴨。而香港的教育方式也被譏爲「塡鴨式」教育。

Yàhnsàm Bātjūk Sèh Tàn Jeuhng
人心不足蛇吞象/
Yàhnsàm Móuh Yimjūk 人心冇厭足

Yàhnsàm Bātjūk Sèh Tàn Jeuhng/Yàhnsàm Móuh Yimjūk

I.E. very greedy, not contented
貪得無厭

e.g. Kàhmyaht sìnji máaihjó ga chè béi kéuih, gàmyaht kéuih yauh wah yiu
禽日 先至 買咗 架 車 俾 佢， 今日 佢 又 話 要
yātchàhng láu, jànhaih yàhnsàm bātjūk sèh tàn jeuhng.
一層 樓，眞係 人心 不足 蛇 吞 象。
(I just bought him a car yesterday, and he asks for a flat today. He's never contented.)
（昨天才給他買了汽車，今天他又要求買樓，眞貪心。）

Once there was a child named A-Jeuhng (lit. elephant). One day he picked up an egg and took it home. After a few days, a small snake emerged from the egg. A-Jeuhng kept it a secret. Sometimes he played with it. They enjoyed themselves very much. One year later, the snake had grown very big. It was becoming a dragon. It could no longer live with A-Jeuhng in such a small house. Before it left, it said to A-Jeuhng, "You've been so nice to me. I will surely repay your kindness someday. If you want to see me, you can go to the east seashore to look for me."

Unfortunately, A-Jeuhng's mother fell sick. The doctor said that she needed dragon's meat to cure her. Therefore he went to look for the snake which had now grown into a dragon. It let A-Jeuhng cut a piece of meat from it.

After that, A-Jeuhng came to ask "The snake" for help again and again. He cut its tongue and its eyes. Finally A-Jeuhng wanted some of its liver to heal the sickness of the king. "The snake" said, "O.K." It opened its mouth wide so that A-Jeuhng could go inside its stomach. But A-Jeuhng was too greedy. He cut too much of the snake's liver. The snake was in so much pain that it could not help but close its mouth, and A-Jeuhng was smothered to death.

有個叫阿象的小孩，一天拾到個蛋，帶回家裏玩。幾天後，那蛋孵出條小蛇來，阿象就偷偷養着牠，又跟牠玩耍，兩個的感情很好。一年後，那蛇長得很大，要變做龍，不能再住在阿象的小屋子了。臨別時，蛇對象說：「你對我有恩，將來我一定盡力報答你。你想見我，只要去東邊的海邊找我就行了。」不幸地，阿象的母親病了，醫生說要吃龍的肉才會痊愈，於是阿象走去找着「蛇」——牠已經變做龍——「蛇」讓阿象割走身上的一塊肉。這之後，阿象一次又一次地要求，割了「蛇」的舌頭和眼睛。到最後，阿象要求割「蛇」的肝給皇帝治病，「蛇」說：「好吧。」就張開大口，讓阿象鑽進肚裏去割。可是阿象太貪心了，他割肝時割得太多，「蛇」痛得忍不住合上了口，阿象就給窒息死了。

Hàahmyú Fàansàang 鹹魚翻生

Hàahmyú Fàansàang

I.E.   good luck falls on a man in bad luck (lit. a salted fish comes to life again)
一個倒霉的人運氣突然轉好

e.g.   Ngóh jungjó luhkhahpchói! Gàmchi hàahmyú fàansàang lo.
我　中咗　六合彩，今次　鹹魚　翻生　咯。

(I have won the Mark Six! Fortune comes to me after I have suffered from poverty for a long time.)
（我買中了彩票，這次走運哩。）

Hàahmyú is a dead fish preserved in salt. It is therefore also used to mean "corpse". It is recorded in *The Historical Records* that the First Emperor of Chin died in 210 B.C. when he was on his way to the east to conduct an inspection. Léih Sī, the prime minister, conspired with Jiuh Gòu, the eunuch, to hide the truth. They didn't announce the death of the emperor, and put the body inside a carriage with a cover. It just happened that the weather was very hot then. The corpse began to smell. Léih Sī told someone to buy a cart of salted fish and let it go after the cart of the emperor so that the smell of the salted fish would cover that of the dead body. Later, Léih Sī made a false imperial decree to put the second son of the emperor on the throne.

「鹹魚」，用鹽醃的魚；廣東話裏也指「死屍」。

《史記》記載：秦始皇往東方巡遊，死在道路上。丞相李斯和宦官趙高合謀，隱瞞了始皇的死訊，而把他的屍體收藏在有蓋的車子內。那時天氣暑熱，屍首發臭，李斯便叫人買了一車子鹹魚，跟在始皇的車的後面，用來掩飾那股臭味。後來李斯矯詔立了秦二世皇帝。

Daaihtàuhhā 大頭蝦；Sātwàhnyú 失魂魚

Daaihtàuhhā

N/SV　an absent-minded person; absent-minded [M: go, jek]
　　　善忘的人；善忘

Sātwàhnyú

N　　an absent-minded person [M: go, tìuh]
　　　比喻善忘的人

e.g.　Kéuih jingyāt daaihtàuhhā/sātwàhnyú, sèhngyaht m̀geidāk nīyeuhng,
　　　佢　正一　　大頭蝦/　失魂魚，　成日　唔記得　呢樣，
　　　m̀geidāk góyeuhng.
　　　唔記得　嗰樣。
　　　(He is really very absent-minded. He always forgets this or that.)
　　　（他真健忘，一天到晚，不是忘了這，就是忘了那。）

Daaihtàuhhā (lit. a big headed shrimp) looks very imposing with its big head and long antennas, but its body is quite small. If we make soup with it, we have to take away the head leaving very little flesh. Formerly, we used Daaihtàuhhā to describe those who looked dignified but have no inner talent. Now it refers to absent-minded people who have a head but no brain.

Sātwàhnyú is a scared fish. It is said that if a fish is scared or jolted when being transported from one place to another, it becomes not good to eat. Now the phrase depicts a person who does not concentrate and always makes mistakes.

　　　大頭蝦，是一種長鬚大頭而蝦身很小的蝦，樣子很威武。但是拿這種蝦來煮湯，去掉了蝦頭，餘下的蝦肉就很少。於是就以「大頭蝦」比喻外表威猛，但沒有內涵的人。現在一般指善忘的人，等於說「頭大無腦」。

　　　失魂魚，指受了驚慌的魚。據說魚受了驚慌（例如在運輸時過分顛簸），牠就變得不好吃。現時用「失魂魚」指那些精神不集中，常常做錯事的人。

Yātháaih Bātyùh Yātháaih 一蟹不如一蟹

Yātháaih Bātyùh Yātháaih

I.E. getting worse and worse
每況愈下

e.g. Yìhgā dī hohksāang yuht làih yuht láahn, jànhaih yātháaih bātyùh
宜家 啲 學生 越 嚟 越 懶, 眞係 一蟹 不如
yātháaih lo.
一蟹 咯。

(Nowadays, the students are becoming lazier and lazier. They are doing much worse.)
（現時學生懶散，情況日差。）

In the Sung dynasty, there was a man called Tòuh Gūk. He was ordered by the government to go to work in the southern part of China. Some people knew that he liked to eat crabs (i.e. Háaih). They got over ten different kinds of crabs for him to eat. The host wanted to play a joke on him. He offered him the largest one first, and then a smaller one, and then an even smaller one.... At last, he offered him one which was as small as a finger nail. Tòuh Gūk smiled and said, "Each crab is not as good as the one before."

　　宋代有個叫陶穀的人，奉命到中國的南方辦公事，有人知道他喜歡吃蟹，便搜羅了十幾種蟹請他品嚐。主人大概想開個玩笑，最先吃的蟹很大，接着的小一點，接着的又小一點……到最後吃到小如手指甲的蟛蜞。陶穀笑着說：「眞是一蟹不如一蟹。」

Gwa Yèuhngtàuh Maaih Gáuyuhk
掛羊頭賣狗肉

Gwa Yèuhngtàuh Maaih Gáuyuhk

I.E. pretend to do legal things superficially but do the opposite secretly
以正當事做掩飾，而暗中幹非法勾當

e.g. Kéuih hòi mauhyihk gùngsi, kèihsaht haih gwa yèuhngtàuh maaih
佢　開　貿易　公司，其實　係　掛　羊頭　賣
gáuyuhk, hòi dóudong.
狗肉，開　賭檔。

(He has a trading firm, but actually he runs gambling business inside.)
(開貿易公司是個幌子，實在經營賭博，幹非法的事。)

During the time of the Spring and Autumn Annals in the state of Chàih, many women liked to put on men's wear when they went out. Duke Gíng wanted to prohibit them from doing so. He first asked his prime minister Ngaanjí for advice. Ngaanjí said, "Your Majesty told the court ladies to wear men's clothing, but you don't allow other women to imitate them. It's just like a man who hangs up an ox head outside of his shop but sells horsemeat inside. If you stop the women from putting on men's wear in the court, then naturally there will not be any woman doing the same." Duke Gíng acted according to what Ngaanjí said. As expected, no woman outside wore men's clothes.

Later, the ox head was replaced by a sheep's head (i.e. Yèuhngtàuh) and horsemeat by dogmeat (i.e. Gáuyuhk). (It's illegal to sell dogmeat in Hong Kong.)

　　春秋時代，齊國有很多女子喜歡穿上男裝走在街上，齊景公想下令禁止，便先問一問宰相晏子。晏子答道：「你叫宮女在王宮裏穿上男裝，但又想禁止其他婦女仿效，這就好像掛起牛頭做招徠，實際賣的卻是馬肉。如果你禁止宮女穿男裝，街上自然沒有男裝打扮的女子了。」景公依晏子的話去辦，果然收到預期的效果。

　　故事裏的「掛牛頭賣馬肉」，後來變了「掛羊頭賣狗肉」（在香港，賣狗肉是犯法的）。

Màhnjéuk 文雀/Sàamjeksáu 三隻手

Màhnjéuk/Sàamjeksáu

N   pickpocket [M: go, tìuh]
     扒手

e.g. Yàhn dò ge deihfòng, síusàm yáuh sàamjeksáu/màhnjéuk.
     人　多嘅　地方，小心　有　三隻手/　文雀。
     (Be aware of pickpockets in crowded places.)
     （擠迫的場合，小心有扒手。）

小手 should be written as 小弄, and also read as "síusáu". Some cunning pickpockets will carry a false hand with them and let it be seen. Then people will not be aware that their third hand is stealing. How pictographic the character is!

   Màhnjéuk is a gentle term for pickpocket. Formerly, the triad gangs were divided into four main groups: 風 (fùng) referred to those who cheated money; 火 (fó), to those who made counterfeit money; 雀 (jéuk), to those who solicited alms and 要 (yiu), to those who blackmailed. Màhnjéuk (lit. a refined bird) refer to birds which would not use violence. They would just peck tiny pieces of grain stealthily.

   「小手」應寫作「小弄」（弄音手）。有些狡猾的扒手在身上裝上一隻假手，故意露在外面，令你不留意他的第三隻手的摸竊活動。「弄」字很形象化呢！

   「文雀」是對扒手的文雅的稱呼。舊日江湖中人分為四類：「風」指行騙錢財的；「火」指假造錢幣的；「雀」指化緣募捐的；「要」指借端要挾的。「文雀」意思是斯文的雀，不會動粗強搶，只會像雀仔(小鳥)一樣，偷偷啄一點穀米。

Tiufūi 跳灰；Tòhdéi 陀地

Tiufūi

FV   to sell heroin
販賣海洛英

Tòhdéi

N   the triad gangs who occupy a certain site [M: go, tìuh]
指佔據某地盤的黑幫分子

e.g.   Góbàan laahn'gwái yauh tiufūi yauh sàu tòhdéifai.
嗰班　爛　鬼　又　跳灰　又　收　陀地費。

(Those rotten guys sell heroin and blackmail people for protection fee.)
（那幫流氓既販毒，又勒索「保護費」。）

Very few people can understand the rarely used characters or the characters only used in ancient times. Instead, we borrow a frequently used homophone to replace it. For example, 粜 (tiu, to sell rice), people will simply use 跳 (tiu, to jump) for it. Fūi, ash, is now used to stand for heroin.

Tòh is the ancient pronoun for "he" or "she". Deih is a suffix indicating plural. So Tòhdéi means the same as "kéuihdeih" (i.e. they, them). When a triad gang member is going to blackmail you, he will always start with, "I got some fellows. They are badly in need of money for a meal..." Those triad gangs who occupy a certain site are thus called Tòhdéi.

　　有些古字或僻字，現在很少人懂，我們往往用一個常見的同音字來代替它。例如「粜」（也寫作「糶」，音跳，意思是「賣米」）。我們乾脆就以「跳」代替。所以「跳灰」其實是「粜灰」。「灰」指「白粉」，即海洛英。

　　「陀」是「佗」的誤寫，即「他」的古字。「地」是表示眾數的詞。所以「陀地」即「他等/他們」。黑社會分子要勒索「保護費」時總是說：「我有班兄弟，他們急於要錢開飯……。」而那些佔據地盤的黑幫也被稱為「陀地」。

Gam Jegū 揼鷓鴣；
Jūk Wòhnggeuk Gāi 捉黃腳雞

Gam Jegū

VO to blackmail someone because he is so careless
乘人一時疏忽來進行敲詐

Jūk Wòhnggeuk Gāi

VO to blackmail someone by using a woman to seduce him
利用女色引誘，然後捉姦而勒索

e.g. Kéuih béi yàhn jūk wòhnggeuk gāi/gam jegū,
佢 俾 人 捉 黃腳 雞/揼鷓鴣，

mìginjó géisahp maahn.
唔見咗 幾十 萬。

(He was blackmailed because he was careless enough to be caught when committing adultery. He lost several hundred thousand dollars for this.)
（他被人捉姦勒索，損失幾十萬元。）

Jegū, partridge, is a kind of wild bird about the size of a pigeon. It is also a kind of tonic food. Triads like to call those who do not belong to any secret societies Jegū. Gam Jegū means to set a trap to make the Jegū come. Then they catch him and snatch his money. Also, Jegū is pronounced very close to "jegu": to look for a chance; intentionally.

Jūk Wòhnggeuk Gāi is almost the same as Gam Jegū. People use a hen to seduce a cock which has a pair of Wòhnggeuk (i.e. yellow feet). Then they can catch it once it comes close to the hen.

鷓鴣是一種野鳥，像鴿子大小，吃了可以補身。幫會中人把外人稱作「鷓鴣」。「揼鷓鴣」就是設計陷阱，引誘「鷓鴣」來，乘機捉住他，搶他的錢。「鷓鴣」亦是「借故」的諧音。

「捉黃腳雞」與「揼鷓鴣」差不多。用母雞引誘公雞（即黃腳雞）走來，乘機捉住牠。

Years of the Dynasties in Chinese History

Shang 商	1766–1122 B.C.
Chou 周	1122–770 B.C.
Spring and Autumn Annals 春秋	770–476 B.C.
Warring States 戰國	475–221 B.C.
Chin 秦	221–202 B.C.
Han 漢	
Western Han 西漢	202 B.C.–A.D. 25
Eastern Han 東漢	25–220
Three Kingdoms 三國	220–265
Tsin 晉	265–420
South and North Dynasties 南北朝	420–589
Sui 隋	581–618
Tang 唐	618–906
Sung 宋	960–1279
Yuan 元	1279–1368
Ming 明	1368–1644
Ching 清	1644–1911

References

A Bibliography of Yue Dialect Studies. Hong Kong: Linguistic Society of Hong Kong, 1993.
Ann, T. K. *Cracking the Chinese Puzzles*. Hong Kong: Stockflows Co., Ltd. 1987.
Balazs, Etienne and Hervouet, Yves. *A Sung Bibliography*. Hong Kong: The Chinese University Press, 1978.
Best Chinese Idioms. Hai Feng Publishing Co., 1991.
Bynner, Witter. *Three Hundred Poems of the Tang Dynasty 618-906*. Hong Kong: Chi Man Press.
Chao, Y. R. *A Grammar of Spoken Chinese*. Berkeley and Los Angeles: University of California Press, 1968.
Ch'en, Shou-yi. *Chinese Literature: A Historical Introduction*. New York: The Ronald Press Co.,1961.
Cheung, H. N. Samuel. "A Study of Xie-hou-yu Expressions in Cantonese." *Tsing Hua Journal of Chinese Studies*. 1982
Chin, Ann-ping and Freeman, Mansfield. *Tai Chen on Mencius*. Yale University Press, 1990.
Chinese Festivals. Hong Kong: The Chartered Bank, 1978.
Damen, Louise. *Culture Learning: The Fifth Dimension in the Language Classroom*. US: Addison-Wesley, 1987.
Defrancis, John. *Chinese Language: Fact and Fantasy*. University of Hawaii Press, 1984.
Eberhard Wolfram. *A Dictionary of Chinese Symbols*. London and New York: Routledge, 1983.
Egan, C. Ronald. *Word, Image and Deed in the Life of Su Shi*. The Council on East Asian Studies, Harvard University and the Harvard-Yenching Institute, 1994.
Greenberg, H. Joseph. *A New Invitation to Linguistics*. New York: Anchor Books, 1977.
Hudson, R. A. *Sociolinguistics*. Malta: Cambridge University Press 1993.
Kwan, Choi-wah. *The Right Word in Cantonese*. Hong Kong: Commercial Press, 1989.
Kwan, Kit-choi. *A Dictionary of Cantonese Colloquialisms in English*. Hong Kong: Commercial Press, 1990.
Lee, Wai-Mun. *Chinese Chess*. Hong Kong: C&W Publishing Co., 1985.
Matthews, Stephen and Yip, Virginia. *Cantonese: A Comprehensive Grammar*. London and New York: Routledge, 1994.
Nienhauser, William. *Indiana Companion to Traditional Chinese Literature*. Bloomington: Indiana University Press, 1986.

Rohsenow, S. John. *A Chinese-English Dictionary of Enigmatic Folk Similes*. US: University of Arizona Press, 1991.

Savidge, Joyce. *This is Hong Kong: Temples*. Hong Kong: Hong Kong Government Publication, 1977.

Shih, Yu-chung Vincent. *The Literary Mind and the Carving of Dragons*. Hong Kong: The Chinese University Press, 1983.

Taylor, C. H. Brewitt. *San Kuo (Romance of the Three Kingdoms)*. The Press of Kelly & Walsh Ltd., 1925.

Wei, Henry. *The Authentic I-Ching*. California: The Borgo Press, 1987.

Wong, S. L. *A Chinese Syllabary Pronounced According to the Dialect of Canton*. Chung Hua Book Co., Ltd. 1957.

《中國戲曲曲藝詞典》。上海辭書出版社，1985。
《嶺南掌故》。廣東旅遊出版社。1987。
孔仲南。《廣東俗語考》。上海文藝出版社，1992。
王建輝、易學金編。《中國文化知識精華》。湖北人民出版社，1989。
丘學強。《妙語方言》。中華書局，1989。
石人。《廣東話趣譚》。博益出版社，1983。
任學良，《漢語造詞法》，中國社會科學出版社。北京，1981。
朱琳。《洪門志》。河北人民出版社，1990。
俞敏，《反語》，中國大百科全書之語言文字，中國大百科全書出版社，北京‧上海，1988。
耿守忠。《萬事萬物溯源辭典》。吉林人民出版社，1991。
高莫野編。《中國成語大辭典》。香港上海印書館，1982。
高華年著。《廣州方言研究》。商務印書館（香港）1980。
張日昇，《香港廣州話英語音譯借詞的聲調規律》，中國語文，第一期（1986）。
郭錫良。《漢字古音手冊》。北京大學出版社，1986。
黃錫凌。《粵音韻彙》。中華書局，1957。
楊蔭深。《中國文學家列傳》。香港光華書店出版，1962。
葉蜚聲、徐通鏘著。《語言學綱要》。北京大學出版社，1990。
劉涌泉、趙世開編。《英漢語言學詞匯》。中國社會科學出版社，1979。
廣州博物館編。《廣州文物與古迹》。文物出版社，1987。
戴冰。《詞語典故菁萃》。廣東高等教育出版社，1990。
關傑才。《英譯廣東口語詞典》。商務印書館，1990。
關漢、韋軒。《廣東民間故事選》。花城出版社，1982。

Index of Expressions by Pronunciation

A-Chà 阿差 18
A-Fūk 阿福 16
Āauwū 丫烏 171
Baahk Beihgō 白鼻哥 134
Baatgwa 八卦 42
Baatpòh 八婆 4
Báauséi 飽死 158
Báauséi Hòhlāan Dáu 飽死荷蘭豆 158
Baingai 蔽翳 179
Bīuchēng 標青 123
Bòlòhgāi→Kaau Chì 波羅雞→靠黐 99
Bunyeh Chèuhn (Chàh) 半夜巡（茶） 80
Chaathàaih 擦鞋 172
Cháau Yàuhyú 炒魷魚 203
Chè Daaihpaau 車大炮 71
Chéngchēung 請槍 164
Chésin 扯線 183
Chètīn Chèdeih 車天車地 71
Chèuigūk 催谷 205
Chēutmāau 出貓 197
Chídeih Mòuh Ngàhn Sàambaak Léung 此地無銀三百兩 189
Chìhnsai M̀sàu 前世唔修 186
Chìhnsai 前世 186

Chìhntòuh Chíh Gám 前途似噉（錦）	90
Chóh Láahngbáandang 坐冷板櫈	177
Chyun 串/寸	70
Daahngālóu Dájiu→Móuh Tàahn 蛋家佬打醮→冇壇（彈）	92
Daaihgū 大姑	2
Daaihlóu 大佬	6
Daaihmòuh Sīyeuhng 大模尸樣	110
Daaihtàuhhā 大頭蝦	210
Daaihyíhlūng 大耳窿	18
Dái (PN) Séi 抵（某人）死	152
Dáiséi 抵死	152
Dálaahn Sàpùhn Mahndou Dūk 打爛砂盤問（璺）到篤	91
Dàudūk Jèunggwān 兜篤將軍	130
Dauhdēng 豆丁	8
Deihséui 地水	48
Dínggwāgwā 頂呱呱	54
Diugá 丟架	170
Dohkkíu 度喬	138
Dùnggwā Dauhfuh 冬瓜豆腐	50
Fáandáu 反斗	22
Fèihlóu 肥佬	56
Fèimchēut Ngóh Sáujíla 飛唔出我手指罅	185
Fógei 伙記	10
Fósìu Kèihgōn→Chèuhng Taan 火燒旗桿→長炭（嘆）	92

Index of Expressions by Pronunciation

Fótáu 伙頭	10
Fuhngjí Sìhngfàn 奉子(旨)成婚	91
Fūktàuh 福頭	16
Gagāi Chèuih Gāi, Gagáu Chèuih Gáu 嫁雞隨雞，嫁狗隨狗	200
Gam Jegū 撳鷓鴣	215
Gàmtùhng Yuhk (Néuih) 金童玉(女)	80
Gànhùhng Díngbaahk 跟紅頂白	133
Gātngūk 吉屋	52
Gáulàuh 九流	117
Gèngchēng 驚青	123
Gīgī Gahtgaht 嘰嘰吃吃	157
Giuh Chèuhnggeuk 撬牆腳	129
Gòudau 高竇	34
Gùhòhn 孤寒	28
Gùnjih Léuhnggo Háu 官字兩個口	66
Gwāchàaih 瓜柴	49
Gwādauh 瓜豆	49
Gwā Lóuhchan 瓜老襯	49
Gwa Yèuhngtàuh Maaih Gáuyuhk 掛羊頭賣狗肉	212
Gwojó Hói Jauh Haih Sàhnsin 過咗海就係神仙	187
Hàahmsāp 鹹濕	36
Hàahmyú Fàansàang 鹹魚翻生	209
Haapchou 呷醋	132
Hàau Jūkgong 敲竹槓	96
Hahmbahlaahng 冚唪唥	58

Hahpsaai Hòhchē 合晒合尺	136
Háu Gahtgaht 口吃吃	157
Jaahpbālāng (Jaahpbālāang) 雜崩能	58
Jáamlaahm 斬纜	95
Jadai 詐帝	156
Jaidākgwo 濟得過	46
Jaìmgwo 濟唔過	46
Jai M̀jai 濟唔濟	46
Jāplāp 執笠	111
Jáugāi 走雞(機)	91
Jáu Hauhmún 走後門	173
Jengdáu 正斗	159
Jeukhéi Lùhngpòuh Dōu M̀chíh Taaijí 著起龍袍都唔似太子	104
Jèung (PN) Gwàn 將(某人)軍	131
Jí Héui Jàugùn Fongfó, Bātjéun Baaksing Dímdāng 只許州官放火，不准百姓點燈	116
Jìsih 滋事	42
Jìsih Baatgwa 滋事八卦	42
Jìyàuh 滋油	20
Jítìn Dūkdeih 指天篤地	154
Jiujik 招嘖	27
Johngbáan 撞板	136
Jouh Chēungsáu 做槍手	164
Jouhdou Jek Kehk Gám 做到隻屐噉	144
Jouhdūng 做東	112

Index of Expressions by Pronunciation

Jouh Galéung 做架樑	129
Jūk Wòhnggeuk Gāi 捉黃腳雞	215
Jyūleih 豬脷	52
Jyūyihsíng 朱義盛	95
Kàhmchēng (Kàhmkàhmchēng) (Kàhmkámchēng) 噚青	123
Kèh Làuhwòhngmáh 騎劉皇馬	166
Laaimāau 賴貓	194
Lāausūnglóu 咾鬆佬	59
Lahkdau 笏竇	34
Lātsōu 甩鬚	170
Lāttō 甩拖	95
Lèihpóu 離譜	136
Lìhngse 零舍	150
Lìhngse M̀tùhng 零舍唔同	150
Lódáu 攞豆	51
Lohkbāt Dá Sàamgāang 落筆打三更	120
Lohksáu Dá Sàamgāang 落手打三更	120
Louhchēut Máhgeuk 露出馬腳	175
Lóuhfú Tàuhseuhng Dèng Sātná 老虎頭上釘虱乸	181
Lóuhgéui 老舉	60
Lóuhsyú Làaigwāi→Móuhdehng Màaihsáu 老鼠拉龜→冇定埋手	82
Lóuhyìhbāt 老而不	80
Maaih Jyūjái 賣豬仔	100
Maaihyùhlóu Sáisàn→Móuhsaai Sènghei 賣魚佬洗身→冇晒腥(聲)氣	92

Màauhgānjūk 茅根竹 ... 77

Māfù 馬虎 ... 38

Màhlātlóu 麻甩佬 ... 12

Mahnbūi 問杯 ... 128

Màhngsāk 萌塞 ... 26

Màhnjéuk 文雀 ... 213

M̀jìcháu 唔知醜 ... 146

Mōkgwòng Jyū / Mōk Gwòngjyū 剝光豬 ... 195

Mōlōchà (Mōlōchàai) 摩囉差 ... 18

M̀sàam M̀sei 唔三唔四 ... 44

M̀sái Mahn A-Gwai 唔使問阿貴 ... 140

Nàih Pòuhsaat Gwogōng→Jihsàn Nàahnbóu
泥菩薩過江→自身難保 ... 86

Néih Jouh Chòyāt, Ngóh Jouh Sahpńgh
你做初一，我做十五 ... 120

Ngaahnggéng 硬頸 ... 32

Ngàaihdou Gàmjìng Fó'ngáahn 捱到金睛火眼 ... 185

Ngāauwū 丫烏 ... 171

Ngàhyīn 牙煙 ... 106

Ngàuhgéng 牛頸 ... 32

Ngàuh Séi Sung Ngàuh Sōng 牛死送牛喪 ... 201

Ngàuhyāt 牛一 ... 64

Ńghhàhng Him Dá 五行欠打 ... 39

Ngoihgōnglóu 外江佬 ... 59

Paaktō 拍拖 ... 95

Pèitàuh Sáan (Faat) 披頭散（髮） ... 80

Index of Expressions by Pronunciation

Pòuhtàuh 浦頭	62
Sàamchèuhng Léuhngdyún 三長兩短	50
Sàamgū Luhkpòh 三姑六婆	4
Sàamjeksáu 三隻手	213
Sàanyàhn Jih Yáuh Miuhgai 山人自有妙計	68
Sahpnìhn (Dōu) M̀fùhng Yātyeuhn 十年(都)唔逢一閏	119
Sailóu 細佬	6
Sailouh 細路	6
Sàinàahm Yih Baakfú 西南二伯父	99
Sàjí 沙紙	56
Sàmpóuh 心抱	62
Sātwàhnyú 失魂魚	213
Sauchói Sáugān→Bàau Syù 秀才手巾→包書(輸)	93
Sá Fàchēung 耍花槍	135
Sáuméih 手尾	75
Séingàuh Yātbihn Géng 死牛一便頸	32
Séuigwái Sìng Sìhng'wòhng 水鬼升城隍	191
Séuipèih 水皮	64
Séui Wàih Chòih 水爲財	127
Sìfó 私伙	10
Sihdaahn 是但	80
Sih Gāp Máh Hàahng Tìhn 事(士)急馬行田	90
Sihk Chāt Gam Sihk 食七咁食	108
Sihk Gáu Daaih Gwái 食九大簋	104
Sihk Mòuhchìhnggāi 食無情雞	203
Sihk Séimāau 食死貓	196

Sihyàuh Lòufaahn→Jíngsīk (Jíng) Séui
豉油撈飯→整色(整)水 87
Sīk Jih Tàuhseuhng Yātbá Dōu 色字頭上一把刀 66
Sīk Yìnghùhng Juhng Yìnghùhng 識英雄重英雄 162
Singgwā 勝瓜 52
Sòujàusí 蘇州屎 75
Sūkgwāt 縮骨 24
Syùngēungkíuh 酸薑蕎 78
Taaiseui Tàuhseuhng Duhng Tóu 太歲頭上動土 181
Taaitáai 太太 2
Tìhnngáap 塡鴨 207
Tipcho Mùhnsàhn 貼錯門神 114
Tiufūi 跳灰 214
Tòhdéi 陀地 214
Tok Daaihgeuk 托大腳 172
Tòuh Gújéng 淘古井 74
Wahtdaht 核突 178
Wàih Lóuh Bātjyùn, Gaauwaaih Jísyùn
為老不尊，教壞子孫 82
Waihsihkmāau 為食貓 196
Wán Jàugùng 搵周公 22
Wán Kaausàan 搵靠山 126
Wòhng Daaih Sīn→Yáuh Kàuh Bīt Ying 黃大仙→有求必應 .. 89
Wòhng Máh'kwá 黃馬褂 134
Wòhsihlóuh 和事老 14
Wùhlèihjīng 狐狸精 1

Index of Expressions by Pronunciation

Wūlēi Dàandōu 烏利單刀 102

Wùlúng 烏龍 21

Yàhnsàm Bātjūk Sèh Tàn Jeuhng 人心不足蛇吞象 209

Yàhnsàm Móuh Yimjūk 人心有厭足 209

Yahpmàaih (PN) Sou 入埋（某人）數 142

Yàuhpéhng Jái / Néui 油瓶仔/女 17

Yāt Bātjouh, Yih Bātyāu 一不做，二不休 148

Yātgo Yuhn Dá, Yātgo Yuhn Ngàaih 一個願打，一個願捱 . . 168

Yātháaih Bātyùh Yātháaih 一蟹不如一蟹 211

Yātlàuh 一流 118

Yātmaht Jih Yātmaht, Nohmáih Jih Muhksāt
    一物治一物，糯米治木虱 40

Yātméi Kaau Jí 一味靠指 154

Yāttàuh Mouhséui 一頭霧水 72

Yātyàhn Dākdouh, Gài'hyún Gàai Sìng
    一人得道，雞犬皆升 203

Yáuh Fànchyun 有分寸 143

Yáuh Fànsou 有分數 143

Yáuh Mòuh Yáuh Yihk 有毛有翼 76

Yàyàwū (Yàhyàhwū) 吔吔烏 54

Yìhhèi 兒戲（兒嬉） 30

Yihsaijóu 二世祖 13

Yìngtòuh Síu (Háu) 櫻桃小（口） 80

Index of Expressions in Chinese

一畫

一人得道，雞犬皆升 Yātyàhn dākdouh, Gài'hyún Gàai Sìng . . 202

一不做，二不休 Yāt Bātjouh, Yih Bātyàu 148

一味靠指 Yātméi Kaau Jí 154

一物治一物，糯米治木虱 Yātmaht Jih Yātmaht,
　　Nohmáih Jih Muhksāt 40

一流 Yātlàuh 117

一個願打，一個願捱 yātgo Yuhn Dá, Yātgo Yuhn Ngàaih . . 168

一頭霧水 Yāttàuh Mouhséui 72

一蟹不如一蟹 Yātháaih Bātyúh Yātháaih 211

二畫

九流 Gáulàuh 117

二世祖 Yihsaijóu 13

人心不足蛇吞象 Yàhnsàm Bātjūk Sèh Tàn Jeuhng 207

人心冇厭足 Yàhnsàm Móuh Yimjūk 207

入埋（某人）數 Yahpmàaih (PN) Sou 142

八卦 Baatgwa 42

八婆 Baatpòh 4

十年（都）唔逢一閏 Sahpnìhn (Dōu) M̀fùhng Yātyeuhn 118

三畫

三姑六婆　Sàamgū Luhkpòh 4
三長兩短　Sàamchèuhng Léuhngdyún 50
三隻手　Sàamjeksáu 213
丫烏　Āauwū/Ngāauwū 171
口吃吃　Háu Gahtgaht 157
大耳窿　Daaihyíhlūng 18
大佬　Daaihlóu 6
大姑　Daaihgū 2
大模尸樣　Daaihmòuh Sīyeuhng 110
大頭蝦　Daaihtàuhhā 210
山人自有妙計　Sàanyàhn Jih Yáuh Miuhgai 68

四畫

五行欠打　Ńghhàhng Him Dá 39
反斗　Fáandáu 22
太太　Taaitáai 2
太歲頭上動土　Taaiseui Tàuhseuhng Duhng Tóu 181
心抱　Sàmpóuh 62
手尾　Sáuméih 75
文雀　Màhnjéuk 213
水皮　Séuipèih 64
水爲財　Séui Wàih Chòih 126
水鬼升城隍　Séuigwái Sìng Sìhng'wòhng 191
火燒旗桿→長炭（嘆）　Fósiu Kèihgōn→
　　Chèuhng Taan 94

Index of Expressions in Chinese

牙煙 Ngàhyīn 106
牛一 Ngàuhyāt 64
牛死送牛喪 Ngàuh Séi Sung Ngàuh Sōng 199
牛頸 Ngàuhgéng 32

五畫

冬瓜豆腐 Dùnggwā Dauhfuh 50
出貓 Chēutmāau 197
半夜巡（茶）Bunyeh Chèuhn (Chàh) 80
冚辦冷 Hahmbahlaahng 58
只許州官放火，不准百姓點燈 Jí Héui Jàugùn Fongfó,
　　Bātjéun Baaksing Dímdāng 115
外江佬 Ngoihgōnglóu 59
失魂魚 Sātwàhnyú 210
打爛砂盤問（璺）到篤 Dálaahn Sàpùhn Mahndou Dūk 91
正斗 Jengdáu 160
瓜老襯 Gwā Lóuhchan 49
瓜豆 Gwādauh 49
瓜柴 Gwāchàaih 49
甩拖 Lāttō 95
甩鬚 Lātsōu 170
白鼻哥 Baahk Beihgō 134

六畫

丟架 Diugá 170
伙記 Fógei 10

伙頭 Fótáu	10
吉屋 Gātngūk	52
合晒合尺 Hahpsaai Hòhchē	136
地水 Deihséui	48
托大腳 Tok Daaihgeuk	172
有分寸 Yáuh Fànchyun	143
有分數 Yáuh Fànsou	143
有毛有翼 Yáuh Mòuh Yáuh Yihk	76
朱義盛 Jyūyihsíng	95
此地無銀三百兩 Chídeih Mòuh Ngàhn Sàambaak Léung	189
吔吔烏 Yàyàwū(Yàhyàhwū)	54
死牛一便頸 Séingàuh Yātbihn Géng	32
老而不 Lóuhyìhbāt	82
老虎頭上釘虱乸 Lóuhfú Tàuhseuhng Dèng Sātná	181
老鼠拉龜→冇定埋手 Lóuhsyú Làaigwāi→ Móuhdehng Màaihsáu	84
老舉 Lóuhgéui	60
色字頭上一把刀 Sīk Jih Tàuhseuhng Yātbá Dōu	66
西南二伯父 Sàinàahm Yih Baakfú	99

七畫

串/寸 Chyun	70
你做初一，我做十五 Néih Jouh Chòyāt, Ngóh Jouh Sahpngh	121
坐冷板櫈 Chóh Láahngbáandang	177
扯線 Chésin	183

Index of Expressions in Chinese

沙紙 Sàjí	56
私伙 Sìfó	10
秀才手巾→包書(輸) Sauchói Sáugān→Bàau Syù	94
豆丁 Dauhdēng	8
走後門 Jáu Hauhmún	173
走雞(機) Jáugāi	91
車大炮 Chè Daaihpaau	71
車天車地 Chètīn Chèdeih	71

八畫

事(士)急馬行田 Sih Gāp Máh Hàahng Tìhn	91
兒戲(兒嬉) Yìhhèi	30
呷醋 Haapchou	132
和事老 Wòhsihlóuh	14
奉子(旨)成婚 Fuhngjí Sìhngfàn	91
孤寒 Gùhòhn	28
官字兩個口 Gùnjih Léuhnggo Háu	66
招嘖 Jìujik	27
披頭散(髮) Pèitàuh Sáan (Faat)	80
拍拖 Paaktō	96
抵(某人)死 Dái (PN) Séi	152
抵死 Dáiséi	152
泥菩薩過江→自身難保 Nàih Pòuhsaat Gwogōng→ Jihsàn Nàahnbóu	85
波羅雞→靠黐 Bòlòhgāi→Kaau Chì	99
油瓶仔/女 Yàuhpéhng Jái / Néui	17

炒魷魚　Cháau Yàuhyú 203

狐狸精　Wùhlèihjìng 1

肥佬　Fèihlóu 56

金童玉(女)　Gàmtùhng Yuhk (Néuih) 80

陀地　Tòhdéi 214

阿差　A-chà 18

阿福　A-fūk 16

九畫

前世　Chìhnsai 186

前世唔修　Chìhnsai M̀sàu 186

前途似嗽(錦)　Chìhntòuh Chíh Gám 91

度喬　Dohkkíu 138

指天篤地　Jítìn Dūkdeih 154

是但　Sihdaahn 80

咾鬆佬　Lāausūnglóu 59

耍花槍　Sá Fàchēung 135

茅根竹　Màauhgānjūk 78

飛唔出我手指罅　Fèimchēut Ngóh Sáujíla 185

食七咁食　Sihk Chāt Gam Sihk 108

食九大簋　Sihk Gáu Daaih Gwái 104

食死貓　Sihk Séimāau 194

食無情雞　Sihk Mòuhchìhnggāi 203

十畫

剝光豬　Mōkgwòng Jyū / Mōk Gwòngjyū 193

Index of Expressions in Chinese 237

唔三唔四 M̀sàam M̀sei 44
唔使問阿貴 M̀sái Mahn A-Gwai 140
唔知醜 M̀jìcháu 146
捉黃腳雞 Jūk Wòhnggeuk Gāi 215
核突 Wahtdaht 178
浦頭 Pòuhtàuh 62
烏利單刀 Wūlēi Dàandōu 102
烏龍 Wùlúng 21
馬虎 Māfù 38
高竇 Gòudau 34

十一畫

做到隻屐噉 Jouhdou Jek Kehk Gám 144
做東 Jouhdūng 112
做架樑 Jouh Galéung 128
做槍手 Jouh Chēungsáu 164
兜篤將軍 Dàudūk Jèunggwān 130
問杯 Mahnbūi 127
執笠 Jāplāp 111
將(某人)軍 Jèung PN Gwàn 130
捱到金睛火眼 Ngàaihdou Gàmjìng Fó'ngáahn ... 184
掛羊頭賣狗肉 Gwa Yèuhngtàuh Maaih Gáuyuhk ... 212
斬纜 Jáamlaahm 95
淘古井 Tòuh Gújéng 74
細佬 Sailóu 6
細路 Sailouh 6

蛋家佬打醮→冇壇（彈） Daahngālóu Dájiu→
　　Móuh Tàahn 92
豉油撈飯→整色（整）水 Sihyàuh Lòufaahn→
　　Jíngsīk (Jíng) Séui 86
頂呱呱 Dínggwāgwā 54
痳甩佬 Màhlātlóu 12

十二畫

勝瓜 Singgwā 52
滋事 Jìsih 42
滋事八卦 Jìsih Baatgwa 42
滋油 Jìyàuh 20
硬頸 Ngaahnggéng 32
著起龍袍都唔似太子 Jeukhéi Lùhngpòuh Dōu
　　M̀chíh Taaijí 104
萌塞 Màhngsāk 26
詐帝 Jadai 156
貼錯門神 Tipcho Mùhnsàhn 114
黃大仙→有求必應 Wòhng Daaih Sīn→
　　Yáuh Kàuh Bīt Ying 89
爲老不尊，教壞子孫 Wàih Lóuh Bātjyùn,
　　Gaauwaaih Jísyùn 82
爲食貓 Waihsihkmāau 194
黃馬褂 Wòhng Máh'kwá 134

十三畫

催谷 Chèuigūk 205

Index of Expressions in Chinese   239

搵周公　Wán Jàugùng 22
搵靠山　Wán Kaausàan 125
填鴨　Tìhnngáap 205
嫁雞隨雞，嫁狗隨狗　Gagāi Chèuih Gāi,
　　Gagáu Chèuih Gáu 200
落手打三更　Lohksáu Dá Sàamgāang 119
落筆打三更　Lohkbāt Dá Sàamgāang 119
跟紅頂白　Gànhùhng Díngbaahk 133
跳灰　Tiufūi 214
過咗海就係神仙　Gwojó Hói Jauh Haih Sàhnsīn ... 187
零舍　Lìhngse 150
零舍唔同　Lìhngse M̀tùhng 150
飽死　Báauséi 158
飽死荷蘭豆　Báauséi Hòhlāan Dáu 158

十四畫

敲竹杠　Hàau Jūkgong 97
福頭　Fūktàuh 16
酸薑蕎　Syùngēungkíuh 78

十五畫

嘰嘰吃吃　Gīgī Gahtgaht 157
摩囉差　Mōlōchà（Mōlōchàai） 18
撞板　Johngbáan 136
撬牆腳　Giuh Chèuhnggeuk 129
標青　Biuchēng 123

蔽翳 Baingai 178

請槍 Chéngchēung 164

賣魚佬洗身→冇晒腥（聲）氣 Maaihyùhlóu Sáisàn→
　　　　Móuhsaai Sènghei 92

賣豬仔 Maaih Jyūjái 100

十六畫

豬脷 Jyūleih 52

搿鷓鴣 Gam Jegū 215

噙青 Kàhmchēng (Kàhmkàhmchēng) (Kàhmkámchēng) 123

賴貓 Laaimāau 194

十七畫

擦鞋 Chaathàaih 172

濟唔過 Jaimgwo 46

濟唔濟 Jai M̀jai 46

濟得過 Jaidākgwo 46

縮骨 Sūkgwāt 24

簕竇 Lahkdau 34

十八畫

雜崩能 Jaahpbālāng (Jaahpbālāang) 58

騎劉皇馬 Kèh Làuhwòhngmáh 166

十九畫

識英雄重英雄 Sik Yìnghùhng Juhng Yìnghùhng 162

Index of Expressions in Chinese

離譜　Lèihpóu 136

二十畫

蘇州屎　Sòujàusí 75
鹹魚翻生　Hàahmyú Fàansàang 209
鹹濕　Hàahmsāp 36

二十一畫

櫻桃小(口)　Yìngtòuh Síu (Háu) 80
露出馬腳　Louhchēut Máhgeuk 176

二十二畫

驚青　Gèngchēng 123
攞豆　Lódáu 51